Assessment *FOR* Learning
An Action Guide for School Leaders

Second Edition

Stephen Chappuis, Richard Stiggins, Judith Arter, and Jan Chappuis

Assessment Training Institute
Portland, OR

Assessment *for* Learning

An Action Guide for School Leaders

© 2005 Assessment Training Institute
Portland, OR

Project Coordinator: Barbara Carnegie
Editor: Robert L. Marcum, editorbob.com
Cover Design: Brass Design
Page Layout: Anita Jones, Another Jones Graphics

The authors and publisher have made every effort to identify and cite the copyright holders of all material
reproduced from other sources, and to obtain permission for their reproduction. Anyone identifying
outstanding copyright attribution issues is invited to contact the publisher, who will be happy to make
any necessary corrections in future editions or reprints of this work.

Many of the Activities and Resources in this book appeared, some in substantially different form,
in J. A. Arter and K. U. Busick, *Practice with Student-Involved Classroom Assessment,*
Portland, OR: Assessment Training Institute, 2001. Reprinted and adapted by permission.

Library of Congress Control Number: 2003106332

ISBN-10: 0-9655101-6-6
ISBN-13: 978-0-9655101-6-5

Printed in the USA

Acknowledgements

This guide represents years of experience that has helped us (1) form our vision of excellence in assessment, and (2) understand the nature of assessment change and how to help schools use assessment to improve student learning. Along the way we have benefited from others who have worked to understand sound assessment more clearly, who applied our ideas and shared successful implementation stories, and those who have helped us teach others about quality assessment. We wish to thank them all. Those who have helped us deepen our own understanding of quality assessment and school leadership include Paul Black and Dylan Wiliam and their associates in the Assessment Reform Group of the United Kingdom, Kathy Busick, Anne Davies, Rick DuFour, Linda Elman, Heidi Hayes-Jacobs, Jim Popham, Lorrie Shepard, Susan Brookhart, Janet Barry, Michael Fullan, and Ruth Sutton.

Practicing school leaders who have implemented our ideas and permitted us to watch and learn include Dan Duke of The University of Virginia; Bob Nielsen of Bloomington, Illinois; Jay Linksman of the Professional Development Alliance in Illinois; Steve Price of Middletown, Ohio; Doug Christensen and Pat Rochewski of the Nebraska Department of Education; and Bruce Herzog and Joni Heutink of Nooksack Valley, Washington.

To help us share our ideas with practitioners, we thank ATI associates Carol Commodore and Ken O'Connor.

We also welcome once again the contributions made by freelance editor Robert L. Marcum, which improved the clarity of ideas and activities presented in this book. His enthusiasm for the subject, attention to detail, and understanding of the big picture helped to unify the work of four authors. Our thanks also to Anita Jones, design consultant, for helping present both text and artwork with the reader in mind.

We believe that the vision building and strategies for change we describe in this guide can lead any school district to excellence in assessment. We acknowledge the commitment of those who are willing to try.

The Assessment Training Institute Staff
April, 2005

Contents

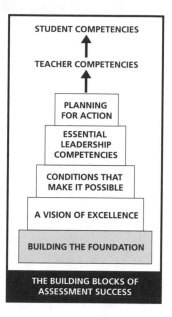

THE BUILDING BLOCKS OF
ASSESSMENT SUCCESS

*Attaining any vision of assessment excellence
requires that certain conditions be in place.
Those conditions include well-defined learning
targets for students, supportive school and
district policies, clear communication systems,
and most important, assessment-literate
teachers and administrators.*

Part One

BUILDING
THE
FOUNDATION

To succeed in standards-based school improvement we must be clear about what students need to know and be able to do, and we need to be skillful in how we teach. To be certain that students have learned what we intend for them to learn, we must develop balanced assessment systems that provide data on how students are progressing, and that also use the classroom assessment process to promote greater learning. What we teach, how we teach it, how well we assess, and how we use assessment to improve student achievement will all determine the success of our efforts, and ultimately, how we are judged.

Evidence suggests that the culture we create in our schools can positively influence student success. Collaborative cultures emphasizing teamwork and continuous learning and improvement are positioned to deliver the necessary professional support teachers need, support aimed at demonstrable results in student achievement. Research evidence continues to grow showing the difference effective school leaders can have on student learning. (Waters, Marzano, & McNulty, 2003). The role of the leader continues to be studied, with scholars and practitioners alike working to translate research into practice, describing what effective leadership looks and sounds like. The number of websites, books, articles, and conferences devoted to the subject of school leadership makes it clear that we are in yet another cycle of examination and study, looking at the topic with multiple lenses from a variety of angles. We may not yet be at the apex; Fullan (2004) predicts that leadership will be to this decade what standards-based reform was to the last.

This recent focus on the role and effectiveness of the school leader provides new understandings about the nature of leadership, and is in part influenced by thinking outside of education. Earlier contributions from business management (Covey, 1989; Peters & Waterman, 1982; Senge, 1990) and from human psychology/motivation (Blanchard & Johnson, 1982) are now joined by current thinking and insight (Collins, 2001; Goleman, Boyatzis, & McKee, 2003; Gladwell, 2000). All share a common foundation in that they describe principles and values by which leaders can live and work, principles more complex than simply following a checklist of behaviors or practices applied in isolation from a set of core beliefs.

Today's standards-based environment is a very different one from when the focus was on effective schools research, when instructional leadership and teacher supervision were the popular topics in principal training programs. Today, with school improvement taking on more urgency due to the federal accountability mandated in the No Child Left Behind Act (NCLB) and the resulting need to raise test scores, improving leadership knowledge and skill is being leveraged as one more strategy directly aimed at raising student achievement.

The current reality for most school administrators is dominated by the implementation of state standards and the need to demonstrate improvement as measured through the AYP (adequate yearly progress) requirement of NCLB. We have written this guide from our belief that quality assessment in the classroom is the foundation for school improvement. It provides a structure through which you can refine your vision of excellence in assessment for your school or district, examine the skills and knowledge needed to support your vision, and develop an action plan to turn your vision into reality. By using this guide in study teams with other school administrators and teacher leaders, you can achieve a balanced, instructionally relevant local assessment system in which both classroom assessments *for* learning and standardized assessments *of* learning effectively serve their intended purposes. Both are important. Although we emphasize in this guide what leaders can do to take advantage of the power of assessment *for* learning to improve student achievement, we believe that all uses of assessment can and should help students learn, and therefore assessments *of* learning also contribute to a balanced assessment system. We will explore this distinction in depth later in this guide.

Beyond working at the systems level for achieving assessment balance and quality, this action guide also helps you as a school leader analyze your individual knowledge about assessment and prepares you to plan your own continuing learning about sound assessment practices. By completing the work presented in the accompanying activities and resources, you will develop your own assessment literacy. Your team will acquire the tools needed to set your staff on the path to assess accurately, to increase student motivation to learn, and to use assessment to improve learning. The key to completing that journey is sustained support of the collaborative learning process and school culture necessary to turn your vision into everyday reality in the classroom.

This guide will help you and your team do the following:

- Create your own vision for assessment balance and quality.
- Begin to understand what classroom assessment *for* learning is, and its relationship to student achievement.
- Understand the need to balance the assessment system between large-scale assessment *of* learning and classroom assessment *for* learning.
- Identify assessment needs relevant to your own school or district and prioritize those needs.
- Develop an action plan for realizing your vision of assessment excellence.
- Analyze your own assessment knowledge and leadership skills relative to a set of 10 assessment competencies for school leaders.

Contents of This Guide

The graphic on page 1 shows the building blocks of assessment success. It also maps our journey through this action guide. To help you and your leadership team develop a deep understanding of each of the building blocks, we've divided this guide into five parts.

- Part 1 introduces the guide's purpose and goals, describes both its print and media contents, and explains its optimal use in the context of a school or district leadership study team. We encourage the same model of professional development for this action guide that we advocate for teachers to become assessment literate. All it requires is a small group of school leaders willing to meet regularly and invest the necessary time in their own professional growth and in the improvement of their local system. By acquiring certain understandings, considering important issues, and planning for the future as a team, we demonstrate the commitment to learning we seek in all aspects of school culture.

- Part 2 outlines our vision of excellence in assessment and describes the essential ingredients necessary to develop an assessment system rooted in balance, quality, and student involvement. Here we balance assessment *of* and *for* learning.

- The third part asks leadership teams to analyze the current status of their school/district assessment system to see if essential conditions are in place for the vision to be realized. Those conditions include well-defined learning targets for students, supportive school/district policies, clear communication systems, and most important, assessment-literate teachers and administrators.

- In Part 4 we shift emphasis from analyzing organizational and institutional assessment excellence to examining the knowledge and skills that individual leaders must master in order to create and sustain assessment excellence. A further examination of the knowledge and skills needed by classroom teachers is also contained in Part 4, as well as ideas for how school leaders can help teachers gain the skills and support them in their classroom practice.

- In the fifth and final part we help leadership teams understand why and how developing a sound assessment system lays a strong foundation for other local improvement initiatives. We help you create the action plan that will lead to assessment balance and quality.

Each section puts forth ideas and suggestions about the use of assessment in schools. From time to time, we will pause and ask your team to discuss and reflect on the ideas and their application in your local context. We have included two different learning aids to help you consider and clarify the ideas, along with suggestions on how to use them to advance your understanding and application of the concepts:

Thinking About Assessment pages present activities for your leadership team to complete as part of your processing and understanding the contents of this guide.

Applying the Skills pages are resources you can use at any time to advance individual or group knowledge about assessment issues, or help your team prepare for and organize successful implementation of balanced assessment. Some are best suited for use with the leadership team; others can be used as faculty meeting or inservice activities with teachers.

These resources are aimed at helping leaders understand what they can do to ensure balance and quality in local assessment systems. It is important to point out, however, that the *teacher* plays the pivotal role in achieving quality assessment. The skills and knowledge that teachers need to apply the principles of assessment *for* learning, although introduced in this book for leaders, are not explicitly taught. The heart of the professional development program offered by ATI for teachers is our text, *Classroom Assessment* for *Student Learning: Doing It Right—Using It Well.*

This guide also includes a compact disc (CD-ROM) and a digital video disc (DVD), found in plastic sleeves just inside the back cover. The CD-ROM contains the activities and resources previously described, tools for leaders to use with other educators when working through the assessment ideas and issues presented here.

The DVD, a key component in one of the first leadership team activities, contains *New Mission, New Beliefs,* a 50-minute presentation with a viewer's study guide featuring Rick Stiggins explaining the distinction between assessment *of* learning and assessment *for* learning, and identifying beliefs about the role of assessment that are likely to promote student learning.

Getting Ready

We think it is important to build your knowledge and understanding of quality assessment and balanced local systems by following the sequence of reading and activities as outlined in this guide. In Part 2 we outline our vision for the perfect assessment system. The first two Thinking About Assessment activities will get you started in developing a foundation for understanding excellence in assessment, including understanding a key concept referred to throughout the guide, the difference between assessment *of* and assessment *for* learning.

Thinking About Assessment

Activity 1: Building the Foundation for Understanding Quality Assessment

Purpose: This first activity helps you understand the "big ideas" of balance in assessment, assessment quality, the power of student involvement in assessment, and assessment *of* and *for* learning. Throughout this guide our goal is to have you think about a vision of assessment excellence, read papers and/or view videos, consider the concepts and ideas presented, and refine your vision as necessary. We'll ask you to work as a leadership team to progressively shape your vision. Then we'll ask your team to compare the current status of your local assessment system to your vision to see if they line up, and identify what you must adjust to make them match.

Time: A 2-hour meeting

Meeting Agenda:

- Working as a team, based on your current level of understanding of important assessment issues, outline your vision of a high-quality assessment system. Do this by taking a half hour to brainstorm and refine your team's answers to the following two questions. Take time to think this through pretty thoroughly, as the results will become very important.

  1. What do you want your assessment system to accomplish? What will be its key objectives?
  2. How will your system accomplish these things? What will be its key components?

- Next, read "Inside the Black Box," by Paul Black and Dylan Wiliam, pages 10–21. Then collect your individual thoughts on the most important lessons and implications of this research. Finally, work as a team to reaffirm, or to rethink and revise as appropriate, your initial vision of excellence in assessment. Refine your vision as needed to reflect any ideas or values learned from Black and Wiliam.

- Next, again as a team, view the ATI DVD, *New Mission, New Beliefs*. This presentation details both the differences in and the need for synergy between assessment *of* and *for* learning and explains why the principles of assessment *for* learning are so powerful. A series of discussion questions is built into the presentation, and you will be asked to pause from time to time and reflect on these. Please take this time as you watch.

After Viewing the "New Mission, New Beliefs presentation":

- Read Table 1-1 (pp. 22–23), contrasting assessment *of* and *for* learning, discussing the nuances of each and how they compare, as needed to be sure everyone on your team understands how they relate.
- Now go back a third time and review the evolving vision you developed at the start of your meeting and revised after reading the Black and Wiliam article. Using Table 1-1, Table 1-2 (p. 24), and the content of the video presentation, once again make adjustments as needed to your vision of excellence in assessment. What do you want it to do for you and how will it help you accomplish those things? Continue to analyze these things as a team, striving for consensus.

Inside the Black Box:

Raising Standards Through Classroom Assessment

BY PAUL BLACK AND DYLAN WILIAM

Firm evidence shows that formative assessment is an essential component of classroom work and that its development can raise standards of achievement, Mr. Black and Mr. Wiliam point out. Indeed, they know of no other way of raising standards for which such a strong prima facie case can be made.

RAISING the standards of learning that are achieved through schooling is an important national priority. In recent years, governments throughout the world have been more and more vigorous in making changes in pursuit of this aim. National, state, and district standards; target setting; enhanced programs for the external testing of students' performance; surveys such as NAEP (National Assessment of Educational Progress) and TIMSS (Third International Mathematics and Science Study); initiatives to improve school planning and management; and more frequent and thorough inspection are all means toward the same end. But the sum of all these reforms has not added up to an effective policy because something is missing.

Learning is driven by what teachers and pupils do in classrooms. Teachers have to manage complicated and demanding situations, channeling the personal, emotional, and social pressures of a group of 30 or more youngsters in order to help them learn

PAUL BLACK is professor emeritus in the School of Education, King's College, London, where DYLAN WILIAM is head of school and professor of educational assessment.

immediately and become better learners in the future. Standards can be raised only if teachers can tackle this task more effectively. What is missing from the efforts alluded to above is any direct help with this task. This fact was recognized in the TIMSS video study: "A focus on standards and accountability that ignores the processes of teaching and learning in classrooms will not provide the direction that teachers need in their quest to improve." [1]

In terms of systems engineering, present policies in the U.S. and in many other countries seem to treat the classroom as a black box. Certain *inputs* from the outside—pupils, teachers, other resources, management rules and requirements, parental anxieties, standards, tests with high stakes, and so on—are fed into the box. Some *outputs* are supposed to follow: pupils who are more knowledgeable and competent, better test results, teachers who are reasonably satisfied, and so on. But what is happening inside the box? How can anyone be sure that a particular set of new inputs will produce better outputs if we don't at least study what happens inside? And why is it that most of the reform initiatives mentioned in the first paragraph are not aimed at giving direct help and support to the work of teachers in classrooms?

The answer usually given is that it is up to teachers: they have to make the inside work better. This answer is not good enough, for two reasons. First, it is at least possible that some changes in the inputs may be counterproductive and make it harder for teachers to raise standards. Second, it seems strange, even unfair, to leave the most difficult piece of the standards-raising puzzle entirely to teachers. If there are ways in which policy makers and others can give direct help and support to the everyday

Source: Reprinted from *Phi Delta Kappan*, October 1998, vol. 80, pp. 139–148. Reprinted by permission.

classroom task of achieving better learning, then surely these ways ought to be pursued vigorously.

This article is about the inside of the black box. We focus on one aspect of teaching: formative assessment. But we will show that this feature is at the heart of effective teaching.

THE ARGUMENT

We start from the self-evident proposition that teaching and learning must be interactive. Teachers need to know about their pupils' progress and difficulties with learning so that they can adapt their own work to meet pupils' needs—needs that are often unpredictable and that vary from one pupil to another. Teachers can find out what they need to know in a variety of ways, including observation and discussion in the classroom and the reading of pupils' written work.

We use the general term *assessment* to refer to all those activities undertaken by teachers—and by their students in assessing themselves—that provide information to be used as feedback to modify teaching and learning activities. Such assessment becomes *formative assessment* when the evidence is actually used to adapt the teaching to meet student needs.[2]

There is nothing new about any of this. All teachers make assessments in every class they teach. But there are three important questions about this process that we seek to answer:

● Is there evidence that improving formative assessment raises standards?

● Is there evidence that there is room for improvement?

● Is there evidence about how to improve formative assessment?

In setting out to answer these questions, we have conducted an extensive survey of the research literature. We have checked through many books and through the past nine years' worth of issues of more than 160 journals, and we have studied earlier reviews of research. This process yielded about 580 articles or chapters to study. We prepared a lengthy review, using material from 250 of these sources, that has been published in a special issue of the

journal *Assessment in Education*, together with comments on our work by leading educational experts from Australia, Switzerland, Hong Kong, Lesotho, and the U.S.[3]

The conclusion we have reached from our research review is that the answer to each of the three questions above is clearly yes. In the three main sections below, we outline the nature and force of the evidence that justifies this conclusion. However, because we are presenting a summary here, our text will appear strong on assertions and weak on the details of their justification. We maintain that these assertions are backed by evidence and that this backing is set out in full detail in the lengthy review on which this article is founded.

We believe that the three sections below establish a strong case that *governments, their agencies, school authorities, and the teaching profession should study very carefully whether they are seriously interested in raising standards in education.* However, we also acknowledge widespread evidence that fundamental change in education can be achieved only slowly—through programs of professional development that build on existing good practice. Thus we do not conclude that formative assessment is yet another "magic bullet" for education. The issues involved are too complex and too closely linked to both the difficulties of classroom practice and the beliefs that drive public policy. In a final section, we confront this complexity and try to sketch out a strategy for acting on our evidence.

DOES IMPROVING FORMATIVE ASSESSMENT RAISE STANDARDS?

A research review published in 1986, concentrating primarily on classroom assessment work for children with mild handicaps, surveyed a large number of innovations, from which 23 were selected.[4] Those chosen satisfied the condition that quantitative evidence of learning gains was obtained, both for those involved in the innovation and for a similar group not so involved. Since then, many more papers have been published describing similarly careful quantitative experiments. Our own review has selected at least 20 more studies. (The number depends on how rigorous a set of selection criteria are applied.) All these studies show that innovations that include strengthening the practice of formative assessment produce significant and often substantial learning gains. These studies range over age groups from 5-year-olds to university undergraduates, across several school subjects, and over several countries.

For research purposes, learning gains of this type are measured by comparing the average improvements in the test scores of pupils involved in an innovation with the range of scores that are found for typical groups of pupils on these same tests. The ratio of the former divided by the latter is known as the *effect size*. Typical effect sizes of the formative assessment experiments were between 0.4 and 0.7. These effect sizes are larger than most of those found for educational interventions. The following examples illustrate some practical consequences of such large gains.

● An effect size of 0.4 would mean that the average pupil involved in an innovation would record the same achievement as a pupil in the top 35% of those not so involved.

● An effect size gain of 0.7 in the recent international comparative studies in mathematics[5] would have raised the score of a nation in the middle of the pack of 41 countries (e.g., the U.S.) to one of the top five.

Many of these studies arrive at another important conclusion: that improved formative assessment helps low achievers more than other students and so reduces the range of achievement while raising achievement overall. A notable recent example is a study devoted entirely to low-achieving students and students with learning disabilities, which shows that frequent assessment feedback helps both groups enhance their learning.[6] Any gains for such pupils could be particularly important. Furthermore, pupils who come to see themselves as unable to learn usually cease to take school seriously. Many become disruptive; others resort to truancy. Such young people are likely to be alienated from society and to become the sources and the victims of serious social problems.

Thus it seems clear that very significant learning gains lie within our grasp. The fact that such gains have been achieved by a variety of methods that have, as a common feature, enhanced formative assessment suggests that this feature accounts, at least in part, for the successes. However, it does not follow that it would be an easy matter to achieve such gains on a wide scale in normal classrooms. Many of the reports we have studied raise a number of other issues.

● All such work involves new ways to enhance feedback between those taught and the teacher, ways that will require significant changes in classroom practice.

● Underlying the various approaches are assumptions about what makes for effective learning —in particular the assumption that students have to be actively involved.

● For assessment to function formatively, the results have to be used to adjust teaching and learning; thus a significant aspect of any program will be the ways in which teachers make these adjustments.

● The ways in which assessment can affect the motivation and self-esteem of pupils and the benefits of engaging pupils in self-assessment deserve careful attention.

IS THERE ROOM FOR IMPROVEMENT?

A poverty of practice. There is a wealth of research evidence that the everyday practice of assessment in classrooms is beset with problems and shortcomings, as the following selected quotations indicate.

● "Marking is usually conscientious but often fails to offer guidance on how work can be improved. In a significant minority of cases, marking reinforces underachievement and underexpectation by being too generous or unfocused. Information about pupil performance received by the teacher is insufficiently used to inform subsequent work," according to a United Kingdom inspection report on secondary schools.[7]

● "Why is the extent and nature of formative assessment in science so impoverished?" asked a research study on secondary science teachers in the United Kingdom.[8]

• "Indeed they pay lip service to [formative assessment] but consider that its practice is unrealistic in the present educational context," reported a study of Canadian secondary teachers.[9]

• "The assessment practices outlined above are not common, even though these kinds of approaches are now widely promoted in the professional literature," according to a review of assessment practices in U.S. schools.[10]

The most important difficulties with assessment revolve around three issues. The first issue is *effective learning*.

• The tests used by teachers encourage rote and superficial learning even when teachers say they want to develop understanding; many teachers seem unaware of the inconsistency.

• The questions and other methods teachers use are not shared with other teachers in the same school, and they are not critically reviewed in relation to what they actually assess.

• For primary teachers particularly, there is a tendency to emphasize quantity and presentation of work and to neglect its quality in relation to learning.

The second issue is *negative impact*.

• The giving of marks and the grading function are overemphasized, while the giving of useful advice and the learning function are under-emphasized.

• Approaches are used in which pupils are compared with one another, the prime purpose of which seems to them to be competition rather than personal improvement; in consequence, assessment feedback teaches low-achieving pupils that they lack "ability," causing them to come to believe that they are not able to learn.

The third issue is the *managerial role* of assessments.

• Teachers' feedback to pupils seems to serve social and managerial functions, often at the expense of the learning function.

• Teachers are often able to predict pupils' results on external tests because their own tests imitate them, but at the same time teachers know too little about their pupils' learning needs.

• The collection of marks to fill in records is given higher priority than the analysis of pupils' work to discern learning needs; furthermore, some teachers pay no attention to the assessment records of their pupils' previous teachers.

Of course, not all these descriptions apply to all classrooms. Indeed, there are many schools and classrooms to which they do not apply at all. Nevertheless, these general conclusions have been drawn by researchers who have collected evidence—through observation, interviews, and questionnaires—from schools in several countries, including the U.S.

An empty commitment. The development of national assessment policy in England and Wales over the last decade illustrates the obstacles that stand in the way of developing policy support for formative assessment. The recommendations of a government task force in 1988[11] and all subsequent statements of government policy have emphasized the importance of formative assessment by teachers. However, the body charged with carrying out government policy on assessment had no strategy either to study or to develop the formative assessment of teachers and did no more than devote a tiny fraction of its resources to such work.[12] Most of the available resources and most of the public and political attention were focused on national external tests. While teachers' contributions to these "summative assessments" have been given some formal status, hardly any attention has been paid to their contributions through formative assessment. Moreover, the problems of the relationship between teachers' formative and summative roles have received no attention.

It is possible that many of the commitments were stated in the belief that formative assessment was not problematic, that it already happened all the time and needed no more than formal acknowledgment of its existence. However, it is also clear that the political commitment to external testing in order to promote competition had a central priority, while the commitment to formative assessment was marginal. As researchers the world over have found, high-stakes external tests always dominate teaching and assessment. However, they give teachers poor models for formative assessment because of their limited function of providing overall summaries of achievement rather than helpful diagnosis. Given this fact, it is hardly surprising that numerous research studies of the implementation of the education reforms in the United Kingdom have found that formative assessments is "seriously in need of development."[13] With hindsight, we can see that the failure to perceive the need for substantial support for formative assessment and to take responsibility for developing such support was a serious error.

In the U.S. similar pressures have been felt from political movements characterized by a distrust of teachers and a belief that external testing will, on its own, improve learning. Such fractured relationships between policy makers and the teaching profession are not inevitable—indeed, many countries with enviable educational achievements seem to manage well with policies that show greater respect and support for teachers. While the situation in the U.S. is far more diverse than that in England and Wales, the effects of high-stakes state-mandated testing are very similar to those of the external tests in the United Kingdom. Moreover, the traditional reliance on multiple-choice testing in the U.S.—not shared in the United Kingdom—has exacerbated the negative effects of such policies on the quality of classroom learning.

HOW CAN WE IMPROVE FORMATIVE ASSESSMENT?

The self-esteem of pupils. A report of schools in Switzerland states that "a number of pupils . . . are content to 'get by.' . . . Every teacher who wants to practice formative assessment must reconstruct the teaching contracts so as to counteract the habits acquired by his pupils."[14]

The ultimate user of assessment information that is elicited in order to improve learning is the pupil. There are negative and positive aspects of this fact. The negative aspect is illustrated by the preceding quotation. When the classroom culture focuses on rewards, "gold stars," grades, or class ranking, then pupils look for ways to obtain the best marks rather than to improve their learning. One reported consequence is that, when they have any choice,

pupils avoid difficult tasks. They also spend time and energy looking for clues to the "right answer." Indeed, many become reluctant to ask questions out of a fear of failure. Pupils who encounter difficulties are led to believe that they lack ability, and this belief leads them to attribute their difficulties to a defect in themselves about which they cannot do a great deal. Thus they avoid investing effort in learning that can lead only to disappointment, and they try to build up their self-esteem in other ways.

The positive aspect of students' being the primary users of the information gleaned from formative assessments is that negative outcomes—such as an obsessive focus on competition and the attendant fear of failure on the part of low achievers—are not inevitable. What is needed is a culture of success, backed by a belief that all pupils can achieve. In this regard, formative assessment can be a powerful weapon if it is communicated in the right way. While formative assessment can help all pupils, it yields particularly good results with low achievers by concentrating on specific problems with their work and giving them a clear understanding of what is wrong and how to put it right. Pupils can accept and work with such messages, provided that they are not clouded by overtones about ability, competition, and comparison with others. In summary, the message can be stated as follows: *feedback to any pupil should be about the particular qualities of his or her work, with advice on what he or she can do to improve, and should avoid comparisons with other pupils.*

Self-assessment by pupils. Many successful innovations have developed self- and peer-assessment by pupils as ways of enhancing formative assessment, and such work has achieved some success with pupils from age 5 upward. This link of formative assessment to self-assessment is not an accident; indeed, it is inevitable.

To explain this last statement, we should first note that the main problem that those who are developing self-assessments encounter is not a problem of reliability and trustworthiness. Pupils are generally honest and reliable in assessing both themselves and one another; they can even be too hard on themselves. The main problem is that pupils can assess themselves only when they have a sufficiently clear picture of the targets that their learning is meant to attain. Surprisingly, and sadly, many pupils do not have such a picture, and they appear to have become accustomed to receiving classroom teaching as an arbitrary sequence of exercises with no overarching rationale. To overcome this pattern of passive reception requires hard and sustained work. When pupils do acquire such an overview, they then become more committed and more effective as learners. Moreover, their own assessments become an object of discussion with their teachers and with one another, and this discussion further promotes the reflection on one's own thinking that is essential to good learning.

Thus self-assessment by pupils, far from being a luxury, is in fact *an essential component of formative assessment.* When anyone is trying to learn, feedback about the effort has three elements: recognition of the *desired goal*, evidence about *present position*, and some understanding of a *way to close the gap* between the two.[15] All three must be understood to some degree by anyone before he or she can take action to improve learning.

Such an argument is consistent with more general ideas established by research into the way people learn. New understandings are not simply swallowed and stored in isolation; they have to be assimilated in relation to preexisting ideas. The new and the old may be inconsistent or even in conflict, and the disparities must be resolved by thoughtful actions on the part of the learner. Realizing that there are new goals for the learning is an essential part of this process of assimilation. Thus we conclude: *if formative assessment is to be productive, pupils should be trained in self-assessment so that they can understand the main purposes of their learning and thereby grasp what they need to do to achieve.*

The evolution of effective teaching. The research studies referred to above show very clearly that effective programs of formative assessment involve far more than the addition of a few observations and tests to an existing program. They require careful scrutiny of all the main components of a teaching plan. Indeed, it is clear that instruction and formative assessment are indivisible.

To begin at the beginning, the choice of tasks for classroom work and homework is important. Tasks have to be justified in terms of the learning aims that they serve, and they can work well only if opportunities for pupils to communicate their evolving understanding are built into the planning. Discussion, observation of activities, and marking of written work can all be used to provide those opportunities, but it is then important to look at or listen carefully to the talk, the writing, and the actions through which pupils develop and display the state of their understanding. Thus we maintain that *opportunities for pupils to express their understanding should be designed into any piece of teaching, for this will initiate the interaction through which formative assessment aids learning.*

Discussions in which pupils are led to talk about their understanding in their own ways are important aids to increasing knowledge and improving under-standing. Dialogue with the teacher provides the opportunity for the teacher to respond to and reori-ent a pupil's thinking. However, there are clearly recorded examples of such discussions in which teachers have, quite unconsciously, responded in ways that would inhibit the future learning of a pupil. What the examples have in common is that the teacher is looking for a particular response and lacks the flexibility or the confidence to deal with the unexpected. So the teacher tries to direct the pupil toward giving the expected answer. In manipulating the dialogue in this way, the teacher seals off any unusual, often thoughtful but unorthodox, attempts by pupils to work out their own answers. Over time the pupils get the message: they are not required to think out their own answers. The object of the exercise is to work out—or guess—what answer the teacher expects to see or hear.

A particular feature of the talk between teacher and pupils is the asking of questions by the teacher. This natural and direct way of checking on learning is often unproductive. One common problem is that, following a question, teachers do not wait long enough to allow pupils to think out their answers. When a teacher answers his or her own question after only two or three seconds and when a minute of silence is not tolerable, there is no possibility that a pupil can think out what to say.

There are then two consequences. One is that, because the only questions that can produce answers in such a short time are questions of fact, these predominate. The other is that pupils don't even try to think out a response. Because they know that the answer, followed by another question, will come along in a few seconds, there is no point in trying. It is also generally the case that only a few pupils in a class answer the teacher's questions. The rest then leave it to these few, knowing that they cannot respond as quickly and being unwilling to risk making mistakes in public. So the teacher, by lowering the level of questions and by accepting answers from a few, can keep the lesson going but is actually out of touch with the understanding of most of the class. The question/answer dialogue becomes a ritual, one in which thoughtful involvement suffers.

There are several ways to break this particular cycle. They involve giving pupils time to respond; asking them to discuss their thinking in pairs or in small groups, so that a respondent is speaking on behalf of others; giving pupils a choice between different possible answers and asking them to vote on the options; asking all of them to write down an answer and then reading out a selected few; and so on. What is essential is that any dialogue should evoke thoughtful reflection in which all pupils can be encouraged to take part, for only then can the formative process start to work. In short, the dialogue between pupils and a teacher should be *thoughtful, reflective, focused to evoke and explore understanding, and conducted so that all pupils have an opportunity to think and to express their ideas.*

Tests given in class and tests and other exercises assigned for homework are also important means of promoting feedback. A good test can be an occasion for learning. It is better to have frequent short tests than infrequent long ones. Any new learning should first be tested within about a week of a first encounter, but more frequent tests

are counterproductive. The quality of the test items—that is, their relevance to the main learning aims and their clear communication to the pupil—requires scrutiny as well. Good questions are hard to generate, and teachers should collaborate and draw on outside sources to collect such questions.

Given questions of good quality, it is essential to ensure the quality of the feedback. Research studies have shown that, if pupils are given only marks or grades, they do not benefit from the feedback. The worst scenario is one in which some pupils who get low marks this time also got low marks last time and come to expect to get low marks next time. This cycle of repeated failure becomes part of a shared belief between such students and their teacher. Feedback has been shown to improve learning when it gives each pupil specific guidance on strengths and weaknesses, preferably without any overall marks. Thus the way in which test results are reported to pupils so that they can identify their own strengths and weaknesses is critical. Pupils must be given the means and opportunities to work with evidence of their difficulties. For formative purposes, a test at the end of a unit or teaching module is pointless; it is too late to work with the results. We conclude that *the feedback on tests, seatwork, and homework should give each pupil guidance on how to improve, and each pupil must be given help and an opportunity to work on the improvement.*

All these points make clear that there is no one simple way to improve formative assessment. What is common to them is that a teacher's approach should start by being realistic and confronting the question, "Do I really know enough about the understanding of my pupils to be able to help each of them?"

Much of the work teachers must do to make good use of formative assessment can give rise to difficulties. Some pupils will resist attempts to change accustomed routines, for any such change is uncomfortable, and emphasis on the challenge to think for yourself (and not just to work harder) can be threatening to many. Pupils cannot be expected to believe in the value of changes for their learning before they have experienced the benefits of such changes. Moreover, many of the initiatives that are needed take more class time, particularly when a central purpose is to change the outlook on learning and the working methods of pupils. Thus teachers have to take risks in the belief that such investment of time will yield rewards in the future, while "delivery" and "coverage" with poor understanding are pointless and can even be harmful.

Teachers must deal with two basic issues that are the source of many of the problems associated with changing to a system of formative assessment. The first is *the nature of each teacher's beliefs about learning.* If the teacher assumes that knowledge is to be transmitted and learned, that understanding will develop later, and that clarity of exposition accompanied by rewards for patient reception are the essentials of good teaching, then formative assessment is hardly necessary. However, most teachers accept the wealth of evidence that this transmission model does not work, even when judged by its own criteria, and so are willing to make a commitment to teaching through interaction. Formative assessment is an essential component of such instruction. We do not mean to imply that individualized, one-on-one teaching is the only solution; rather we mean that what is needed is a classroom culture of questioning and deep thinking, in which pupils learn from shared discussions with teachers and peers. What emerges very clearly here is the indivisibility of instruction and formative assessment practices.

The other issue that can create problems for teachers who wish to adopt an interactive model of teaching and learning relates to *the beliefs teachers hold about the potential of all their pupils for learning.* To sharpen the contrast by overstating it, there is on the one hand the "fixed I.Q." view—a belief that each pupil has a fixed, inherited intelligence that cannot be altered much by schooling. On the other hand, there is the "untapped potential" view—a belief that starts from the assumption that so-called ability is a complex of skills that can be learned. Here, we argue for the underlying belief that all pupils can learn more

effectively if one can clear away, by sensitive handling, the obstacles to learning, be they cognitive failures never diagnosed or damage to personal confidence or a combination of the two. Clearly the truth lies between these two extremes, but the evidence is that *ways of managing formative assessment that work with the assumptions of "untapped potential" do help all pupils to learn and can give particular help to those who have previously struggled.*

POLICY AND PRACTICE

Changing the policy perspective. The assumptions that drive national and state policies for assessment have to be called into question. The promotion of testing as an important component for establishing a competitive market in education can be very harmful. The more recent shifting of emphasis toward setting targets for all, with assessment providing a touchstone to help check pupils' attainments, is a more mature position. However, we would argue that *there is a need now to move further, to focus on the inside of the "black box" and so to explore the potential of assessment to raise standards directly as an integral part of each pupil's learning work.*

It follows from this view that several changes are needed. First, policy ought to start with a recognition that the prime locus for raising standards is the classroom, so that the overarching priority has to be the promotion and support of change within the classroom. Attempts to raise standards by reforming the inputs to and measuring the outputs from the black box of the classroom can be helpful, but they are not adequate on their own. Indeed, their helpfulness can be judged only in light of their effects in classrooms.

The evidence we have presented here establishes that a clearly productive way to start implementing a classroom-focused policy would be to improve formative assessment. This same evidence also establishes that in doing so we would not be concentrating on some minor aspect of the business of teaching and learning. Rather, we would be concentrating on several essential elements: the quality of teacher/pupil interactions, the stimulus and help for pupils to take active responsibility for their own learning, the particular help needed to move pupils out of the trap of "low achievement," and the development of the habits necessary for all students to become lifelong learners. Improvements in formative assessment, which are within the reach of all teachers, can contribute substantially to raising standards in all these ways.

Four steps to implementation. If we accept the argument outlined above, what needs to be done? The proposals outlined below do not follow directly from our analysis of assessment research. They are consistent with its main findings, but they also call on more general sources for guidance.[16]

At one extreme, one might call for more research to find out how best to carry out such work; at the other, one might call for an immediate and large-scale program, with new guidelines that all teachers should put into practice. Neither of these alternatives is sensible: while the first is unnecessary because enough is known from the results of research, the second would be unjustified because not enough is known about classroom practicalities in the context of any one country's schools.

Thus the improvement of formative assessment cannot be a simple matter. There is no quick fix that can alter existing practice by promising rapid rewards. On the contrary, if the substantial rewards promised by the research evidence are to be secured, each teacher must find his or her own ways of incorporating the lessons and ideas set out above into his or her own patterns of classroom work and into the cultural norms and expectations of a particular school community.[17] This process is a relatively slow one and takes place through sustained programs of professional development and support. This fact does not weaken the message here; indeed, it should be seen as a sign of its authenticity, for lasting and fundamental improvements in teaching and learning must take place in this way. A recent international study of innovation and change in education, encompassing 23 projects in 13 member countries of the Organisation for Economic Co-operation and Development, has arrived at exactly the same conclusion with regard to effective policies for change.[18] Such arguments lead us to propose a four-point scheme for teacher development.

1. *Learning from development.* Teachers will not take up ideas that sound attractive, no matter how extensive the research base, if the ideas are presented as general principles that leave the task of translating them into everyday practice entirely up to the teachers. Their classroom lives are too busy and too fragile for all but an outstanding few to undertake such work. What teachers need is a variety of living examples of implementation, as practiced by teachers with whom they can identify and from whom they can derive the confidence that they can do better. They need to see examples of what doing better means in practice.

So changing teachers' practice cannot begin with an extensive program of training for all; that could be justified only if it could be claimed that we have enough "trainers" who know what to do, which is certainly not the case. The essential first step is to set up a small number of local groups of schools—some primary, some secondary, some inner-city, some from outer suburbs, some rural—with each school committed both to a school-based development of formative assessment and to collaboration with other schools in its local group. In such a process, the teachers in their classrooms will be working out the answers to many of the practical questions that the evidence presented here cannot answer. They will be reformulating the issues, perhaps in relation to fundamental insights and certainly in terms that make sense to their peers in other classrooms. It is also essential to carry out such development in a range of subject areas, for the research in mathematics education is significantly different from that in language, which is different again from that in the creative arts.

The schools involved would need extra support in order to give their teachers time to plan the initiative in light of existing evidence, to reflect on their experience as it develops, and to offer advice about training others in the future. In addition, there would be a need for external evaluators to help the teachers with their development work and to collect evidence of its effectiveness. Video studies of classroom work would be essential for disseminating findings to others.

2. *Dissemination.* This dimension of the implementation would be in low gear at the outset—offering schools no more than general encouragement and explanation of some of the relevant evidence that they might consider in light of their existing practices. Dissemination efforts would become more active as results and resources became available from the development program. Then strategies for wider dissemination—for example, earmarking funds for inservice training programs—would have to be pursued.

We must emphasize that this process will inevitably be a slow one. To repeat what we said above, *if the substantial rewards promised by the evidence are to be secured, each teacher must find his or her own ways of incorporating the lessons and ideas that are set out above into his or her own patterns of classroom work.* Even with optimum training and support, such a process will take time.

3. *Reducing obstacles.* All features in the education system that actually obstruct the development of effective formative assessment should be examined to see how their negative effects can be reduced. Consider the conclusions from a study of teachers of English in U.S. secondary schools:

> Most of the teachers in this study were caught in conflicts among belief systems and institutional structures, agendas, and values. The point of friction among these conflicts was assessment, which was associated with very powerful feelings of being overwhelmed, and of insecurity, guilt, frustration, and anger. . . . This study suggests that assessment, as it occurs in schools, is far from a merely technical problem. Rather, it is deeply social and personal.[19]

The chief negative influence here is that of short external tests. Such tests can dominate teachers' work, and, insofar as they encourage drilling to produce right answers to short, out-of-context questions, they can lead teachers to act against their own better judgment about the best ways to develop the learning of their pupils. This is not to argue that all such tests are unhelpful. Indeed, they have an important role to play in securing public confidence in the accountability of schools. For the immediate future, what is needed in any development program for formative assessment is to study the interactions between these external tests and formative assessments to see how the models of assessment that external tests can provide could be made more helpful.

All teachers have to undertake some summative assessment. They must report to parents and produce end-of-year reports as classes are due to move on to new teachers. However, the task of assessing pupils summatively for external purposes is clearly different from the task of assessing ongoing work to monitor and improve progress. Some argue that these two roles are so different that they should be kept apart. We do not see how this can be done, given that teachers must have some share of responsibility for the former and must take the leading responsibility for the latter.[20] However, teachers clearly face difficult problems in reconciling their formative and summative roles, and confusion in teachers' minds between these roles can impede the improvement of practice.

The arguments here could be taken much further to make the case that teachers should play a far greater role in contributing to summative assessments for accountability. One strong reason for giving teachers a greater role is that they have access to the performance of their pupils in a variety of contexts and over extended periods of time.

This is an important advantage because sampling pupils' achievement by means of short exercises taken under the conditions of formal testing is fraught with dangers. It is now clear that performance in any task varies with the context in which it is presented. Thus some pupils who seem incompetent in tackling a problem under test conditions can look quite different in the more realistic conditions of an everyday encounter with an equivalent problem. Indeed, the conditions under which formal tests are taken threaten validity because they are quite unlike those of everyday performance. An outstanding example here is that collaborative work is very important in everyday life but is forbidden by current norms of formal testing.[21] These points open up wider arguments about assessment systems as a whole—arguments that are beyond the scope of this article.

4. *Research.* It is not difficult to set out a list of questions that would justify further research in this area. Although there are many and varied reports of successful innovations, they generally fail to give clear accounts of one or another of the important details. For example, they are often silent about the actual classroom methods used, the motivation and experience of the teachers, the nature of the tests used as measures of success, or the outlooks and expectations of the pupils involved.

However, while there is ample justification for proceeding with carefully formulated projects, we do not suggest that everyone else should wait for their conclusions. Enough is known to provide a basis for active development work, and some of the most important questions can be answered only through a program of practical implementation.

Directions for future research could include a study of the ways in which teachers understand and deal with the relationship between their formative and summative roles or a comparative study of the predictive validity of teachers' summative assessments versus external test results. Many more questions could be formulated, and it is important for future development that some of these problems be tackled by basic research. At the same time, experienced researchers would also have a vital role to play in the evaluation of the development programs we have proposed.

ARE WE SERIOUS ABOUT RAISING STANDARDS?

The findings summarized above and the program we have outlined have implications for a variety of responsible agencies. However, it is the responsibility of governments to take the lead. It would be premature and out of order for us to try to consider the relative roles in such an effort, although success would clearly depend on cooperation among government agencies, academic researchers, and school-based educators.

The main plank of our argument is that standards can be raised only by changes that are put into direct effect by teachers and pupils in classrooms. There is a body of firm evidence that formative assessment is an essential component of classroom work and that its development can raise standards of achievement. We know of no other way of raising standards for which such a strong prima facie case can be made. Our plea is that national and state policy makers will grasp this opportunity and take the lead in this direction.

1. James W. Stigler and James Hiebert, "Understanding and Improving Classroom Mathematics Instruction: An Overview of the TIMSS Video Study," *Phi Delta Kappan,* September 1997, pp. 19–20.

2. There is no internationally agreed-upon term here. "Classroom evaluation," "classroom assessment," "internal assessment," "instructional assessment," and "student assessment" have been used by different authors, and some of these terms have different meanings in different texts.

3. Paul Black and Dylan Wiliam, "Assessment and Classroom Learning," *Assessment in Education*, March 1998, pp. 7–74.

4. Lynn S. Fuchs and Douglas Fuchs, "Effects of Systematic Formative Evaluation: A Meta-Analysis," *Exceptional Children*, vol. 53, 1986, pp. 199–208.

5. See Albert E. Beaton et al., *Mathematics Achievement in the Middle School Years* (Boston: Boston College, 1996).

6. Lynn S. Fuchs et al., "Effects of Task-Focused Goals on Low-Achieving Students with and Without Learning Disabilities," *American Educational Research Journal*, vol. 34, 1997, pp. 513–543.

7. OFSTED (Office for Standards in Education), *Subjects and Standards: Issues for School Development Arising from OFSTED Inspection Findings 1994–5: Key Stages 3 and 4 and Post-16* (London: Her Majesty's Stationery Office, 1996), p. 40.

8. Nicholas Daws and Birendra Singh, "Formative Assessment: To What Extent Is Its Potential to Enhance Pupils' Science Being Realized?," *School Science Review*, vol. 77, 1996, p. 99.

9. Clement Dassa, Jes's Vazquez-Abad, and Djavid Ajar, "Formative Assessment in a Classroom Setting: From Practice to Computer Innovations," *Alberta Journal of Educational Research*, vol. 39, 1993, p. 116.

10. D. Monty Neill, "Transforming Student Assessment," *Phi Delta Kappan*, September 1997, pp. 35–36.

11. *Task Group on Assessment and Testing: A Report* (London: Department of Education and Science and the Welsh Office, 1988).

12. Richard Daugherty, *National Curriculum Assessment: A Review of Policy, 1987–1994* (London: Falmer Press, 1995).

13. Terry A. Russell, Anne Qualter, and Linda McGuigan, "Reflections on the Implementation of National Curriculum Science Policy for the 5–14 Age Range: Findings and Interpretations from a National Evaluation Study in England," *International Journal of Science Education*, vol. 17, 1995, pp. 481–492.

14. Phillipe Perrenoud, "Towards a Pragmatic Approach to Formative Evaluation," in Penelope Weston, ed., Assessment of Pupils' Achievement: Motivation and School Success (Amsterdam: Swets and Zeitlinger, 1991), p. 92.

15. D. Royce Sadler, "Formative Assessment and the Design of Instructional Systems," Instructional Science, vol. 18, 1989, pp. 119–144.

16. Paul J. Black and J. Myron Atkin, Changing the Subject: Innovations in Science, Mathematics, and Technology Education (London: Routledge for the Organisation for Economic Co-operation and Development, 1996); and Michael G. Fullan, with Suzanne Stiegelbauer, The New Meaning of Educational Change (London: Cassell, 1991).

17. See Stigler and Hiebert, pp. 19–20.

18. Black and Atkin, op. cit.

19. Peter Johnston et al., "Assessment of Teaching and Learning in Literature-Based Classrooms," *Teaching and Teacher Education*, vol. 11, 1995, p. 359.

20. Dylan Wiliam and Paul Black, "Meanings and Consequences: A Basis for Distinguishing Formative and Summative Functions of Assessment," *British Educational Research Journal*, vol. 22, 1996, pp. 537–548.

21. These points are developed in some detail in Sam Wineburg, "T. S. Eliot, Collaboration, and the Quandaries of Assessment in a Rapidly Changing World," *Phi Delta Kappan*, September 1997, pp. 59–65.

Table 1-1

Comparing Assessment *of* and *for* Learning:
Overview of Key Differences

	Assessment for Learning	*Assessment of Learning*
Reasons for Assessing	Promote increases in achievement to help students meet more standards; support ongoing student growth; improvement	Document individual or group achievement or mastery of standards; measure achievement status at a point in time for purposes of reporting; accountability
Audience	Students about themselves	Others about students
Focus of Assessment	Specific achievement targets selected by teachers that enable students to build toward standards	Achievement standards for which schools, teachers, and students are held accountable
Place in Time	Process during learning	Event after learning
Primary Users	Students, teachers, parents	Policy makers, program planners, supervisors, teachers, students, parents
Typical Uses	Provide students with insight to improve achievement; help teachers diagnose and respond to student needs; help parents see progress over time; help parents support learning	Certify competence or sort students according to achievement for public relations, gatekeeper decisions, grading, graduation, or advancement

	Assessment for Learning	*Assessment of Learning*
Teacher's Role	Transform standards into classroom targets; inform students of targets; build assessments; adjust instruction based on results; involve students in assessment	Administer the test carefully to ensure accuracy and comparability of results; use results to help students meet standards; interpret results for parents; teachers also build assessments for report card grading
Student's Role	Self-assess and contribute to setting goals; act on classroom assessment results to be able to do better next time	Study to meet standards; take the test; strive for the highest possible score; avoid failure
Primary Motivator	Belief that success in learning is achievable	Threat of punishment, promise of rewards
Examples	Using rubrics with students; student self-assessment; descriptive feedback to students	Achievement tests; final exams; placement tests, short cycle assessments

Source: Adapted from *Understanding School Assessment* (pp. 17 and 18), by J. Chappuis and S. Chappuis,, 2002, Portland, OR: Assessment Training Institute. Adapted by permission.

Table 1-2
Purposes for (Users and Uses of) Assessment

Assessment User	Assessment *for* Learning	Assessment *of* Learning
Students	Am I improving over time? Do I know what it means to succeed? What should I do next? What help do I need?	Am I succeeding at the level that I should be? Am I capable of success? How am I doing in relationship to my classmates? Is the learning worth the effort?
Teachers	What does this student need? What do these students need? What are student strengths to build on? How should I group my students? Am I going too fast? Too slow? Too far? Not far enough?	What grade do I put on the report card? What students need to be referred for special service? What will I tell parents?
Parents	What can we do at home to support learning? Is my child learning new things?	Is my child keeping up? Is this teacher doing a good job? Is this a good school? District?
Principal		Is instruction producing results? Are our students ready for the workplace or the next step in learning? How shall we allocate building resources to achieve success?
Superintendent		Are our programs of instruction producing desired results? Is each building producing results? Which schools need additional resources? How shall we allocate district resources to achieve success?
State Department of Education		Are programs across the state producing results? Are individual districts producing results? Who is making adequate yearly progress and who is not? How shall we allocate district resources to achieve success?
Citizens		Are our students achieving in ways that prepare them to become productive workers and citizens?

Source: Adapted from *Student-Involved Assessment FOR Learning,* 4th ed. (pp. 22, 24, 25), by R. J. Stiggins, 2005, Upper Saddle River, NJ: Merrill/Prentice Hall. Copyright ©2005 by Pearson Education, Inc. Adapted by permission of Pearson Education, Inc.

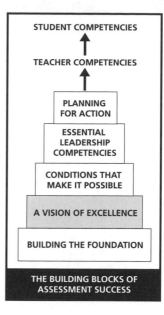

STUDENT COMPETENCIES

TEACHER COMPETENCIES

PLANNING
FOR ACTION

ESSENTIAL
LEADERSHIP
COMPETENCIES

CONDITIONS THAT
MAKE IT POSSIBLE

A VISION OF EXCELLENCE

BUILDING THE FOUNDATION

THE BUILDING BLOCKS OF
ASSESSMENT SUCCESS

*A balanced assessment system takes advantage of assessment **of** learning and assessment **for** learning; each can make essential contributions. When both are present in the system, assessment becomes more than just an index of school success. It also serves as the cause of that success.*

Part Two

A VISION
OF THE
PERFECT
ASSESSMENT
SYSTEM

American education has been unable to agree on the role and effective use of standardized testing since the middle of the twentieth century. We have had difficulty agreeing on what to assess, why to assess it, how to assess it, and how to use the results to assist learning. It is testimony to our failure to come to terms with the relationship between assessment and school improvement that, in the year 2005, little evidence exists to show that 60 years of standardized testing has contributed significantly to the improvement of our educational system. This in spite of the fact that we have spent billions of dollars over the past six decades developing and administering college admissions, district, state, national, and international assessments. Yet, even so, in 2001 we adopted our first-ever national every-pupil examination system with the unprecedented testing requirements of the No Child Left Behind Act. In so doing, we once again demonstrated our societal belief in assessment *of* learning as a school improvement tool, especially when coupled with accountability sanctions and rewards.

We are now at a time when standards-based schools and NCLB require us to help all students learn well. We need to analyze our assessment systems once and for all, figure out the roadblocks to our effective use of assessment to improve student achievement, and implement programs that help educators help students learn using assessment as good teaching, not just as a measurement tool.

The purpose of this section of the guide is to introduce school leaders to the components needed for an effective assessment system. Here we provide our own vision of excellence in assessment. With this vision in mind, and with the added detail and school/district analysis activity provided in Part 3, educators can determine where they are now and develop a plan to achieve a sound, balanced, and instructionally supportive assessment system.

The Perfect Assessment System

Assessment is the process of gathering evidence of student learning to inform instructional decisions. To work effectively, local assessment systems must produce accurate evidence and deliver it in a timely and understandable form into the hands of all instructional decision makers, so they can use it to support student learning. The perfect assessment system helps all assessment users take advantage of both the process and its results to keep students confident and striving to learn.

We advocate for an assessment system that is *perfect* because to do anything else would seem to allow students to continue to be harmed by assessment when it is done poorly. So to work effectively, the perfect assessment system must be developed and implemented by educators who hold certain beliefs about students, learning, and assessment. Without those beliefs and values, the system is not likely to tap the full potential of assessment as a school improvement tool.

At the school and/or district level, we think the leadership required to make all of this possible must meet the following criteria:

- Have a vision of excellence in assessment that is in balance and that meets the information needs of *all* users, from students and teachers to board members and legislators.
- Understand the conditions, including the assessment competencies of administrators, that must be in place for a balanced vision to be attained; that is, know the path that leads from where the district or school is now to an assessment system that is in balance.
- Understand the research on classroom assessment, recognizing that assessment quality and accuracy, descriptive feedback, and student involvement are essential to realizing the student achievement gains research tells us occur when principles of assessment *for* learning are applied in the classroom.
- Be willing to secure and allocate the resources needed to remove barriers to assessment competence.

Fundamental Beliefs and Values

A local school district assessment system must arise from and reflect the following guiding beliefs.

☐ *The mission of school is to maximize student success at meeting specified academic achievement standards.*

In standards-driven schools, success is determined by the proportion of students who meet standards. The greater that proportion, the more effective is the school. This is different from the past, when *effectiveness* meant that schools produced a rank order of students, from the highest to lowest achiever, by the end of high school. Today's schools must help *all* students develop established reading, writing, and math problem-solving proficiencies. Society expects this: attainment of standards sets students up to survive in and contribute to an increasingly complex society.

☐ *All students can learn.*

To maximize success students, teachers, student families, and school administrators must truly believe that all students can, if they try, hit achievement targets appropriate for them. The foundation of every student's belief that they are a capable learner is their prior academic record of success at learning. Students who expect to succeed in the future are those who have done so in the past. They are confident. Those who have experienced chronic failure can lose confidence, become hopeless about ever succeeding, and stop trying. If they have not yet met standards, this becomes a huge problem, and it is part of our job to prevent this from happening. Our learning and assessment systems must be built to promote confidence, optimism, and more learning for all students.

☐ *But students will not all learn at the same rate.*

One of the realities is that, while all students can learn, they will not all start at the same place, learn at the same rate, or reach the same ultimate level of proficiency. This is because of differences in academic ability, interests, and commitments. The perfect assessment system will accommodate these by providing a continuous-progress curriculum and then by relying on assessment, record keeping, and communication processes that provide accurate information that adjusts to student needs.

This need to accommodate certainly manifests itself with those students who bring special needs to the classroom. Those with learning challenges are entitled to assessment procedures that are consistent with the stipulations of their individual educational plans. This entitlement is granted to them as a matter of law. But in a perfect assessment system, there is more.

For example, in a perfect system, students with learning disabilities are never held accountable for meeting standards that they have no hope of achieving. Specifically, that means that they are never given a test consisting of exercises on which they are doomed to fail. For instance, when they are given test exercises that they cannot even read, let alone respond to, hopelessness results. When the test is written in a language that they don't speak, discouragement follows. The effect of doing these kinds of things can be devastating to their confidence in themselves as learners, and can bring an end to their willingness to risk trying to learn. To counter this, in a perfect system, these students complete standardized tests when everyone is sure they are ready to demonstrate competence. Thus, the assessment is intended to *corroborate what is already known* about the student's achievement.

Accommodations also are needed for those who bring diverse cultural or linguistic backgrounds to the classroom. In assessment contexts, the danger of bias is strong. Accurate assessment is only possible if exercises and scoring procedures are developed and applied in ways that ensure the collection of dependable information.

For all students, from those most academically challenged to the most gifted, the perfect assessment system accommodates their rate of achievement, always presenting opportunities to demonstrate immediately success at learning—not before or long after.

In a perfect assessment system, periodic standardized assessments *of* learning and continuous classroom assessments *for* learning—each reflective of enabling achievement targets or standards—feed information about individual students' achievement into an information management system that shows where each is at any point in time relative to state standards. This reservoir of information is used in calculated ways—in its entirety or in summary form—to help decision makers keep all students believing that they can keep learning if they keep trying—regardless of the pace of their development or how other students are progressing. In all cases, student, teacher, and family remain in touch with the student's improvement over time.

Periodically, evidence of achievement is aggregated across students to reflect group performance for public reporting. That evidence can be presented in both criterion- and norm-referenced ways and will influence important programmatic decisions. But once again, the evidence is interpreted in terms of how performance today compares to previous performance. Only then can the public see viable evidence of school effectiveness.

☐ *Communities must understand and support sound assessment practices.*

In the perfect assessment system, those stakeholders in school quality who are not professional educators, such as parents, taxpayers, and politicians, also know and understand sound assessment practice. While they are not able to apply those practices as teachers and administrators can, they understand that assessments gather evidence of student learning for purposes of instructional planning—not just to assign grades and raise annual test scores (although these will be among the effects of implementing sound practices). It is only with this kind of understanding that community members will sign off on implementing sound practices in ways that permit their use in the classroom and school.

☐ *The desire to learn must come from within the learner.*

Learners, not teachers, are in charge of learning. If students don't want to learn or don't feel able to succeed at learning, there will be no learning. In the past, schools have operated on the belief that, if I judge you to have failed or threaten to do so, it will cause you to try harder. This is only true if students believe that trying harder is likely to result in success. Absent this belief, the threat is hollow and cannot enhance learning. Often when it comes to assessment, we also have believed that, if a little intimidation doesn't work, use a lot of intimidation. Similarly, many teachers believed that to maximize learning, they must maximize learners' anxiety.

This blind societal faith in a relationship among tougher challenges, greater effort, and more learning has manifested itself in politicians' desire to "raise the bar" by adopting "world-class standards" mapped onto "high-stakes tests." These are attempts to tap the motivational power of assessment by using it to turn up the heat.

In fact, increased intimidation and anxiety work to drive up learning only if learners possess and can muster the inner reserves of confidence and intellectual power needed to respond productively. For students on extended losing streaks in the classroom, increasing intimidation and anxiety will have exactly the opposite effect: it will cause them to give up. As a challenged learner, if I see standards going even higher and assessments becoming even tougher than the ones I already have been failing at for years, I am most likely to feel defeated, not

31

energized. Our learning and assessment systems must honor these differences in academic histories and dispositions among our students if they are to promote hope for all.

☐ *Intellectual capabilities are not fixed within learners; rather, capacity to learn can be improved with proper interventions and experiences.*

Instituting accountability for learning cannot by itself create good schools. Merely instructing educators and students that annual test scores must go up and then applying punitive consequences if they do not does only so much to improve the quality of schools. As the saying goes, you don't fatten the hog merely by weighing it. Rather, we must intervene in the system to cause change to happen. We didn't put men on the moon by building a great telescope through which to watch them land. We built, tested, and implemented systems to put them there, continually evaluating and adjusting their progress. Doctors don't cure patients just by checking lab tests. They intervene with pharmacological treatments and use the lab tests to see if the treatments are working. Schools will not maximize learning merely by testing it frequently. We get good schools by intervening in the classroom to promote greater achievement. In the perfect system, we use assessment to check for achievement, to be sure. But we also use assessment as good instruction to promote learning.

☐ *All assessment users are important.*

There is a way in which assessment can contribute to developing effective schools that has been largely ignored in the evolution of the standards, assessment, and accountability scenario described here. We combine our high-stakes standardized assessments *of* learning with other assessments to be used *for* learning (Assessment Reform Group, 1999). Whereas assessment *of* learning as described provides an index of school success, assessment *for* learning serves to help students learn more. Assessment becomes more than an index of school success, it becomes a cause of school success. The crucial distinction is between *assessment to determine the status of learning* and *assessment to promote greater learning.*

☐ *The professional environment surrounding assessment in schools of the past cannot be the environment of the future.*

We have established a need to shift the culture of assessment in schools in three important ways.

- We have used assessment almost exclusively as an accountability tool, but now we seek to supplement that with efforts to use assessment to support learning.
- In that same sense, we have favored standardized tests, but now wish to assign classroom assessment its role in school improvement.
- Finally, we have favored the information needs of adult users and now wish to honor the needs of all assessment users, young and old, in the service of student success.

In addition, there is one more important cultural shift needed in the manner in which we address assessment in schools. Historically, neither teachers nor administrators have been trained in, nor have they been expected to understand, the principles of sound assessment practice. As a result, we remain largely a national faculty unable to fulfill our assessment responsibilities. For this reason, in a very real sense, practicing teachers and administrators have been victimized by an assessment environment over which they have little influence. Regardless of state licensing requirements for competence in assessment or previous coverage of assessment competencies in preservice preparation programs, practicing educators must take responsibility for learning about and routinely applying principles of sound practice. Without this professional leadership, we will not achieve the deep cultural shifts needed to balance assessment in all key ways.

What Is "Assessment *for* Learning"?

It is tempting to equate this concept with the more common term, *formative assessment.* They are not the same. Assessment *for* learning is about far more than testing more frequently or providing teachers with evidence so they can revise instruction, although these are part of it. Assessment *for* learning must actively involve students.

When they assess *for* learning, teachers use classroom assessment and the continuous flow of information about student achievement that it provides to advance, not merely check on, student learning. They accomplish this by doing the following:

- Understanding and articulating *in advance of teaching* the achievement targets that their students are to hit.

- Informing their students about those learning goals *in terms that students understand* from the very beginning.

- Becoming assessment literate so they can transform those expectations into assessment exercises and scoring procedures that *accurately reflect student achievement.*

- Using classroom assessments *to build student confidence* in themselves as learners, helping them take responsibility for their own learning so as to lay a foundation for lifelong learning.

- Translating classroom assessment results into *frequent, descriptive (versus judgmental) feedback* for students, providing them with specific insights regarding their strengths as well as how to improve.

- Continuously *adjusting instruction* based on the results of classroom assessments.

- Engaging students in *regular self-assessment* with standards held constant so they can watch themselves grow over time and thus learn to become in charge of their own success.

- Actively *involving students in communicating* with their teachers and their families about their achievement status and improvement.

- Making sure that students understand *how the achievement targets* that they strive to hit now *relate to those that will come after.*

As presented in the accompanying DVD and in Table 1-1, we can use assessment to support and to verify learning—assessment *of* and *for* learning. In the assessment *of* learning context, it has been our habit to think of adults as the primary instructional decision makers—as the primary assessment users in school improvement. To be sure, parents, teachers, school leaders, and other grownups do make critically important instructional decisions. Further, these decisions have more positive impact when they are informed by evidence of the current state of student learning.

But students are important data-based instructional decision makers, too. They read the continuous flow of evidence of their own success and use it to decide whether, how, and under what conditions to continue or discontinue the effort associated with learning. For this reason, our learning and assessment systems must honor their information needs, along with those of adults (for instruction and accountability), by ensuring timely delivery of understandable information into students' hands. This is the foundation of our concept of assessment *for* learning.

The Active Ingredients

Excellence in assessment requires that the values and beliefs stated here be transformed into assessment program components, each of which makes its contribution to the system while at the same time interacting to enhance the power of the others. (In Part 3 we define each program component in more detail.)

Carefully Defined Achievement Expectations

The starting place for articulating achievement expectations must be achievement standards, whether state, local, or classroom. Ultimately our assessments *of* learning must bring us information about how each student has performed on each standard.

Next, to lay the foundation for assessments *for* learning, schools and/or districts must deconstruct each standard into the classroom-level achievement targets that students must master over time on their journey up to that standard. To determine the ascending levels of proficiency, local curriculum developers and teachers must start with a clear understanding of the standard and then ask the following questions:

- What must students know and understand when the time comes to demonstrate that they have mastered this standard? What are the knowledge foundations of success here?
- What patterns of reasoning, if any, must students be capable of applying at that time when they are called on to demonstrate mastery of this standard? How must they be ready to use their knowledge to figure something out?
- What performance skills, if any, must they have mastered to be ready to demonstrate mastery of this standard when that time comes?

35

- What products must they be ready to create, if any, to demonstrate mastery of this standard?

All standards can be analyzed in this manner to design the written curriculum that maps the ongoing sequence of learning targets and assessments *for* and *of* learning that will guide student learning in standards-driven schools. Such curriculum maps are needed to guide learning both within and across grade levels.

Finally, as teachers, we must transform each enabling classroom learning target (knowledge, reasoning, skills, or products) into student-friendly terms and share them with learners from the very beginning of learning. We accomplish this by translating each target into familiar vocabulary and grammatical contexts and by pairing those descriptions with models of strong and weak work that we also share with students.

Honoring All Users and Uses

If *assessment* is the process of gathering information to facilitate instructional decision making, then the question here is, What are those decisions and who is making them? Each assessment must be built and used to help someone do something that improves learning. We cannot help with information unless and until we know who needs what help.

We already have established that a variety of different people need access to a variety of different kinds of information at different times and in different forms to do their jobs. For instance, there are classroom-level users: students, teachers, and parents. Sometimes teachers use evidence to support learning of individual students or small groups, other times they use it to verify learning among their students for accountability purposes. They use assessment *for* learning and so need access to a continuous flow evidence of learning.

There also are users at levels of instructional support, as well as policy and resource allocation, whose decisions are less frequent and generally more far reaching, affecting the learning of large numbers of students. They need less precise evidence less frequently. These are accountability decisions—the purview of assessment *of* learning.

Dependable Evidence of Learning

To inform instructional decisions appropriately, the perfect assessment system must provide decision makers with accurate information about student achievement. Whether used to support learning or to verify it, the system is only as good as the evidence it generates.

Creating a dependable assessment involves four specific design decisions. First, the creator must select a proper assessment method. Four categories of methods are available: selected response (multiple choice, true/false, etc.), written response (essay), performance assessments (observation and judgment), and direct personal interaction with students (questions and answers during instruction, for example). These methods are not interchangeable. Each works better as reflections of some kinds of achievement than of others. Accuracy turns, in part, on finding a strong match of target to method.

Second, the creator must develop enough items, tasks, or exercises for the assessment to provide a sufficient sample of student performance to lead to a confident conclusion about proficiency. Any test includes a sample of all the questions we could have asked but didn't have time for. The assessor must include enough to permit a generalization from student performance on this sample to the broad domain of achievement that it samples.

Third, the assessment items, tasks, or exercises must be of high quality in their own right. We need good multiple-choice items, essay exercises and scoring guides, or performance tasks and rubrics. Vague, poorly worded, or imprecise questions or directions can keep learners from showing what they know and can do.

Finally, even if the creator selects a proper method and samples sufficiently with quality items, other sources of interference can bias or distort the results. For instance, distracting problems can arise during administration of the assessment, such as noise or other attention grabbers; students may become ill or emotionally upset; or evaluator bias may distort scoring. Accurate assessment requires that assessors anticipate as many such factors as possible and act to keep them from distorting results.

Effective Management and Communication of Results

Thinking in terms of the total educational system, the active ingredients start with a clear sense of the kind(s) of achievement to be assessed and a clear sense of who is going to use the results and how. These get translated into accurate assessments. To complete the picture, once the assessment results are in, they need to find their way into the hands of their intended users in a timely and understandable form. This presents information management and communication challenges.

Evidence must accumulate within the system in ways that permit it to be shared in a variety of forms with a variety of intended users. For instance, in assessment *for* learning environments, where students and teachers are managing student progress to mastering standards, the system must reveal changes in achievement over time in terms that both student and teacher understand. Because of the focus on individual student learning, this evidence need not always be comparable across schools, classrooms, or even students, as long as it supports the learning of each student it is intended to guide.

With assessment *of* learning, when the purpose is to verify learning at a particular point in time, the system must specify which students have met which standards. Or in a different assessment *of* learning context, policy makers and resource appropriators must know how many or what proportion of students met which standards. These results do need to be comparable so scores can be aggregated as appropriate for reporting.

Certain principles must be observed to ensure that assessment results are effectively communicated to intended users. For example, both those delivering evidence and those receiving it must hold a common understanding of the achievement to be mastered. If they hold different definitions of what it means to succeed, they will have difficulty communicating about student performance on any assessment. This also means they must share a common meaning of any symbols used to share information, such as test scores, report card grades, work samples, and so on. If each understands these shorthand symbols differently, miscommunication is assured.

The Promise of Balanced Assessment Systems

The overlooked school improvement question is this: What would happen to standardized test scores if we brought classroom assessment *for* learning online as a full partner in support of school improvement? Published reviews of research reveal the encouraging answer.

Research Results

In 1984, Bloom provided a summary of research on the impact of mastery learning models comparing standard whole-class instruction (the control condition) with two experimental interventions, a mastery learning environment and one-on-one tutoring of individual students. One hallmark of both experimental conditions was use of classroom assessment as a key part of instruction. The analyses showed differences ranging from one to two standard deviations in student achievement favoring the classroom assessment experimental conditions.

You will recall the 1998 research review presented in Part 1. Black and Wiliam examined the research literature on assessment worldwide, asking if there is evidence that improving the quality and effectiveness of use of formative (classroom) assessments raises student achievement as reflected in summative assessments. If so, they asked, what kinds of improvements in classroom assessment practice are likely to yield gains in achievement?

They collected and then synthesized over 250 articles that addressed these issues. Of these, several dozen directly addressed the question of impact on student learning with sufficient scientific rigor and experimental control to permit firm conclusions. Pooling the information on the estimated effects of improved formative assessment on summative test scores, they discovered unprecedented positive effects on student achievement. They report effect sizes of a half to a full standard deviation. Further, Black and Wiliam (1998) report that "improved formative assessment helps low achievers more than other students and so reduces the range of achievement while raising achievement overall." *This result has direct implications for districts seeking to reduce achievement gaps between minorities and other students.* We know of no other school improvement intervention that can claim effects of this nature or this size.

This research tells us that these achievement gains are maximized in contexts where educators do the following:

- Increase the accuracy and quality of classroom assessments
- Provide students with frequent descriptive feedback (versus evaluative feedback)
- Involve students in classroom assessment, including record keeping and communication, especially with low-achieving students

In short, students learn more when teachers apply the principles of assessment *for* learning as a matter of routine in their classrooms.

Summary: Balance Is Essential

The perfect assessment system is set up and managed by those who believe that the mission of school is to ensure all students learn well. They know that all students can learn, and are prepared to accommodate differences in the rate of learning. They understand that productive learning environments help students improve their capacity to learn and so seek learning and assessment interventions to support that growth. Educators in these systems operate on the belief that the desire to learn must come from within the learner and they know that this desire can be triggered and supported by balancing assessment *of* learning with assessment *for* learning, as depicted in Figure 2-1. These system developers and users understand and acknowledge the historic gap in teachers' and administrators' training in sound assessment practices that has made it impossible for practitioners to take responsibility for making classroom assessment work well for them and their students, and they fill that gap with professional development around sound practices.

Figure 2-1

Assessment Synergy

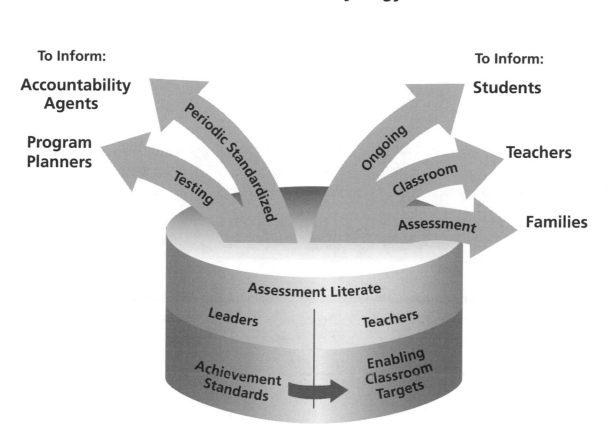

Thinking About Assessment

Activity 2: "Emily's Story"

Purpose: To illustrate high-quality assessment in action in the lives of real students, teachers, administrators, and policy makers.

Time: 40 minutes after reading and discussing Part 2 of this guide.

Directions: Read the story of Emily, reflecting on the keys to success: What conditions needed to be in place for Emily and her classmates, Ms. Weathersby and her colleagues, school leaders, and the community to facilitate this success?

Brainstorm lists of those necessary conditions by answering the following questions:

- What conditions needed to be in place in Ms. W's classroom?
- What conditions needed to be in place in the English Department and the high school?
- What contribution did the district need to make for this success to happen?
- What contribution did the school board and community need to make?

As a leadership team, then, address the following questions:

- To what extent are these conditions satisfied in your classrooms, schools, district, and community?
- Do you need to change or add to your team's vision of assessment excellence as a result of reading this story?

A STORY OF CLASSROOM SUCCESS

Emily's Story

A Vision of Success

At a local school board meeting, the English faculty from the high school presents the results of their evaluation of the new writing instruction program that they had implemented over the past year. The audience includes a young woman named Emily, a junior at the local high school, sitting in the back of the room with her parents. She knows she will be a big part of the presentation. She's only a little nervous. She understands how important her role is. It has been quite a year for her, unlike any she has ever experienced in school before. She also knows her parents and teacher are as proud of her as she is of herself.

As part of their preparation for this program, the English faculty attended a summer institute on assessing writing proficiency and integrating such assessments into their teaching and their students' learning. The teachers were confident that this kind of professional development and their subsequent program revisions would produce much higher levels of writing proficiency.

As the first step in presenting program evaluation results, the English department chair, Ms. Weathersby, who also happens to be Emily's English teacher, distributes a sample of student writing to the board members (with the student's name removed), asking them to read and evaluate this writing. They do so, expressing their dismay aloud as they go. They are less than complimentary in their commentary on these samples of student work. One board member reports with some frustration that, if these represent the results of that new writing program, the new program clearly is not working. The board member is right. This is, in fact, a pretty weak piece of work. Emily's mom puts her arm around her daughter's shoulder and hugs her.

But Ms. Weathersby urges patience and asks the board members to be very specific in stating what they don't like about this work. As the board registers its complaints, a faculty member records the criticisms on chart paper for all to see. The list is long, including everything from repetitiveness to disorganization to short, choppy sentences and disconnected ideas.

Next, Ms. Weathersby distributes another sample of student writing, asking the board to read and evaluate it. Ah, now this, they report, is more like it! This work is much better! But be specific, she demands. What do you like about this work? They list positive aspects: good choice of words, sound sentence structure, clever ideas, and so on. Emily is ready to burst! She squeezes her mom's hand.

The reason she's so full of pride at this moment is that this has been a special year for her and her classmates. For the first time ever, they became partners with their English teachers in managing their own improvement as writers. Early in the year, Ms. Weathersby ("Ms. W," they all call her) made it crystal clear to Emily that she was, in fact, not a very good writer and that just trying hard to get better was not going to be enough. She expected Emily to improve—nothing else would suffice.

Ms. W. started the year by working with students to implement new state writing standards, including understanding quality performance in word choice, sentence structure, organization, and voice, and by sharing some new "analytical scoring guides" written just for students. Each scoring guide explained the differences between good and poor-quality writing in understandable terms. When Emily and her teacher evaluated her first two pieces of writing using these standards, she received very low ratings. Not very good. . . .

Source: Reprinted from *Student-Involved Assessment FOR Learning,* 4th ed. (pp. 6–11), by R. J. Stiggins, 2005, Upper Saddle River, NJ: Merrill/Prentice Hall. Copyright ©2005 by Pearson Education, Inc. Reprinted by permission of Pearson Education, Inc.

But she also began to study samples of writing Ms. W. provided that Emily could see were very good. Slowly, she began to understand why they were good. The differences between these and her work started to become clear. Ms. W. began to share examples and strategies that would help her writing improve one step at a time. As she practiced and time passed, Emily and her classmates kept samples of their old writing to compare to their new writing, and they began to build portfolios. Thus, she literally began to watch her own writing skills improve before her very eyes. At midyear, her parents were invited in for a conference at which Emily, not Ms. Weathersby, shared the contents of her portfolio and discussed her emerging writing skills. Emily remembers sharing thoughts about some aspects of her writing that had become very strong and some examples of things she still needed to work on. Now, the year was at an end and here she sat waiting for her turn to speak to the school board about all of this. What a year!

Now, having set the board up by having them analyze, evaluate, and compare these two samples of student work, Ms. W. springs a surprise. The two pieces of writing they had just evaluated, one of relatively poor quality and one of outstanding quality, were produced by the same writer at the beginning and at the end of the school year! This, she reports, is evidence of the kind of impact the new writing program is having on student writing proficiency.

Needless to say, all are impressed. However, one board member wonders aloud, "Have all your students improved in this way?" Having anticipated the question, the rest of the English faculty joins the presentation and produces carefully prepared charts depicting dramatic changes in typical student performance over time on rating scales for each of six clearly articulated dimensions of good writing. They accompany their description of student performance on each scale with actual samples of student work illustrating various levels of proficiency.

Further, Ms. W. informs the board that the student whose improvement has been so dramatically illustrated with the work they have just analyzed is present at this school board meeting, along with her parents. This student is ready to talk with the board about the nature of her learning experience. Emily, you're on!

Interest among the board members runs high. Emily talks about how she has come to understand the truly important differences between good and bad writing. She refers to differences she had not understood before, how she has learned to assess her own writing and to fix it when it doesn't "work well," and how she and her classmates have learned to talk with her teacher and each other about what it means to write well. Ms. W. talks about the improved focus of writing instruction, increase in student motivation, and important positive changes in the very nature of the student–teacher relationship.

A board member asks Emily if she likes to write, and she answers, "I do now!" This board member turns to Emily's parents and asks their impression of all of this. They report with pride that they had never seen so much evidence before of Emily's achievement and most of it came from Emily herself. Emily had never been called on to lead the parent-teacher conference before. They had no idea she was so articulate. They loved it. Their daughter's pride in and accountability for her achievement has skyrocketed in the past year.

As the meeting ends, it is clear to all in attendance that evening that this application of student-involved classroom assessment had contributed to important learning. The English faculty accepted responsibility for student learning, shared that responsibility with their students, and everybody won. There are good feelings all around. One of the accountability demands of the community was satisfied with the presentation of credible evidence of student success, and the new writing program was the reason for improved student achievement. Obviously, this story has a happy ending.

Success from the Student's Point of View

The day after the board meeting, I interviewed Emily about the evening's events. As you read, think about how our conversation centers on what really works for Emily.

"You did a nice job at the school board meeting last night, Emily," I started.

"Thanks," she replied. "What's most exciting form me is that, last year, I could never have done it."

"What's changed from last year?"

"I guess I'm more confident. I knew what had happened for me in English class and I wanted to tell them my story."

"You became a confident writer."

"Yeah, but that's not what I mean. Last night at the board meeting I was more than a good writer. I felt good talking about my writing and how I'd improved. It's like, I understand what had happened to me and I have a way to describe it."

"Let's talk about Emily the confident writer. What were you thinking last night when the board members were reacting to your initial writing sample—you know, the one that wasn't very good? Still confident?"

"Mom helped. She squeezed my hand and I remember she whispered in my ear, "You'll show 'em!" That helped me handle it. It's funny, I was listening to their comments to see if they knew anything about good writing. I wondered if they understood as much about it as I do—like, maybe they needed to take Ms. Weathersby's class."

"How did they do?" I asked, laughing.

"Pretty well, actually, Em replied. "They found some problems in my early work and described them pretty well. When I first started last fall, I wouldn't have been able to do that. I was a terrible writer."

"How do you know that, Em?

"No I understand where I was then, how little I could do. No organization. I didn't even know my own voice. No one had ever taken the time to show me the secrets. I'd never learned to analyze my writing. I wouldn't have known what to look for or how to describe it or how to change it. That's part of what Ms. W. taught us."

"How did she do that?"

"To begin with, she taught us to do what the board members did last night: analyze other people's writing. We looked at newspaper editorials, passages from books we were reading, letters friends had sent us. She wanted us to see what made those pieces work or not work. She would read a piece to us and then we'd brainstorm what made it good or bad. Pretty soon, we began to see patterns—things that worked or didn't work. She wanted us to begin to see and hear stuff as she read out loud."

"Like what?" I asked.

"Well, look, here's my early piece from the meeting last night. See, just read it!"

(Please read the Beginning of the Year Sample in Figure 2-2.)

Figure 2-2

BEGINNING OF THE YEAR Writing Sample

Computers are a thing of the future. They help us in thousands of ways. Computers are a help to our lives. They make things easier. They help us to keep track of information.

Computers are simple to use. Anyone can learn how. You do not have to be a computer expert to operate a computer. You just need to know a few basic things.

Computers can be robots that will change our lives. Robots are really computers! Robots do a lot of the work that humans used to do. This makes our lives much easier. Robots build cars and do many other tasks that humans used to do. When robots learn to do more, they will take over most of our work. This will free humans to do other kinds of things. You can also communicate on computers. It is much faster than mail! You can look up information, too. You can find information on anything at all on a computer.

Computers are changing the work and changing the way we work and communicate. In many ways, computers are changing our lives and making our lives better and easier.

Source: Personal writing by Nikki Spandel. Reprinted by permission.

"See, there are no grammar or usage mistakes. So it's 'correct' in that sense. But these short, choppy sentences just don't work. And it doesn't say anything or go anywhere. It's just a bunch of disconnected thoughts. It doesn't grab you and hold your attention. Then it just stops. It just ends. Now look at my second piece to see the difference."

(Please read the End of the Year Sample in Figure 2-3.)

"In this one, I tried to tell about the feelings of frustration that happen when humans use machines. See, I think the voice in this piece comes from the feeling that 'We've all been there.' Everyone who works with computers has had this experience. A writer's tiny problem (not being able to find a good ending) turns into a major problem (losing the whole document). This idea makes the piece clear and organized. I think the reader can picture this poor,

---

Figure 2-3

END OF THE YEAR Writing Sample

So there I was, my face aglow with the reflection on my computer screen, trying to come up with the next line for my essay. Writing it was akin to Chinese water torture, as I could never seem to end it. It dragged on and on, a never-ending babble of stuff.

Suddenly, unexpectedly—I felt an ending coming on. I could wrap this thing up in four or five sentences, and this dreadful assignment would be over. I'd be free.

I had not saved yet, and decided I would do so now. I clasped the slick, white mouse in my hand, slid it over the mouse pad, and watched as the black arrow progressed toward the "File" menu. By accident, I clicked the mouse button just to the left of paragraph 66. I saw a flash and the next thing I knew, I was back to square one. I stared at the blank screen for a moment in disbelief. Where was my essay? My ten-billion-page masterpiece? Gone?! No—that couldn't be! Not after all the work I had done! Would a computer be that unforgiving? That unfeeling? Didn't it care about me at all?

I decided not to give up hope just yet. The secret was to remain calm. After all, my file had to be *somewhere*—right? That's what all the manuals say—"It's in there somewhere." I went back to the "File" menu, much more carefully this time. First, I tried a friendly sounding category called "Find File." No luck there; I hadn't given the file a name.

Ah, then I had a brainstorm. I could simply go up to "Undo." Yes, that would be my savior! A simple click of a button and my problem would be solved! I went to Undo, but it looked a bit fuzzy. Not a good sign. That means there is nothing to undo. Don't panic ... don't panic ...

I decided to try to exit the program, not really knowing what I would accomplish by this but feeling more than a little desperate. Next, I clicked on the icon that would allow me back in to word processing. A small sign appeared, telling me that my program was being used by another user. Another user? What's it talking about? I'm the only user, you idiot! Or at least I'm trying to be a user! Give me my paper back! Right now!

I clicked on the icon again and again—to no avail. Click ... click ... clickclickclickCLICKCLICKCLICK!!!! Without warning, a thin cloud of smoke began to rise from the back of the computer. I didn't know whether to laugh or cry. Sighing, I opened my desk drawer, and pulled out a tablet and pen. It was going to be a long day.

Source: Personal writing by Nikki Spandel. Reprinted by permission.

frustrated writer at her computer, wanting, trying to communicate in a human way—but finding that the computer is just as frustrated with her!"

"You sound just like you did last night at the board meeting."

"I'm always like this about my writing now. I know what works. Sentences are important. So is voice. So are organization and word choice—all that stuff. If you do it right, it works and you know it," she replied with a smile.

"What kinds of things did Ms. W. do in class that worked for you?"

"Well, like, when we were first getting started, Ms. Weathersby gave us a big stack of student papers she'd collected over the years—some good, some bad, and everything in between. Our assignment was to sort them into four stacks based on quality, from real good to real bad. When we were done, we compared who put what papers in which piles and then we talked about why. Sometimes, the discussions got pretty heated! Ms. W. wanted us to describe what we thought were the differences among the piles. Over time, we formed those differences into a set of rating scales that we used to analyze, evaluate, and improve our writing."

"Did you evaluate your own work or each other's?"

"Only our own to begin with. Ms. W. said she didn't want anyone being embarrassed. We all had a lot to learn. It was supposed to be private until we began to trust our own judgments. She kept saying, 'Trust me. You'll get better at this and then you can share.'"

"Did you ever move on to evaluating each other's work?

"Yeah. After a while, we began to trust ourselves and each other. Then we were free to ask classmates for opinions. But Ms. W. said, no blanket judgments—no saying just, this is good or bad. And we were always supposed to be honest. If we couldn't see how to help someone improve a piece, we were supposed to say so."

"Were you able to see improvement in your writing along the way?" I wondered.

"Yeah, see, Ms. W. said that was the whole idea. I've still got my writing portfolio full of practice, see? It starts out pretty bad back in the fall and slowly gets pretty good toward spring. This is where the two pieces came from that the board read last night. I picked them. I talk about the changes in my writing in the self-reflections in here. My portfolio tells the whole story. Want to look through it?"

"I sure do. What do you think Ms. Weathersby did that was right, Emily?"

"Nobody had ever been so clear with me before about what it took to be really good at school stuff. It's like, there's no mystery—no need to psych her out. She said, 'I won't ever surprise you, trust me. I'll show you what I want and I don't want any excuses. But you've got to deliver good writing in this class. You don't deliver, you don't succeed.'

"Every so often, she would give us something she had written, so we could rate and provide her with feedback on her work. She listened to our comments and said it really helped her improve her writing. All of a sudden, *we* became *her* teachers! That was so cool!

"You know, she was the first teacher ever to tell me that it was okay not to be very good at something at first, like, when you're trying to do something new. But we couldn't stay there. We had to get a little better each time. If we didn't, it was our own fault. She didn't want us to give up on ourselves. If we kept improving, over time, we could learn to write well. I wish every teacher would do that. She would say, 'There's no shortage of success around here. You learn to write well, you get an A. My goal is to have everyone learn to write well and deserve an A.'"

"Thanks for filling in the details, Em."

"Thank you for asking!"

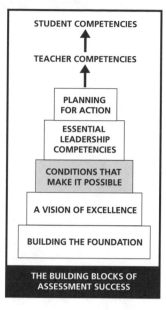

3

Leadership in the pursuit of assessment balance and quality begins with a guiding vision, clearly showing how assessment fits into effective instruction. School leaders must understand the importance of quality assessment at all levels, and must articulate the standards that will guide assessment practices in every classroom.

Part Three

THE PATH:
FIVE DOORS
TO EXCELLENCE
IN ASSESSMENT

Up to this point we've examined a vision of balance, quality, and student involvement in local assessment systems. These big ideas form the core of our vision of a perfect system. Should any of them be missing, we run the risk not just of having systems that are out of balance, but of assessing inaccurately, misrepresenting student achievement, and missing the learning opportunities presented to us through the principles of assessment *for* learning.

At the end of Part 2, in Activity 2, "Emily's Story," we asked your team to consider what conditions would be necessary in the district, school, and classroom to achieve the depicted level of student success. Here in Part 3 we will explain in more detail the conditions necessary for your vision to take hold in your own school or district. To some extent, these conditions may already be in place. Or, you may discover work that needs to be done in some areas but not in others. Whatever the case, without vision, and the leadership necessary to bring it to life, little is likely to change in the name of quality assessment.

Overview of the Path to the Perfect Assessment System

To integrate assessment *for* learning into the instructional program, districts and schools will need to examine five conditions we believe are necessary for excellence in assessment. For convenience, and like the old TV game show, we place them behind five doors that literally need to be opened. Behind each door is a set of tasks to be completed and suggestions for how to complete them. As the school or district accomplishes each task, it removes barriers and moves closer to its desired destination of a perfect assessment system. This is a long-term program of improvement; no district or school will be able to move forward on all five fronts at once. Each organization must establish its own priorities, its own starting places, and its own sequence for completing the work.

Door 1 calls for developing a *clearly articulated and appropriate set of achievement standards for each student* as the foundation for quality assessment. We can assess accurately only those achievement targets we have defined. Even with academic content standards now defined in every state, this remains for many schools and districts a local task that still requires attention.

Door 2 requires a commitment to providing *accurate, understandable, and usable information about student achievement to all users of assessment results*. We will consider how to plan to meet these many needs.

Door 3 requires an *assessment-literate school culture*. All educators must understand the differences between sound and unsound assessment practices as well as the implications of both. We will outline standards for quality assessment, and introduce a set of nine Principles of Assessment *for* Learning. (Please note that in this guide we only introduce the concepts: the practices that teachers need to master through their own professional development are presented for use by teachers in collaborative study teams in *Classroom Assessment* for *Student Learning: Doing It Right—Using It Well* [Assessment Training Institute, 2004].)

Door 4 leads us to reconsider how best to *collect, store, manage, and communicate information about student achievement*. All stakeholders in the educational system deserve information that is timely, accurate, and understandable, and that can lead to continued improvement.

Door 5 asks us to lay a *foundation of assessment policy that supports quality practices*. Some policies must be set at the state level, but most are put in place at the district and school levels. Sound assessment policy guides sound assessment practice. We will consider what that means, and which policies are most likely to lead to an educational environment supportive of quality assessment.

At the end of Part 3 we present a series of rating scales that the leadership of any school or district can use to gauge the current state of their assessment system. If your analysis leads to the conclusion that your assessment house is completely in order, kudos to the teachers, administrators, and communities who made that happen. But sometimes such appraisals also point to needed improvements. In those cases, we offer possible solutions.

DOOR 1

Focusing on Achievement Expectations

To assess student achievement accurately, teachers and administrators must know and understand the content standards that their students are to master. Again, we cannot teach or assess achievement that we have not defined. To establish clear and appropriate achievement expectations, a school district can take three steps.

First, the school community must agree on the meaning of academic success within its schools by asking, *What do we expect successful graduates of our local educational system to know and be able to do?* Now more than ever, in standards-based educational systems, the answer should take the form of high school graduation requirements stated in competency terms, not in credit hours or grade-point averages. Second, district curriculum directors and teachers for all grade levels must decide how that vision of success can be realized within the local curriculum. The result of their work must be a well-defined curriculum, coupled grade to grade and tightly aligned to state standards, that specifies how students progress from kindergarten through high school. Third, leaders must be sure all teachers are confident, competent masters of the achievement standards assigned as their instructional responsibility. We should not just assume that all teachers are, as a result of their preservice training, prepared to teach the content they are assigned.

Let's examine how these three pieces come together.

Agreeing on Achievement Expectations

We assume that effective schools maximize the achievement of the largest possible number of students. They are, or need to become, standards-driven institutions. The place to start is with a statement of achievement expectations for high school graduation. Opinions diverge about what those expectations should be. In almost every state, academic standards have been established that define what teachers should teach and what students should learn. Some are specific, others are broad and do not provide the scaffolding needed for teachers or students to make immediate sense of them in the classroom. Still others stop short of defining learning expectations for the end of high school. Regardless of the nature of the standards in your state, to fully succeed, districts and schools must continue the work begun by the state and integrate the views of at least four segments of the community with these mandated standards.

State content standards are the foundation for a locally established curriculum. But schools should still solicit the opinions of the *family* community—the parents who entrust their children to local schools and the taxpayers who support those schools. In addition, educators must get input from the *business* community—future employers of those successful graduates. Still other advice can come from the *higher education* community—the other destination for our successful graduates. And finally and most importantly, careful consideration should be given to the opinions of those in the *school* community—the teachers who are masters of the disciplines students are to learn.

The process most school districts use to achieve this synthesis of community values and opinions is a combination of community meetings or forums and community surveys of public opinion. Often several iterations of each are needed to reach a consensus on the sense of the community—to work through strongly held differences of opinion. This process is important to producing a rigorous and relevant curriculum that reflects the needs of adult work and life in the twenty-first century and that includes the values and priorities of the local community.

Many school districts have succeeded in assembling these diverse sets of educational objectives into composite portraits of their successful graduates. In doing so they articulate the "characteristics of the learner" they desire each student to exhibit on graduating, characteristics that result from the combined power of the "characteristics of the learning"—the academic standards in the written curriculum.

Creating an Effective Curriculum

Once the school/community vision of ultimate success is completed, the professional education community can add the next ingredient. They must work collaboratively across grade levels to back those end-of-high-school and state achievement standards into the grade-level curriculum so as to map out the routes that students will take from kindergarten to grade 12 to succeed. The result of this work must be a carefully planned, specifically detailed curriculum, linked grade to grade and course to course, that begins with a vision of what desired student performance looks like after K–12 schooling. That means teachers from primary grades, intermediate grades, middle schools or junior high, and high schools within the district must meet and assume and assign responsibility for helping students progress through higher levels of academic attainment. It means that teachers must interact with one another and plan for the contributions to be made by each K–12 team member. It means that a level of specificity not contained in the state standards is fully described in writing in local curricula, guiding teachers in preparing daily lessons.

To illustrate, if students are to become competent writers, educators must specify what writing foundations primary-grade teachers will need to help their students master. How will elementary teachers then build on that foundation? What forms of writing competence will middle school or junior high teachers contribute? And how will high school teachers complete writing competence that launches confident, effective writers into work or college? Not only must each question be thoughtfully answered, each teacher must know how their contribution fits into this big picture, and what comes before and after their own work.

Many districts have found it useful to meet and work in cross-grade-level or vertical teams on a regular basis. These articulation planning teams tap into state standards and grade-level benchmarks to assist in finding appropriate divisions and levels of content. They can also consult, along with the state standards, the standards developed by national teams working within the professional associations, such as the National Council of Teachers of Mathematics, the International Reading Association, and the National Council of Teachers of English.

A locally developed, high-quality curriculum, reflecting state standards and aligned to national standards where appropriate, sufficiently specific, and consistently formatted across subjects and grade levels for easy use, is the foundation of quality assessment, because it states what should be assessed to track student progress. And when made public in a variety of ways and formats, it becomes a guide for all stakeholders to use in helping students learn.

The development of this high-quality curriculum can be challenging for several reasons. Teaching has historically been something teachers do alone. Within general curricular guidelines, they select their own educational objectives and design instruction to achieve those objectives. Given this history, the concept of collaborative planning around teaching a common set of learning expectations can be intimidating and therefore difficult to complete. The movement toward professional learning communities as advocated for by DuFour (2004), Schmoker (2004), and others, is a big step toward creating the norm of collegiality that is needed for the kind of work we are describing.

Once established, ongoing care must be taken to ensure the curriculum is not shelved on the back bookcase. Implementing the curriculum in every classroom so the learning expectations are common for students from one school to the next and one classroom to the next is a leadership challenge, and must be planned carefully. Both what we teach our students and how well we teach them will be reflected in local or state assessment results, and all students deserve exposure to the same high-quality curriculum in order to truly show us what they know and can do. But developing a sufficiently detailed and balanced curriculum may not be enough. We still need to ensure that the written curriculum is also the taught curriculum, that teachers actively use it as their guide for lesson development and delivery. It is essential that schools/districts provide teachers the time to work together to learn the curriculum, plan lessons and assessments, and continue their own learning in the academic disciplines they teach (Schmoker, 2002). See Resource 3 in Part 4 for ideas for how to implement a new curriculum once written.

Teacher Mastery of Student Standards

Districts and schools establish their academic expectations for students by developing a vision of academic success and an articulated K–12 curriculum supporting state standards. But the key to student success in meeting those standards is in the instruction their teachers provide. A further condition must be that teachers are masters of the achievement targets their students are expected to hit. A school district cannot afford even one classroom where this condition is not satisfied. If a single teacher is incapable of helping students master essential achievement targets, that teacher becomes a weak link in a continuous chain that will cause some students to fail later because they will not have mastered prerequisites.

Consequently, once achievement standards are clearly identified at all grade levels in all subjects, school districts must be sure teachers are prepared to help students meet them. This may require content-area professional development for some teachers, or mentors who assist teachers in subject matter knowledge. If willing to help, the high school physics teacher is a treasure trove of knowledge for the elementary teacher who may be teaching motion and energy.

Special attention should be given to those teachers new to the profession. They should receive sample lessons, specialized content training to better understand the standards, and the time needed to plan lessons aligned to the curriculum.

Summary

This first condition for assessment quality requires defining what students must learn to be considered academically successful. This planning is usually completed at the district level in order to provide equally high-quality educational opportunities across buildings. But work can also be done within school buildings, grade levels, and even classrooms. Teachers can examine their educational priorities by auditing their classroom curriculum (what they actually teach) against the written curriculum and adjust their teaching as needed, always focusing on what students need to learn to be able to demonstrate proficiency, either in the classroom or on state-level assessments of learning for accountability purposes (see Activity 16).

DOOR 2

Serving ALL Assessment Users

By definition, assessment results reflect a particular student's attainment of a specified set of achievement standards at a single point in time. Standardized test results provide achievement data summarized across large numbers of students on multiple targets broadly defined for a particular grade level at one point during the school year. These tests, assessments *of* learning, are most useful in providing periodic status reports for the program planning level of decision making, and can also provide information about the overall progress of the system.

Educational decision makers who need only periodic access to achievement information reflecting group performance can use standardized test results effectively to satisfy those needs. Teachers, students, and parents who need ongoing access to high-resolution portraits of individual student achievement receive this information through *classroom* assessments.

Let us restate a critical point: *Because decision makers at these different levels have such diverse information needs, no single assessment can meet all their needs.* In today's testing for accountability environment, we have asked (and in some cases believed) that standardized tests serve double and even triple duty: reporting large group scores, serving diagnostic purposes for individual students, and being an instrument for high-stakes decisions all at once. If we are to administer and use a range of assessments with maximum effectiveness and efficiency, we must plan carefully for their use, understand what information is actually needed, and know whether the assessment can provide the information required for the intended purpose.

Understanding Who the Users Are

In schools, there are three levels of assessment users: classroom, instructional support, and policy. The first column in Table 3-1 identifies the users in each category. Columns two and three identify key questions to be answered and the information needed to help each user. A school district committed to meeting the needs of all assessment users must develop plans for conducting the assessments needed to provide the required information—at all levels.

Users at the classroom level obtain the information they need from the teacher's day-to-day classroom assessments. User needs at the other two levels will be served by standardized assessments. The essential planning question is, *How can we be sure all users receive relevant student achievement information in a timely and understandable form?*

Table 3-1

Users and Uses of Assessment Results

Users	Key Question(s) to Be Answered	Information Needed
Classroom Level		
Student	Am I meeting the teacher's learning expectations? Where do I need help to succeed? How can I best manage my own learning?	Continuous information about individual student attainment of specific instructional requirements
Teacher	Which students need what help? Who among my students should work together? What grade should appear on the report card?	Continuous information about individual student achievement
	Did my teaching strategies work?	Continuous assessment of group performance
Parent	Is my child succeeding in school? What does my child need to succeed? Is/Are my child's teacher(s) monitoring and communicating student progress? Is this school providing the support students need?	Continuous feedback on the student's mastery of required material
Instructional Support Level		
Principal/ Vice Principal	Is instruction in particular areas producing results? Is this teacher effective? What kinds of professional development will help? How shall we spend building resources to be effective?	Periodic assessment of group achievement

Users	Key Question(s) to Be Answered	Information Needed
Instructional Support Level cont.		
Lead/Mentor Teacher	What does this teacher need to do the job?	Periodic assessment of group achievement
Counselor/ Psychologist	Who needs (can have access to) special support services such as remedial programs? What students should be assigned to which teachers to optimize results?	Periodic assessment of individual achievement
Curriculum Director	Is our program of instruction effective?	Periodic assessment of group achievement
Policy Level		
Superintendent	Are programs producing student learning? Is each building producing acceptable results? Which programs need/ deserve more resources?	Periodic assessment of group mastery of district curriculum
School Board	Are students in the district learning? Is the superintendent producing results?	Periodic assessment of group achievement
State Dept. of Education	Are programs across the state producing results?	Periodic assessment of group mastery of state curriculum
Citizen/ Legislator (state or national)	Are students in our schools achieving in ways that will allow them to be effective citizens?	Periodic assessment of group mastery of valued targets

Source: Adapted from *Student-Involved Assessment FOR Learning,* 4th ed. (pp. 22-25), by R. J. Stiggins, 2005, Upper Saddle River, NJ: Merrill/Prentice Hall. Copyright ©2005 by Pearson Education, Inc. Adapted by permission of Pearson Education, Inc.

Planning for Classroom Assessment

To monitor student achievement effectively, we teach classroom teachers to begin each unit of instruction or course of study with a clear vision of the specific achievement targets their students are to hit. Beginning with the curriculum targets of instruction, teachers structure their lessons to lead students to progress over time to demonstrate mastery of state standards. To do this, they answer the following questions: In what order will students master specific content knowledge? How will they learn to use that knowledge to reason and solve problems? What performance skills will they master, and in what sequence? What kinds of achievement products will they be called on to create? With this in mind, then, teachers begin instruction with a predetermined plan for assessing whether, or to what extent, each student has reached the intended learning. We ask that teachers have a written sequence of instructional targets, a plan for the assessments intended to track student progress, and where students are now in relation to both plans.

Additionally, teachers will want to consider how and when the results will be communicated to students and parents so they may also make timely, informed decisions. Since students, like teachers, make decisions of the sorts identified in Table 3-1 on a continuous basis, this communication plan should also reflect ways to allow students to monitor their own progress. In summary, the classroom assessment planning completed by each teacher at the beginning of each program of study asks, *What targets will be assessed, when they will be assessed, and how will the results be used?*

Planning for Standardized Testing

This essential question, *How can we be sure all users receive relevant student achievement information in a timely and understandable form?*, must guide the administration and use of standardized tests at instructional support and policy levels. By compiling a complete inventory of ALL of the standardized tests students take during the course of a year, at both the district and school levels, educators take a critical step in knowing if the needs of all users are being met. This analysis will also show if there are overlaps or duplications in the testing program, if some standards are going unassessed, and how much time the administration of all of the tests takes. *What standardized tests are to be administered at what grade levels, reflecting what standards and/or achievement targets at what point in time?* State tests and district tests are the most obvious, but often there are school tests and grade-level or department tests also administered that should be included to achieve a full and accurate picture. Further, *What specific assessment users are to be served by the results? What decisions will be made on their basis?* This analysis should reveal which standards are being assessed and which are not, as well as whose information needs are being met by these tests and whose are not.

A plan for mapping the district's big standardized assessment picture can take the form of a table with these column headings:

- Name and form of the standardized test (list each test in a battery separately)
- Amount of time required for administering the test
- Students tested (grade level and time of year)
- Specific achievement targets assessed (content knowledge, specific patterns of reasoning, performance skills, product development capabilities or some combination of these?)
- Specific state/district standards assessed through those test items
- Specific assessment method(s) used
- How the results will be reported
- Intended users of results and decisions made based on those results
- Procedures for communicating results to all relevant users and ways to verify that the results were understood, interpreted, and used correctly

This analysis will show how each set of test results fits into the record of each individual student's mastery of achievement standards—how each contributes to the evolving picture of the learner. Here again, assessments that are redundant, fail to align properly with the curriculum, or fail to contribute needed information can be eliminated. It may also become clear that managing the amount of data generated, if it is to be put to optimum use for programmatic improvement and also be communicated to users to help students become better learners, may require specialized software. Districts that have taken advantage of technology to compile, store, manipulate, and report student assessment data both systematically and systemically are able to meet the needs of all users in timely and efficient ways.

This planning, conducted at the classroom, school, and district levels, can contribute to both the efficiency and effectiveness of districts' assessment systems and allow them to operationalize their commitment to all assessment users.

Summary

This second condition for success helps school leaders build their system around the needs of real assessment users. It calls for developing awareness of who those users are and what specific information needs they bring to the table. Periodic standardized tests, including short-cycle, common, or interim assessments, will meet some of those needs; classroom assessments will meet others. Both are essential. If either is not delivering accurate information or is misunderstood by intended users, students are at risk. Schools and districts can discover how to blend the two levels of assessment according to the information needs of those who work to help students learn.

DOOR 3

Developing Assessment Literacy

High-quality, accurate assessments are a must if decision makers are to be able to do their jobs. They must have dependable information about student achievement, and we can deliver that reliable information if we apply standards of quality to all assessments. To apply those standards consistently, teachers and administrators must have the opportunity to learn about and practice using them. In short, they must become assessment literate.

A set of assessment quality standards is outlined here, along with several road-blocks to their implementation and specific strategies for removing those obstacles.

Keys to Quality Classroom Assessment*

Accurate and effective classroom assessments are built on a foundation that includes the following five key dimensions:

- Arise from and be designed to serve the *specific information needs of intended user(s)*
- Arise from clearly articulated and appropriate *achievement targets*
- *Accurately reflect* student achievement
- Yield results that are *effectively communicated* to their intended users
- *Involve students* in classroom assessment, record keeping, and communication

These keys are illustrated in Figure 3.1. This model is built around two components: (1) *assess accurately*; (2) use assessment *to benefit students*, not merely to grade and sort them. Notice that the assessment contexts—*intended users and uses* and *learning targets*—combine to help determine a proper *assessment design*, from which the best mode of *communication* is derived. *Students are involved* at all steps. High-quality classroom assessment equals accurate information—clear purposes, clear learning targets, and an appropriate design—used effectively to help students learn.

---

*This section is adapted from R. J. Stiggins, J. Arter, J. Chappuis, & S. Chappuis, *Classroom Assessment* for *Student Learning: Doing It Right—Using It Well.* (pp. 12–17), Portland, OR: Assessment Training Institute, 2004. Adapted by permission.

Figure 3-1
Keys to Quality Classroom Assessment
Quality Classroom Assessment = Accurate Information, Effectively Used

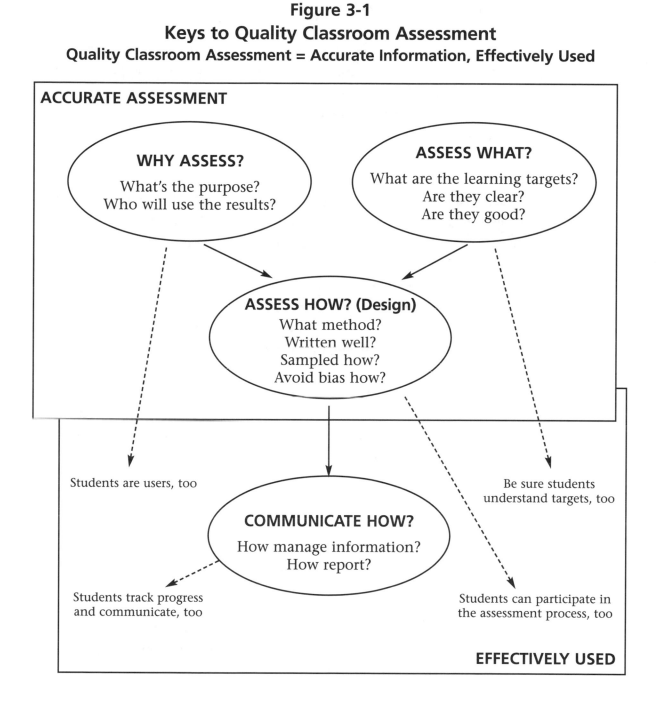

Source: Adapted from *Classroom Assessment for Student Learning: Doing It Right—Using It Well.* (p. 13), by R. J. Stiggins, J. Arter, J. Chappuis, & S. Chappuis, 2004, Portland, OR: Assessment Training Institute. Adapted by permission.

Why Assess? To Serve the User's Information Needs

We assess to gather evidence of student learning that will inform instructional decisions in ways that maximize that learning. As learning progresses, teachers and students both need regular information about what students have and have not yet learned, so they may make instructional decisions that keep those students growing.

Teachers make some decisions frequently, such as when deciding what comes next in student learning within lessons or when trying to discover what's blocking student learning. Typically, these decisions are made day to day in the classroom based on evidence derived from classroom activities and assessments.

Teachers make other decisions periodically, such as when assigning report card grades or identifying students for special services. Here they also rely on classroom assessment evidence accumulated over time and for different purposes, in this case to determine how much learning has occurred up to a point in time.

Other instructional decisions are made less frequently, such as when school districts make adjustments in instructional programs or purchase curriculum materials. Often these decisions turn on results of once-a-year standardized tests reflecting very broad content domains.

It is therefore apparent that different assessments serve a variety of users and uses, centering on achievement defined at a variety of levels, and requiring a variety of kinds of assessment information delivered at different times. All resulting information must be accurate and must be used effectively.

In any assessment context, whether supporting learning while it is happening or checking for it after it has happened, educators must start by understanding the information needs of the intended users, then build assessments to meet those needs. These assessment purposes (users and uses) will influence the form and frequency of assessment, as well as the level and type of detail required in communicating results.

Assess What? Clear Targets

In addition to beginning with a purpose in mind, as teachers, we must also have a clear sense of the achievement expectations we wish our students to master. Obviously, these achievement expectations are what we will be assessing. We can't develop multiple-choice test items, extended response exercises and scoring procedures, or performance assessments of learning targets that we ourselves have not clearly and completely defined. Understanding the important learning targets is the essential foundation of sound assessment, and of good teaching too. Therefore, every teacher's fundamental classroom assessment responsibility is to become a confident, competent master of the academic subjects they are assigned to teach at the grade levels where they teach them. Only then will the achievement targets students are to master be clear.

When these crucial classroom learning targets are clear, the next step is to transform them into student-friendly language. This represents an important insight into how to use assessment to increase student learning. We know that students' chances of success grow markedly when they start their learning with a clear sense of where they are headed and when they play a role in tracking and communicating about their own progress along the way. Teachers help them succeed, therefore, by providing an understandable vision of success with examples of what success will look like when they get there.

Assess How? Assessment Design to Promote Accuracy

Assessments can produce accurate or inaccurate information about student achievement. They can correctly represent or misrepresent learning. Obviously, our goal is accurate assessment in any context.

The previous two sections lay a foundation of accuracy. If teachers start assessment development with a clear sense of the intended user's information needs, they have every hope of serving them well. Starting with a clear sense of the achievement targets to measure lays a foundation from which to accurately assess them. An assessment devised without clear purpose or focus is extremely unlikely to produce accurate information.

Accuracy requires selecting a proper assessment method for each context. Each assessment method has unique strengths and limitations, and works well in some contexts (purposes and learning targets) but not in others. Assessment methods are not interchangeable. The task always is to choose a proper method for the particular situation—the quality of any assessment hinges on this.

Once teachers have chosen methods for their particular context, they must develop their choice and use it well. This means creating high-quality assessment exercises (test questions, extended written response questions, or performance tasks). It means including enough exercises to lead to confident conclusions about student achievement without wasting time gathering more evidence than the context requires. Table 3-2 compares achievement targets and assessment methods, noting which combinations make good matches and which do not.

Finally, every assessment situation brings with it its own list of things that can go wrong and that can render results inaccurate. For instance, a score on any assessment can misrepresent the student's real achievement if the test questions are poorly written, the directions are misleading, the student suffers from extreme test anxiety, or subjective scoring procedures for extended response or performance assessments are conducted carelessly. It is every teacher's responsibility to anticipate what can go wrong in various assessment contexts and prevent those problems when possible.

To ensure accuracy, over and above starting with clear targets and information needs, all involved in any assessment must do the following:

- Rely on proper assessment methods for each particular context.
- Sample student achievement appropriately.
- Rely only on quality exercises and scoring procedures to avoid all potential sources of bias.

Communicate Results How? In a Timely and Understandable Manner

Even if learning targets and information needs are clear and the information gathered is precisely accurate, an assessment can fail to achieve its learning ends if the results are not communicated effectively to the intended user(s). If schools and districts use test scores to convey results and the users don't understand how the score connects to learning or if teachers use symbols such as letter grades on a

Table 3-2

Aligning Achievement Targets to Assessment Methods

Target to Be Assessed	Assessment Method			
	Selected Response	Extended Written Response	Performance Assessment	Personal Communication
Knowledge Mastery	Good match for assessment mastery of elements of knowledge.	Good match for tapping understanding of relationships among elements of knowledge.	Not a good match—too time consuming to cover everything.	Can ask questions, evaluate answers and infer mastery—but a time-consuming option.
Reasoning Proficiency	Good match only for assessing understanding of some patterns of reasoning.	Written descriptions of complex problem solutions can provide a window into reasoning proficiency.	Can watch students solve some problems and infer reasoning proficiency.	Can ask student to "think aloud" or can ask followup questions to probe reasoning.
Skills	Not a good match. Can assess mastery of the knowledge prerequisites to skillful performance, but cannot rely on these to tap the skill itself.		Good match. Can observe and evaluate skills as they are being performed.	Strong match when skill is oral communication proficiency; not a good match otherwise.
Ability to Create Products	Not a good match. Can assess mastery of the knowledge prerequisites to the ability to create products, but cannot assess the quality of products themselves.	Strong match when the product is written. Not a good match when the product is not written.	Good match. Can assess the attributes of the product itself.	Not a good match.

report card when users have a different idea what those symbols mean, they communicate ineffectively and poor-quality decisions, decisions harmful to students, will result.

To prevent such problems, we recommend the following standards of good communication practice:

- Both the message sender and receiver must understand the achievement target in question to be the same thing—if they unwittingly talk about different kinds of achievement, they will miscommunicate.
- The information underpinning the communication must be accurate—inaccurate information leads automatically to miscommunication.
- Both message sender and receiver must understand the symbols being used to convey information to mean the same thing—if they think the scores or grades mean different things, they will miscommunicate.
- The communication must be tailored to the intended audience.

Involve Students—Make Assessment Instruction

Student involvement is a critically important shift in our traditional or conventional perspectives regarding the role of assessment in promoting effective schools: the most important instructional decisions (that is, the decisions that contribute the most to student learning) are made, not by the adults working in the system, but by students themselves. Students decide whether the learning is worth the effort required to attain it. Students decide whether they believe they are capable of reaching the learning targets. It is only after students make these decisions in the affirmative that their teachers can impact their learning lives. So part of every teacher's classroom assessment job is to keep students believing in themselves as learners through the effective use of classroom assessment.

The point is not that we adults don't contribute immensely to student learning. We do. We are critical players in teaching, learning, and assessment. It's just that we are second in the rank order of importance as instructional decision makers.

Table 3-3 summarizes the important aspects of each of the five keys to quality classroom assessment.

Table 3-3
Indicators of Sound Classroom Assessment Practice*

1. Why Assess? **Assessment Processes and Results Serve Clear and Appropriate Purposes**	a. Teachers understand who the users and uses of classroom assessment information are and know their information needs. b. Teachers understand the relationship between assessment and student motivation and craft assessment experiences to maximize motivation. c. Teachers use classroom assessment processes and results formatively (assessment *for* learning). d. Teachers use classroom assessment results summatively (assessment *of* learning) to inform someone beyond the classroom about students' achievement as of a particular point in time. e. Teachers have a comprehensive plan over time for integrating assessment *for* and *of* learning in the classroom.
2. Assess What? **Assessments Reflect Clear and Valued Student Learning Targets**	a. Teachers have clear learning targets for students; they know how to turn broad statements of content standards into classroom-level targets. b. Teachers understand the various types of learning targets they hold for students. c. Teachers select learning targets focused on the most important things students need to know and be able to do. d. Teachers have a comprehensive plan over time for assessing learning targets.
3. Assess How? **Learning Targets Are Translated into Assessments That Yield Accurate Results**	a. Teachers understand what the various assessment methods are. b. Teachers choose assessment methods that match intended learning targets. c. Teachers design assessments that serve intended purposes. d. Teachers sample learning appropriately in their assessments. e. Teachers write assessment questions of all types well. f. Teachers avoid sources of bias that distort results.
4. Communicate How? **Assessment Results Are Managed Well and Communicated Effectively**	a. Teachers record assessment information accurately, keep it confidential, and appropriately combine and summarize it for reporting (including grades). Such summary accurately reflects current level of student learning. b. Teachers select the best reporting option (grades, narratives, portfolios, conferences) for each context (learning targets and users). c. Teachers interpret and use standardized test results correctly. d. Teachers effectively communicate assessment results to students. e. Teachers effectively communicate assessment results to a variety of audiences outside the classroom, including parents, colleagues, and other stakeholders.
5. Involve Students How? **Students Are Involved in Their Own Assessment**	a. Teachers make learning targets clear to students. b. Teachers involve students in assessing, tracking, and setting goals for their own learning. c. Teachers involve students in communicating about their own learning.

*Sound classroom assessment practice = Skill in gathering accurate information + effective use of information and procedures

Source: Reprinted from *Classroom Assessment* for *Student Learning: Doing It Right—Using It Well.* (p. 27), by R. J. Stiggins, J. Arter, J. Chappuis, & S. Chappuis, 2004, Portland, OR: Assessment Training Institute. Reprinted by permission.

Barriers to Accurate Assessment

Even though these five key indicators of sound classroom assessment practice are straightforward and easy to understand, they can at times be difficult to meet. As educators, we face personal, community, and institutional barriers to quality assessment. Let's explore a few such roadblocks, along with a strategy for their removal.

A Lack of Time to Assess Well

Without doubt, the most prominent barrier to quality assessment from the teacher's point of view is the lack of time to assess well. If teachers believe they don't have time to meet the standards of assessment quality, they won't act to do so. Several specific time issues trouble teachers deeply.

One concern is the broadening curriculum, which means teachers must teach and assess an ever-expanding list of student achievement goals. The curriculum is growing to include more achievement targets such as technology and health-related topics, more complexity within the "established" targets (for instance, an enhanced understanding of what it means to be a proficient reader or writer), more learning targets classified as problem solving or reasoning, and more complex ways of integrating the curriculum across disciplines. How can teachers assess even more when they already have too little time to assess current targets?

There is only one answer: Learn to assess more efficiently.

One solution, defined in Door 1, is to start with a vision of 12th-grade achievement and trace that vision back down through the K–12 curriculum to develop a smooth and complete transition from beginning student to competent student. In this way, teachers can remove redundant and irrelevant material and promote efficient instruction and assessment. Finding what is currently taught and assessed that doesn't relate to or support the attainment of the content standards and then eliminating it from the classroom curriculum would add value and time to any classroom teacher's instruction.

Here is another time problem: Many teachers contend that some assessment methods are too labor intensive. For example, in recent years the message many administrators and teachers were receiving was that performance assessment, "authentic" exercises leading to observations and judgments of students, is the best way to assess student achievement. Advocates cited the richness of results they could derive from detailed observations of performance and judgment based on complex performance standards. Hidden between the lines for many teachers was the subliminal message, "lots of hard work and more time required!" Few educators are actively looking for more work to do.

Again, the solution is to learn to assess more efficiently. Too much performance assessment, or any other assessment method, for that matter, can throw the picture out of balance. Performance assessment is not always the best way. In fact, sometimes it isn't even an acceptable way to assess. In certain instances, and with certain achievement targets, other methods such as multiple-choice or true/false tests are better choices. When they fit, these options are always more efficient. When teachers *do* turn to performance assessment, it can also be a powerful source of instruction, with scoring guides being turned into teaching tools and students being taught to self-assess using the rubrics. But a rich knowledge of how to use performance assessments efficiently is required.

A third time problem is that for many districts the only way to store and communicate information about student achievement is the teacher gradebook and report card grades. That process eats huge amounts of time all by itself, leaving neither time nor opportunity to consider alternatives.

If we conceive of record keeping as a teacher-centered activity relying on traditional gradebook methodology, the time demands far outstrip anything a teacher or administrator can manage. Again, the solution to this problem lies in breaking an outdated mold. What worked in the 1920s will not—indeed cannot—meet today's twenty-first century needs in standards-driven schools. Teachers must start with clearly defined achievement targets, thoroughly developed assessment plans, efficient assessment methods, and strategies for record keeping that rely on information management software. But not only do all teachers not have access to this technology, many that do have not become sufficiently assessment literate to use it to its full potential.

An Institutional Barrier to Quality

The accountability objectives of NCLB generally receive more support from educators and administrators than do the methods being used to actually leave no child behind. Teachers across the country are under enormous pressure to improve test scores: nobody wants to work in a "failing" school. But the increased testing and the use of standardized tests that may themselves be flawed at determining school success have consequences beyond potential faulty evaluation of schools. Valued classroom curriculum can be eliminated because it isn't tested, endless drill-and-kill exercises matching the test formats can substitute for and stifle real learning, and the higher the stakes the higher the likelihood of unethical test preparation (Popham, 2005).

The use of even more standardized assessments of learning poses an even stronger threat to assessment balance and quality than ever before. Unless we take the time to ensure that these tests adhere to standards of quality and don't mismeasure what they purport to accurately measure, and until we help ourselves and our communities view the results with a clear understanding of how they can and cannot be used, our assessment systems will not improve teaching and learning in the ways envisioned by the authors of NCLB.

A Community Barrier to Quality

It is not uncommon for parents to define sound assessment practices in terms of their own personal experience when they were in school. The standard they set is this: "Anything you do to my child by way of assessment that I didn't experience in school is unsound practice." If the practices they experienced were sound and appropriate, parents are right to expect their children's teachers to use them. But the problem arises when the practices they expect are, in fact, unsound. Then, this parental resistance or advocacy becomes a barrier to quality.

The only way past this roadblock is for educators to be sufficiently assessment literate to be able to describe their assessment practices in nondefensive and convincing terms to those who question them.

The Ultimate Barrier to Quality

The bottom line: We cannot meet standards of quality if we don't know what those standards are or how to meet them. A lack of assessment literacy is the ultimate barrier to quality. The removal of this barrier sets up the removal of all others.

Removing the Barriers

The vast majority of educators practicing today have not been given the opportunity to learn about the standards or their application. High-quality professional development programs are needed to provide this foundation—especially given our long history of failing to train teachers and administrators in assessment. On the following pages, we outline the objectives of a practitioner-centered professional development program in classroom assessment, along with highly efficient training strategies. Teachers and administrators are prepared to fulfill their ongoing assessment responsibilities when they do the following:

■ Understand essential differences between sound and unsound assessment practices and commit to meeting key quality standards.

■ Know how to meet standards of quality in all classroom, school, and district assessment contexts.

■ Know how to apply the nine Principles of Assessment *for* Learning that follow, using the classroom assessment process as a teaching tool to motivate students to strive for higher levels of learning.

The Nine Principles of Assessment for *Learning*

1. Teachers understand and can articulate in advance of teaching the achievement targets students are to hit.
2. Students are informed regularly about those targets in terms they can understand, in part through the study of the criteria by which their work will be evaluated and samples of high-quality work.
3. Students can describe what targets they are to hit and what comes next in their learning.
4. Classroom teachers can transform those targets into dependable assessments that yield accurate information.
5. Classroom assessment information is used by both teacher and student to revise and guide teaching and learning.

6. Feedback given to students is descriptive, constructive, frequent, and immediate, helping students know how to plan and improve.

7. Students are actively, consistently, and effectively involved in assessment, including learning to manage their own learning through the skills of self-assessment.

8. Students actively, consistently, and effectively communicate with others about their achievement status and improvement.

9. Teachers understand the relationship between assessment and student motivation and use assessment to build student success and confidence rather than failure and defeat.

Organizing Learning Teams for Professional Development in Assessment for Learning

To satisfy these requirements, we recommend a professional development program that relies on a blend of *learning teams* (also referred to as study groups or study teams) and *individual study* and practice by teachers as the basis of interaction and growth. In these teams, a small group of teachers and administrators agree to meet regularly to share responsibility for their mutual professional development.

We believe that collaborative learning teams represent the future of professional development in American schools (see Activity 17). Their effectiveness has been proven over time by hundreds of successful learning teams in schools across the country. They are especially effective in schools embracing a professional learning community approach to school improvement. In the learning team model, teachers are drawn to the promise of time to concentrate on one important topic long enough to internalize some new and useful ideas. This, combined with time to talk with and learn from colleagues (both rare commodities for too many educators), makes this model of professional development attractive. Participants in assessment literacy learning teams often recognize and welcome the "permission" to focus on quality classroom assessment rather than prepping for the state test through the endless use of mini-versions of that test.

Resource 4 in Part 4 goes into more detail on this topic, and describes what principals can do to support learning teams.

Summary

Instruction is most effective when it includes the use of quality assessments. Such assessments are built around users' needs, arise from clearly articulated achievement targets, rely on proper methods, sample student achievement appropriately, avoid sources of bias and distortion that can lead to inaccurate results, involve students in the process, and are communicated accurately.

However, a lack of time and other resources needed to assess well, an educational environment dominated by having students perform well on large-scale accountability measures, and community or parent expectations can present imposing barriers to quality. Removing these potential roadblocks requires developing an assessment-literate school culture.

We have proposed developing a foundation of assessment literacy that places control of professional development in the hands of each practitioner. It calls for an individual commitment to learning about assessment *for* learning but supports that effort with a collaborative team.

DOOR 4

Communicating Effectively About Student Achievement

If schools are to help all students progress toward state standards, and if teachers are to track the progress and development of their students using classroom assessments, our academic record-keeping strategies will have to evolve rapidly. We must communicate effectively about student achievement relative to the written standards. We can take advantage of software programs for generating, storing, retrieving, and delivering information about student achievement.

In other words, a grade on a report card every nine weeks based on a summary of handwritten and often uninterpretable gradebook notations cannot tell the student, teacher, or parent precisely where the student is at any point in time on the path to mastering the standards. Moreover, students charged with tracking and communicating their own improvement need ongoing access to far greater detail about their own achievement than such records can provide. Teachers receiving new students at the beginning of the year or students coming from a different school, and who are expected to take students from where they are to new levels of competence, also require greater detail. A C+ on a transcript or report card does nothing to inform a new teacher what the student has and has not learned. Likewise, parents who desire and expect to see specific information about the progress of their children are not served by grades on a report card every nine weeks. Further, the time required to enter, retrieve, and summarize records by hand, as teachers do with gradebooks, will soon prove too cumbersome to be practical in a standards-based curriculum.

For these reasons, among others, school districts must commit to developing effective information management and communication systems.

To develop such communication systems in standards-driven schools where students are progressing through an articulated curriculum, we recommend that school districts take advantage of information management software systems. These systems can assist teachers and districts with essential assessment activities in a number of ways, including the following:

- Organize the goals and objectives that comprise the curriculum.
- Provide standards-based report card formats.
- Generate assessments using a variety of exercise formats.
- Assist teachers in collecting classroom observational data.
- Print assessments for use in the classroom or permit their administration online.
- Permit instant scanning and scoring of selected response assessments.
- Allow direct scanning of virtually any form of record desired, such as actual samples of student writing or videotapes of student performance.
- Provide long-term dependable and efficient storage of that information and instant retrieval and summary as needed.
- Facilitate immediate access to summative assessment records online by anyone authorized to see them, permitting teachers or parents to obtain instant information about the status of any student or any group of students for conferencing or planning purposes.
- Ensure that all users are assessment literate.

DOOR 5

Creating a Supportive Policy Environment

Another important part of a quality assessment program is a commitment to developing school or district policies that support quality assessment and that make the standards of sound assessment practice clear and understandable. While sound assessment policies don't ensure sound practices, they can contribute by reaffirming a commitment to quality.

To develop such policies at the district level, the superintendent should draft for school board review and approval an assessment philosophy that spells out the assessment responsibilities for district personnel. Sample entries for such a policy are discussed in this section, and others are included in Activity 18.

It has been our experience that district leadership teams do the best job of analyzing and revising assessment policy after they have completed a professional development program in assessment literacy themselves—after they have completed the work of Door 3.

A Sample District Assessment Policy

A district assessment policy should establish the standards by which quality assessment will be judged. Further, it should set an expectation that staff will apply standards of quality in all assessment contexts. This kind of policy might be worded as follows:

The board believes that effective instruction depends on high-quality assessment, and therefore expects all assessments to provide accurate information about student achievement. Each assessment must adhere to standards of quality that all staff know and follow.

The primary purpose of assessment is to improve student learning. It is the expectation of this school district that all assessments will be directly linked to specific instructional targets, use assessment methods appropriate for the type of instructional target, have proper design features, and allow for effective communication of results.

The district acknowledges that assessment can serve as a powerful form of instruction. By involving students in the assessment and evaluation of their own achievement under direct supervision, teachers can use assessment to help students progress toward state achievement standards. All staff will be provided appropriate professional development in order to become assessment literate.

A variety of assessment forms are considered appropriate for use within this district, including the following:

- *Selected response (multiple-choice, true/false, matching, and fill-in)*
- *Essay assessments*
- *Performance assessments (based on observation and judgment)*
- *Direct personal communication with the student*

Any assessments that cannot be linked specifically to student academic well-being through effective decision making or instruction should be discarded. Further, the district will create an assessment and communication system that permits continuous and thorough tracking of student progress.

This is just a sample of the ideas that could be presented in an assessment policy. Other possible topics include beliefs about assessment, guiding principles, more detailed expectations for educators (such as by defining the term *assessment literate*), communication with parents, and so on. In Activity 18 in Part 4 we present a number of assessment policies for review and discussion. One in particular, Policy 2107, may also provide ideas for policies that support quality assessment.

Personnel Policy and Excellence in Assessment

Several dimensions of personnel policy may be in need of revision to ensure the long-term development of an assessment-literate staff. Beginning at the most general level, state licensing requirements should include explicit expectations of assessment competence as a condition for certification in a teacher or administrator role. Similarly, teacher and administrator training programs in higher education institutions should be encouraged to offer coursework that includes relevant assessment training.

Admittedly, neither certification standards nor college course offerings are the responsibility of district superintendents or building principals. But the quality of teaching is, even more so now under the teacher quality provisions of NCLB. Administrators cannot assure their communities of high quality until these aspects of personnel policy change. If new teachers continue to enter the system lacking the needed competence, the requirement for local professional development in assessment—often an expensive proposition—will never go away. For these practical reasons, district superintendents might work through their professional associations to lobby state legislatures and higher education systems to fulfill their responsibilities in developing assessment competence in their students.

Other personnel policy matters hit closer to home. The criteria that districts apply when screening and selecting new teachers and administrators should include an expectation of competence in assessment. The criteria used to evaluate ongoing teacher and administrator performance on the job might be adjusted to include evaluation of the quality of assessments and their use. (Refer to Activity 13 and Activity 15 in Part 4.)

Rethinking Other Relevant Policies

In addition to personnel policy, there are other policy areas that may need reevaluation in pursuing excellence in assessment, including policies on curriculum, lesson planning, homework, graduation requirements, promotion/retention, communicating about student achievement (including grading), and policy related to expenditure of assessment resources.

For example, a school district might specify in policy and regulation its commitment to a standards-based curriculum and to communicating clearly about student achievement. It is not uncommon for district policy manuals to be limited to procedures for report card grading and for conducting parent–teacher conferences. These policy statements might be revamped to reflect the expectation that schools and teachers be accountable for formulating clear, accurate messages about student achievement that are consistent across classrooms, delivering those messages to students and parents in understandable terms, and verifying that the messages got through. Further, communication policy may need to be expanded to permit sharing information about student achievement via portfolios and various student-involved conference formats. In Part 4 we offer a variety of example policies, some good and some not so good, for you to review and consider in terms of how such policies can support assessment *for* learning.

It is not uncommon in school district budgets to find just one entry related to assessment: the allocation of funds for the standardized testing program, sometimes found under a line item labeled "evaluation." Since we now understand that assessment happens at many other levels for many other purposes, resources also need to be allocated for all purposes, including professional development to ensure the quality of classroom assessment *for* learning. Other resources might be needed to create and then maintain an information management system for student achievement data.

Summary

Every school district needs a vision of excellence in assessment to guide its practices, and this calls for a carefully worded district assessment philosophy, approved as policy.

We recommend that districts transform into policy a vision of excellence in assessment that calls for the effective use and balance of high-quality standardized and classroom assessments. This policy should make standards of quality clear and explicit, and should be clear in the expectation that all teachers and administrators consistently meet those standards.

Summarizing the Path to Excellence in Assessment

Leadership in the pursuit of excellence in assessment begins with a guiding vision, clearly showing how assessment fits into and supports instruction. School leaders should understand the importance of quality assessment at all levels and articulate the standards that will guide assessment practices in every classroom. This vision of quality is committed to paper in the form of a plan that guides district practice. In addition, leaders must ensure an assessment-literate staff, both in the classroom and in the principal's office. The school board must establish the districtwide policy environment that will underpin the pursuit of that vision in every classroom and school within the district. Curriculum directors must contribute clear visions of achievement expectations, holding the entire team together to function as a unit across grade levels and disciplines, and ensuring that state, district, and building assessments are used in a coordinated, aligned fashion in support of student achievement. In addition, principals must be prepared to use assessment to show the community how effective their schools are, while at the same time helping teachers develop the assessment literacy needed to create and use high-quality assessments day to day with students in the classroom. By applying the principles of assessment *for* learning, teachers will substantiate clear research findings: using classroom assessment raises student achievement.

Thinking About Assessment

Activity 3: Creating an Assessment Profile for Your School/District

Purpose: This activity is necessary to charting a path toward your assessment vision. When completed, your analysis will show you what work has already been accomplished and what work lies ahead of you. In effect, it helps identify priorities and by doing so, maps the course for achieving balance and quality.

Time: Variable; likely to be 2–4 hours.

Directions: Read through the items in the following self-analysis correlated to the Five Doors described in Part 3. Discuss each item with your team and come to agreement about where you would place your school/district along the item's 5-point continuum. Consider the following as you move through the activity:

■ The larger, more diverse a team you can assemble that is representative of your school/district, the more accurate your profile is likely to be. Expanding participation in this activity to others in your system not part of your leadership study team is beneficial. Or, your team can do the profiling activity first and then repeat it with a larger group to create more understanding of the issues and gain a larger representation of opinion.

■ If a larger district or school team is assembled, coming to consensus about each item may be more difficult because people will bring not only different perspectives but also very different realities. For example, one person's school may deserve a high rating on one item while another school in the district hasn't even considered that scope of work and therefore admittedly gets a lower mark. How can that be reconciled to reflect the work the district needs to accomplish? Or, the district may be doing well overall in one area but that work has not filtered into the schools. How should the team rate the district overall? There is likely to be rich, revealing discussion about many of the issues raised in the profile; staying focused on the status of the level of analysis (school or district) is essential.

■ What we know and don't know at the time we're asked to make judgments or evaluations influences our answers to questions. In this activity and in many others in this guide, the responses from participants are directly related to their level of assessment literacy.

Closure: As we noted at the start of this guide, our intention is to help you in two areas: (1) at an organizational/institutional (school or district) level, and (2) at a personal/professional level, one that considers the necessary knowledge and skills for leading assessment reform. We think it is helpful for teams to revisit this self-analysis profile both before and after reading and doing many of the activities in Part 4. Doing the analysis before going on to Part 4 will help clarify and increase understanding of the 10 competencies for leaders you will encounter there. Coming back after reading Part 4 and reviewing the profile in light of these 10 competencies will produce a deeper, more complete analysis.

SCHOOL/DISTRICT ASSESSMENT SELF-ANALYSIS

Instructions: Rate your local assessment system on each of the performance scales provided.

Door 1: Achievement Standards

Check Appropriate Rating

Everyone acknowledges the need to have clearly identified achievement standards.	__	__	__	__	__	Standards are considered unnecessary or unattainable.
Achievement standards have been designed with a clear vision of desired student performance at the end of K–12 schooling.	__	__	__	__	__	They have not.
Those standards are clearly written, contain the appropriate level of rigor, and reflect the needs of adult work/life in the 21st century.	__	__	__	__	__	They are unclear, etc.
If needed, time and resources have been allocated to make the necessary improvements.	__	__	__	__	__	They have not.
The community is/was involved in developing achievement standards.	__	__	__	__	__	It was not.
Achievement standards are published for all to see, reviewed regularly, and revised as needed.	__	__	__	__	__	They are not.
Local achievement standards have been aligned to state standards.	__	__	__	__	__	They have not been aligned to state standards.
Those standards have been further clarified as grade-level curriculum in every subject and every grade.	__	__	__	__	__	Each teacher develops his/her own curriculum.
The written curriculum has been audited/reviewed to ensure it contains a balance of knowledge, reasoning, skill, and product targets.	__	__	__	__	__	The curriculum has not been audited for this balance.

A curriculum implementation plan has been written describing roles and responsibilities that ensures standards-based instruction is achieved through use of the adopted curriculum.	|——|——|——|——|	There is no plan to ensure standards-based instruction.
There is consistency in achievement expectations across teachers.	|——|——|——|——|	Each teacher has unique expectations.
Teachers are held accountable for teaching the adopted curriculum.	|——|——|——|——|	There is no monitoring of what is taught.
Staff training and support in curriculum implementation are ongoing in all subjects.	|——|——|——|——|	There is little inservice training for staff on teaching to the standards.
New teachers in particular are given specialized assistance understanding and teaching to the standards.	|——|——|——|——|	Mentoring new teachers in the use of the written curriculum is absent.
Teachers are given time to collaboratively plan lessons aimed at accomplishing grade-level expectations.	|——|——|——|——|	Time is not dedicated for this purpose.
Teachers are trained in strategies such as the use of curriculum mapping or vertical teaming as tools for adding clarity and focus to what is taught.	|——|——|——|——|	No training in this area.
Achievement standards are held high for **all** students.	|——|——|——|——|	Expectations vary depending upon the student.
Model lessons linked to the content standards are available and used for professional development.	|——|——|——|——|	No examples are provided.
Each teacher's mastery of her/his assigned content has been verified. Those needing support in developing content area knowledge are provided that support.	|——|——|——|——|	Little is known about this.

Door 2: Commitment to ALL Assessment Users

Check appropriate rating

Educators understand the need to provide information to all users of assessment data.	—	—	—	We have little awareness of the different information interests in the range of users.
The information needs of all users are systematically planned for, differentiating and balancing assessments *of* and *for* learning.	—	—	—	Important needs are overlooked; we are not in balance.
We have a specific plan for how we attend to user needs at these levels:				
Classroom	—	—	—	This level of users has been neglected.
Instructional Support (program evaluation/effectiveness, instructional materials, etc.)	—	—	—	This level of users has been neglected.
Policy (board, legislature, etc.)	—	—	—	This level of users has been neglected.
A technology-based information management system accessible to all users is in place.	—	—	—	We have no way to manage or communicate assessment data from the various levels.
Assessment results for all uses are related back to the content standards.	—	—	—	We assess items not in our written curriculum.

Door 3: Developing Assessment Literacy

Check appropriate rating

Educators are aware of the consequences of inaccurate measurement.	—	—	—	Most are unaware of this or don't believe it is a problem.
We have defined appropriate quality standards for assessments, both *of* and *for* learning.	—	—	—	We have no standards of assessment quality.
Educators are receptive to improving their assessment competence, as needed.	—	—	—	There is disinterest or resistance to doing so.
Teachers understand what assessment methods to use when and how to use them.	—	—	—	Matching the assessment method to the type of learning target is not practiced.

Teachers understand and apply the principles of sound grading practices, assigning report card grades that are accurate, fair, and representative of current achievement status. | —— | —— | —— | No opportunities have been offered to learn these practices.

Assessment is systematically woven into instruction using student involvement and is used formatively to inform teaching and learning. | —— | —— | —— | It is not clear how assessment can be good teaching.

Resources as needed are allocated for learning team–based professional development training in classroom assessment. | —— | —— | —— | No resources have been allocated.

Professional development in subject-area content is part of our professional development program. | —— | —— | —— | Nothing is offered in subject-area content.

The 9 principles of assessment *for* learning are understood and known and integrated by all into daily classroom instruction. | —— | —— | —— | These principles are not known or applied.

If used, common or short-cycle assessments are of high quality. | —— | —— | —— | Common or short-cycle assessments have not been audited for quality.

Educators all understand that the strengths and limitations of assessment data from various levels of assessment can guide curriculum and instruction. | —— | —— | —— | There is not a clear sense in the ways data can and cannot be used from various assessments.

Door 4: Effective Communication

Check appropriate rating

Communication to parents focuses on student progress toward the defined learning expectations in the written curriculum and the criteria used to assess that progress. | —— | —— | —— | This does not routinely happen.

The district has committed to communicating effectively about student achievement. | —— | —— | —— | No priority has been attached to effective communication.

90

Shared understanding of learning targets, including "student-friendly" and "parent-friendly" versions of the curriculum, is a communication priority. ——— | | | ——— This has been neglected.

Accurate assessments of student mastery of the standards are at the heart of the communication plan. ——— | | | ——— This has been neglected.

The district uses a data management system for collecting, storing, retrieving, and communicating achievement data. ——— | | | ——— Is neither investigating or implementing such use.

The school/district verifies receipt of the message. ——— | | | ——— This has been neglected.

Schools report multiple types of data to parents in meaningful and timely ways. ——— | | | ——— They do not.

Students are involved in communicating about their own progress and achievement status. ——— | | | ——— Students play no role in this.

The communication of standardized test results to parents is in clear, understandable terms. ——— | | | ——— We have no plan or procedures for this.

There is agreed meaning of symbols used in communicating student learning. ——— | | | ——— This has been neglected.

Door 5: Creating Supportive Policies Based on Assessment Beliefs

Check appropriate rating

The district has adopted a guiding assessment philosophy, a mission, and beliefs regarding student assessment. ——— | | | ——— District has not adopted assessment philosophy.

Our view of policy is one of opportunity to achieve the vision and to positively impact professional practice rather than one of compliance and regulation.	—	—	—	—	Our policy perspective is mostly one of rules and regulations.
Personnel policies reflect an expectation of assessment competence.	—	—	—	—	Policies do not reflect an expectation of assessment competence.
Hiring policies and procedures require it.	—	—	—	—	Policies and procedures do not require it.
Ongoing staff evaluations require it.	—	—	—	—	Evaluations do not require it.
District professional development policies reflect it.	—	—	—	—	Professional development policies do not reflect it.
Budget allocations assure the quality of both classroom *for* learning and standardized assessment *of* learning.	—	—	—	—	Resources are not allocated for both.
We have identified those policies at the school/district level that contribute to productive assessment practice.	—	—	—	—	We have not.
Our approach to developing and coordinating policies relating to assessment is systemic.	—	—	—	—	It is a random approach.
We routinely evaluate the impact of assessment policies and practices.	—	—	—	—	We do not routinely evaluate them.

Leadership for Assessment Reform

Check appropriate rating

We are committed to academic excellence and this is communicated through a clear vision for the instructional program.	|	|	|	|	We are committed to minimum competence.
This vision defines how assessment fits into effective teaching and learning.	|	|	|	|	It does not.
We define success as high achievement for all learners, not sorting into winners and losers.	|	|	|	|	We define success in terms other than high achievement.
Leaders are assessment literate themselves and are committed to assessment literacy for all.	|	|	|	|	Leaders are not schooled in sound assessment practices and are unaware of or negative about the need for staff literacy throughout.
We are willing to risk changing assessment priorities and practices to achieve excellence and balance.	|	|	|	|	We prefer maintaining the status quo.
The district has developed a written comprehensive assessment action plan.	|	|	|	|	A plan has not been written.
An assessment planning team with representatives from all key stakeholder groups has been established and meets regularly.	|	|	|	|	No planning group exists.
A schedule of assessments given has been established displaying grade level, time of year, type of assessment, subject area, standards assessed, and use of results.	|	|	|	|	This information has not been compiled.
A plan has been developed that coordinates state, district, and building level tests.	|	|	|	|	No written plan exists.

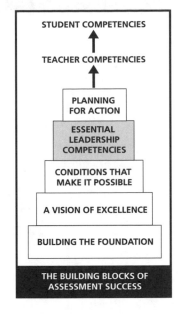

THE BUILDING BLOCKS OF
ASSESSMENT SUCCESS

*Political turmoil and public debate will continue to surround the
No Child Left Behind legislation in the foreseeable future. While
that plays out, most of America's students will come to school
every day wanting to learn, trusting their teachers and schools to
prepare them effectively for success. To meet the challenge, school
leaders must know and do what's right in the area of student
assessment. The school leader's assessment responsibilities can be
met through the application of a set of 10 assessment competencies.*

Part Four

THE REQUIRED SKILLS
FOR ASSESSMENT
BALANCE AND QUALITY
TEN COMPETENCIES FOR EDUCATIONAL LEADERS

So far, we've explored a vision for a balanced, quality assessment system, considered the essential components for such a system, and examined the foundation that needs to be in place for that system to raise student achievement. In Part 4 we turn our attention to the specific competencies school leaders need to develop in order to create local systems that prosper. The 10 competencies we describe help ensure that all assessments are used for their intended purposes and that assessment and its results benefit student learning.

As educational leaders work to understand and comply with the requirements of the No Child Left Behind Act (NCLB), the once-a-year standardized tests that serve as the core of that legislation continue to be called into question. Some cite the current state of testing technology as not being up to the task of tracking students' yearly progress accurately and reliably (Center on Education Policy, 2003). Others point to the long-term disadvantages and harmful effects of high-stakes tests on student learning, citing few achievement gains on independent measures and higher overall dropout rates as an outcome when tests are connected to high stakes (Amrein & Berliner, 2003). In 2005, four years after its passage, political turmoil and public debate continue to surround the legislation.

While the benefits of high-stakes tests for accountability are argued, most of America's students come to school every day wanting to learn, trusting their teachers and schools to prepare them effectively for success. Meeting that challenge requires knowing and doing what's right in the area of student assessment (Stiggins, 2002). Part of knowing what we're doing from an assessment perspective means having the skill to use assessment in ways never envisioned by NCLB. It means using assessment not just to measure and calculate adequate yearly progress, but also to build learner confidence and motivation to learn; to actually be the catalyst for higher student achievement and not merely the dipstick that gauges it.

It will take much more than another test at grades 3 through 8 in every school in every state, every year. This is not an argument against accountability or the use of standardized tests. It is rather an argument for a more comprehensive, balanced, and thoughtful approach to the use of assessment in improving schools, one that doesn't allow the score of a single test to determine what we think is good or bad about students and schools. Standardized tests, constructed far from the classroom, cannot provide the level of specificity about individual student achievement that assessment-literate classroom teachers can produce. Only when balanced with classroom assessment *for* learning, the daily assessments used by teachers that mirror good instruction and allow students to risk learning without being constantly evaluated, will schools do their job in meeting the information needs of all assessment users, including students.

Leading Assessment for Learning

So, as NCLB continues to play out, what can building principals and other administrators do to foster assessment quality and balance? Just as state and district assessment systems need to attend to balancing assessments *of* and *for* learning, leaders can and should attend to issues of quality and balance at the school level. They can begin to create sound assessment practices where they don't exist, and nurture and extend appropriate assessment where it is already in place.

The framework for leaders that follows is specific to *assessment for learning.* Two characteristics distinguish this framework from others, and make it a set of knowledge and skills that leaders should attend to. First, standards-driven reform has created new knowledge requirements and responsibilities for school leaders. In today's systems the bell curve is being replaced by the goal that *all* students learn well. Instead of a teacher-centered curriculum, learning standards are public and what counts is that each child attain those standards. Assessing the standards, not just through large-scale accountability tests or even local short-cycle or common assessments, but day to day in the classroom, where standards, instruction, and assessment are all pages in the same book, is a requirement for effective of standards-based reform. Without specific leadership knowledge linked to intentional action to ensure assessment quality and effective use, how can we expect success?

The second reason this framework is relevant for standards-based school reform is the reward in improved student learning brought about by the use of classroom assessment *for* learning. Described by Fullan (2004) as "a high yield strategy," the research reported on the topic (discussed in Part 1) helps explain why leadership knowledge and skill specific to it would be beneficial (see Table 1-1). Because of that, assessment *for* learning has implications not just for school leaders but also for broader public policy: the research is conclusive, and improved learning lies within the grasp of anyone wishing to apply it.

The 10 competencies shown in Table 4-1 have been revised from a framework designed for educational leaders (Arter, Stiggins, Duke, & Sagor, 1993). Research on assessment to support learning (Black & Wiliam, 1998), and the need to achieve balance between standardized and classroom assessment (Stiggins, 2002) have both influenced the revisions.

Table 4-1

1. The leader understands the standards of quality for student assessments and how to ensure that these standards are met in all assessments.

2. The leader understands the principles of assessment *for* learning and works with staff to integrate them into classroom instruction.

3. The leader understands the necessity of clear academic achievement standards, aligned classroom-level achievement targets, and their relationship to the development of accurate assessments.

4. The leader knows and can evaluate teachers' classroom assessment competencies and helps teachers learn to assess accurately and use the results productively.

5. The leader can plan, present, or secure professional development activities that contribute to the use of sound assessment practices.

6. The leader analyzes student assessment information accurately, uses the information to improve curriculum and instruction, and assists teachers in doing the same.

7. The leader develops and implements sound assessment and assessment-related policies.

8. The leader creates the conditions necessary for the appropriate use and reporting of student achievement information, and can communicate effectively with all members of the school community about student assessment results and their relationship to improving curriculum and instruction.

9. The leader understands the attributes of a sound and balanced assessment system.

10. The leader understands the issues related to the unethical and inappropriate use of student assessment and protects students and staff from such misuse.

What does it look like when school leaders demonstrate competence in each of the 10 areas? The activities and resources that follow will help you as leaders to master and apply these competencies. Our intent is not to offer an exhaustive list—there are more ways to work toward the 10 competencies than space allows us in this book—but rather to provide a catalyst for you to think about how you fulfill your leadership role in assessment. From there, you can reflect on what you already know and can do, and on what you need to do or learn next to implement a quality, balanced student assessment system at your local level.

Competency 1

The leader understands the standards of quality for student assessments and how to ensure that these standards are met in all assessments.

Part of the teacher's professional competence includes knowing how to apply standards of quality to classroom assessment development or selection, and it is part of the school leader's assessment responsibility to be able to judge whether an assessment adheres to these standards. Even though most teachers lack training in classroom assessment, they still develop a majority of their own assessments. Further, selecting ready-made assessments these days is easier than picking questions from the back of the textbook or from other supplementary material. Websites on the Internet offer test items and tasks to teachers in many subjects in many grade levels, and test item banks remain popular software purchases for teacher test construction.

Principals and other school leaders can evaluate any assessment developed or selected by teachers according to the following quality standards:

1. *Clear and appropriate purposes*: Sound assessments arise from specific information needs. Always know why you are giving an assessment *before* you administer it.
2. *Clear targets*: What is being assessed should arise from well-defined content standards.
3. *Accurately reflect achievement:* Sound assessments contain high-quality items, match the appropriate method to the type of learning target, and control for bias and samples appropriately.
4. *Effectively communicate results:* Report results clearly and manage and store them effectively.
5. *Involve students*: Students have a role in all aspects of assessment.

These standards of quality ensure the accuracy of classroom assessments. The Black and Wiliam (1998) research described in Part 1 points to the positive effects on learning when assessment quality improves.

To help teachers meet these standards, school leaders can become assessment literate themselves and by doing so ensure that all assessments provide accurate information. However, too often the assessment job of classroom teachers has been removed from their hands. In place of helping teachers become assessment literate, schools and districts may substitute ready-made assessments narrowly designed to prepare for state tests or to generate additional assessment *of* learning data.

Classroom assessment is not about teachers creating or using mini-versions of the state test. And even though they may be used well in formative ways, it also isn't about conducting short-cycle assessments that may or may not adhere to standards of design quality. Classroom assessment is about giving students information about their own learning on their way to state standards. It enables students to reach the standard on a state test because the scaffolding of learning has been in place in classroom instruction and assessment, allowing them to gain the knowledge and skills necessary to demonstrate that mastery on that test. All assessments along this path, formative and summative, need to reflect standards of quality.

Large-scale assessments also must adhere to standards of quality if they are to be accurate and reliable. Items of poor quality and errors in scoring procedures on state tests are common reports in the media and raise public concern about test quality and the credibility of scores. In 2001, the Commission on Instructionally Supportive Assessment (CISA) released a set of nine requirements that large-scale assessments must adhere to if they are to maximize their usefulness in supporting instruction. Although these guidelines are aimed at state-level accountability tests and therefore are not relevant to classroom assessment, some of the guidelines may have some usefulness for districts constructing assessments to complement the state testing system (pp. iv–v):

1. A state's content standards must be prioritized to support effective instruction and assessment.
2. A state's high-priority content standards must be clearly and thoroughly described so that the knowledge and skills students need to demonstrate competence are evident.

3. The results of a state's assessment of high-priority content standards should be reported standard-by-standard for each student, school, and district.

4. A state must provide educators with optional classroom assessment procedures that can measure students' progress in attaining content standards not assessed by state tests.

5. A state must monitor the breadth of the curriculum to ensure that instructional attention is given to all content standards and subject areas, including those that are not assessed by state tests.

6. A state must ensure that all students have the opportunity to demonstrate their achievement of state standards; consequently, it must provide well-designed assessments appropriate for a broad range of students, with accommodations and alternate methods of assessment available for students who need them.

7. A state must generally allow test developers a minimum of three years to produce statewide tests that satisfy Standards for Educational and Psychological Testing and similar test-quality guidelines.

8. A state must ensure that educators receive professional development focused on how to optimize children's learning based on results of instructionally supportive assessments.

9. States should continually track progress to ensure that tests are
   a) appropriate for the accountability purposes for which they are used,
   b) appropriate for determining whether students have attained state standards, c) appropriate for enhancing teaching, and d) not the cause of negative consequence.

Thinking About Assessment

Activity 4: ATI Interactive Video: *Evaluating Assessment Quality: Hands-on Practice*

Purpose: This interactive video/DVD provides guided practice auditing classroom assessments for quality on four of the five Keys to Quality Classroom Assessment (see Door 3 in Part 3 of this guide). What does it look like when an assessment has (or doesn't have) clear purposes, is (or is not) based on clear targets, is (or is not) designed well, and includes (or doesn't include) student involvement? This video provides checklists and rubrics to use with seven sample classroom assessments in various subject areas, grade levels, and levels of quality.

Description: The video begins with a short overview of the five Keys to Quality. The first activity is to compare two assessments using a checklist based on the Keys. In the next segment, Rick Stiggins and Judy Arter compare the two assessments against each Key. Subsequent segments examine each Key to Quality, ask users to compare two assessments using a Key-specific rubric, and then analyze the assessments based on that Key.

Timing: About 2–3 hours

Directions: Obtain a copy of the video or DVD and follow the directions provided.

Thinking About Assessment

Activity 5: Analyze Classroom Assessments for Clear Targets

Purpose: One of the first places a classroom assessment's accuracy goes astray is in the match to the intended learning. Creating or selecting a test without having a test plan can result in mismatches between instruction and assessment. The assessment probably will not measure what you intended it to measure, which is known as a *validity* problem. If you have ever faced an exam yourself that did not match what you thought were the most important aspects of the course you were taking, you know what that feels like from the student's point of view. When we make a plan for an assessment, whether we intend to create the assessment or just copy it, we are making the advance decisions about validity—what the test will cover and how much weight each learning target will get. In the following activity, teachers will analyze a test they have given to determine its match to the intended learning targets.

Timing: 30 to 60 minutes

Directions: Ask teachers to bring a selected response or extended written response test they have given to students in the past, or one they plan to give in the near future. Then have them follow these steps to audit it for clear targets.

1. *Analyze your test item by item.*
   Identify and write down what learning each item assesses. Describe the learning in whatever terms you want. If two or more items address the same learning, use the same terms to describe that learning.

2. *Organize the learning targets into a test plan.*
   Transfer the information from Step 1 to this chart. Use the example that follows as your guide.

*This activity is adapted from R. J. Stiggins, J. Arter, J. Chappuis, & S. Chappuis, *Classroom Assessment* for *Student Learning: Doing It Right—Using It Well* (pp. 108–109), Portland, OR: Assessment Training Institute, 2004. Adapted by permission. If you have access to this text, you will find a blank of the form used in Step 2 on the accompanying CD, in the Chapter 4 file, "Analyze for Clear Targets."

Learning Target	Item #s	# of points

Example of Step 2 for an Elementary Math Test

Learning Target	Item #s	# of points
Number Sense: Place value	1, 5, 9, 11, 16	10
Representation	2	4
Number Operations: Fractions, multiply by 2, subtract with borrowing	4, 12	5
Problem Solving/Add with carrying	3	3
Measurement: Identify correct units	7, 10, 14, 15	7
Data Analysis & Probability: Tables, charts, and graphs	13	3
Algebra: number patterns, number sentences	6, 8	4

3. *Question your test plan: Is this a representative sample of what you taught and what you expected students to learn? How does it relate to standards?*
   - Does the number of points for each learning target represent its relative importance within the whole? If not, which ones are out of balance? Are some learning targets overrepresented? If so, which one(s)? Are some learning targets underrepresented? If so, which one(s)?
   - Does the number of points for each learning target represent the amount of time you spent on it relative to the whole? If not, which ones are out of balance?
   - Are some of the important learning targets you taught left out? If so, which one(s)?
   - How does your assessment reflect content standards?

4. *Adjust your test plan.*
   As needed, adjust the numbers in the "# of points" column on the chart in Step 2 to reflect both the amount of time you spent teaching each learning target and each target's relative importance to the content as a whole.

As needed, add or delete learning targets to reflect what you taught and what you deemed most important to learn and assess.

5. *Draw conclusions about your assessment.*
   What does this tell you about the matches among what's written in your curriculum, what you taught, and what you assessed?

Closure: Ask teachers to complete this sentence with whatever comes to mind:

Without clear targets . . .

Or, you could use this phrase:

Without knowing what each question on a test measures, we can't . . .

You may wish to have them write their thoughts in one or two minute, collect them, and read them aloud (using no names) to end the session. Here are some likely (and not so likely, but true) answers:

Without clear targets, or without knowing what each question on a test measures, we can't . . .

- Know if the assessment adequately covers and samples what we taught.
- Correctly identify what students know and don't know and their level of achievement.
- Plan the next steps in instruction.
- Give detailed, descriptive feedback to students.
- Have students self-assess or set goals likely to help them learn more.
- Keep track of student learning target by target or standard by standard.
- Complete a standards-based report card.

Thinking About Assessment

Activity 6: Developmental Continua for Teachers

Purpose: The attached developmental continua describe stages of teacher learning about quality assessment. They parallel the Five Keys to Quality Classroom Assessments: "clear and appropriate purposes," "clear targets," "accurately reflect student achievement (including appropriate match of methods to targets, high-quality items, good sampling, and avoiding potential sources of bias and distortion)," "effectively communicated," and "involve students." The continua can be used in at least two ways.

1. As an activity during professional development for leaders to practice questions to ask teachers (and the answers to listen for) to explore their understanding of high-quality, student-involved classroom assessment.
2. As a resource for teachers to self-assess their own learning development in the area of high-quality, student-involved classroom assessment *for* learning. In this latter use are additional purposes:
   ■ To model self-assessment by students through the use of teacher self-assessment on developmental continua. Teachers who are engaged in studying assessment can use the developmental continua at any time during learning to self-assess status and growth. This information could become part of their professional growth portfolio.
   ■ To help develop teacher understanding of the five Keys to Quality Assessment.
   ■ To practice what we preach. If we want students to self-assess, it helps if we also self-assess. If we want students to apply criteria to their own performance, then we might do so as well. Likewise, as leaders we shouldn't ask teachers to do anything we haven't done. If we want teachers to define criteria for quality and use them with students, we need to provide teachers with criteria for the quality of their work. These developmental continua are designed to do just that.

Background: Practice in auditing classroom assessments for quality is provided in this Activity and on the ATI video, *Evaluating Assessment Quality: Hands-on Practice*. We realize that such auditing requires knowledge and practice. Even if you don't feel comfortable auditing assessments for quality, you can still ask teachers questions and listen to their responses. The attached developmental continua help you key your responses to those typically made by educators at different levels of understanding about classroom assessment. Note that Key 1 includes formative assessment procedures where the teacher uses assessment information to plan instruction. Procedures concerning descriptive feedback to students are in Key 4—Communication. Procedures where students do the thinking and the work are in Key 5—Student Involvement.

Note: These developmental continua are works in progress (as are any other such continua). As such, they can be tinkered with: As you and your colleagues ask teachers questions and note responses, you can add phrases to the continua that exemplify for you levels of understanding and implementation of assessment *for* learning.

Directions: First, read through the attached developmental continua. Then divide into pairs or small groups and assign each group one of the following sets of questions about clear targets, clear users and uses, and so on. Next, each group should brainstorm strong and weak teacher responses to their questions and write them on chart paper. Then, groups do a gallery tour—post the charts around the room and have everyone walk around, reading each group's responses. Finally, have the whole group compare their brainstormed list of teacher responses to the developmental continua. Find matches, discuss questions, and plan next steps.

Here are the questions in each category:

Clear and Appropriate Purposes:
1. How do you use the results of your classroom assessments?

Clear Targets:
1. What are your outcomes (targets) for students in general—overall, what do you hope to accomplish with students this year?
2. Why are these the important outcomes you want to emphasize? *and/or* How do your outcomes for students relate to local content standards?

Accurately Reflect Achievement:
1. What is the range of assessment methods to choose from? How do you decide when to use each assessment method?

2. Do you look at assessment questions to see if they are well written? If so, what do you look for?

3. Do you look at the coverage of questions on an assessment to make sure they cover well the learning targets being assessed? If so, how do you decide?

4. What might go wrong during an assessment that might get in the way of students actually showing what they know and can do? Describe potential sources of bias and distortion (pitfalls) and how these could affect the accuracy of assessment results.

Good Communication:

1. How do you communicate assessment results to parents?

2. How do you communicate assessment results to students?

3. How do you communicate assessment results to administrators and other educational stakeholders?

Student Involvement:

1. How do you involve students in their own assessment?

Developmental Continuum Key 1—Assess Why?

Skilled = I understand the various purposes (users and uses) for classroom assessment and why it is essential to have clear purposes for assessment. I successfully balance various purposes. The following statements tend to describe me:

1. **I can explain** why it is essential to have clear purposes for assessment and **I plan** my assessments specifically with purposes (users and uses) users and uses in mind.
2. **I regularly implement both formative** (assessment *for* learning) **and summative** (assessment *of* learning) **assessment** in my classroom.
3. **I regularly use assessment information** to do such things as plan instruction, set goals for students, track student progress, and reflect on my own teaching.
4. **I have a plan for integrating summative and formative assessment over time** in my classroom and formative assessment purposes are in the majority.
5. **I consciously use assessment procedures and results to improve motivation and maximize achievement.**

Practiced = I understand that it is important to have clear purposes for assessment, I know about the various purposes of classroom assessment, and I am trying out and comparing procedures. The following statements tend to describe me:

1. **I can describe various purposes for classroom assessment**—who uses assessment information and what they use it to do. I understand that users include students as well as parents and other educators. I recognize that the type of information they need might be different from the type I need in the classroom and I am experimenting with designing assessments to meet their needs.
2. **I can define formative** (assessment *for* learning) **and summative** (assessment *of* learning) **assessment** and give examples. I can describe why each is important. I am trying various formative assessment ideas.
3. **I frequently use assessment information** to do such things as plan instruction, set goals for students, track student progress, and reflect on my own teaching.
4. **I am trying out ideas for how best to balance assessment *for* and *of* learning in my classroom.**
5. I can describe the impact assessment has on students and **I am becoming more able to consciously use assessment procedures and results to improve motivation and maximize achievement.**

Learning = I am aware of the need to define clear purposes for assessment, and I am learning more about it. The following statements tend to describe me:

1. **I know that different users need different information,** and I am trying to learn how needs differ so that I can better plan classroom assessments.
2. **I have heard of formative** (assessment *for* learning) **and summative** (assessment *of* learning) **uses of assessments**, and I'm learning about how they differ and am seeking out examples.
3. **I sometimes use assessment information to fine tune instruction,** and I am trying to do more.
4. **I want to develop a better balance of assessment** *for* **and** *of* **learning,** but I'm not entirely sure where to begin.
5. **I am aware of the impact assessment has on students** and I am trying to learn how to consciously use assessment procedures and results to improve motivation and maximize achievement.

Ready to Learn = I have not yet considered various purposes for assessment. The following statements tend to describe me:

1. **I know that there are different purposes for assessment, but I have not considered** if my assessment procedures and results completely meet everyone's needs.
2. **I have heard of formative** (assessment *for* learning) **and summative** (assessment *of* learning) **assessment,** but I haven't yet explored their distinctions.
3. **I use assessment mostly for grading.** I may be uncomfortable about this, but I am unsure about what else to do.
4. **I don't entirely see why rethinking assessment purposes is necessary.**
   I know that assessment affects students, but **I'm not sure how to consciously manipulate procedures to maximize motivation and learning.**

Developmental Continuum Key 2—Assess What?

Skilled = I understand and can articulate the enduring skills and knowledge important for students to master. I am, myself, a master of the learning targets I teach. The following statements tend to describe me:

1. **I can explain why having clear targets is essential** to accurate assessments, and I always plan my assessments to cover specific targets.
2. At any given time, **I can readily describe my** short- and long-term **learning targets for students**.
3. **My learning targets for students represent the best thinking in the field** and I can describe how they form the building blocks for student mastery of local content standards, performance standards, and/or benchmarks.
4. **I can readily explain how each of my learning targets spring from those in earlier grades and lay the foundation** for students' success in later grades.
5. **I use my learning targets to plan instruction and assessments.** I can state the learning targets for **everything** I teach.
6. **I can provide thorough descriptive details** about the student knowledge and skills associated with each of my learning targets. For example, if the learning target is becoming a fluent reader, I can define what a fluent reader knows and is able to do and the stages of development in becoming one.

Practiced = I mostly have clear and appropriate learning targets for students, and am filling out the final details. The following statements tend to describe me:

1. **I can describe different kinds of learning targets** and find specific examples of each kind. I understand why it is important to be able to do this. I am experimenting with ways to ensure my assessments accurately cover my targets.
2. At any given time, **I can usually describe my** short- and long-term **learning targets for students**.
3. **I am working steadily to ensure that my learning targets for students represent the best thinking in the field** and that I understand how they form the building blocks for student mastery of local content standards, performance standards, and/or benchmarks.
4. **I understand how my learning targets mesh over grade levels** and how my targets fit into the bigger scheme.
5. **I mostly use my learning targets to plan instruction and assessments,** but sometimes I plan activities first and then go back to identify which learning targets are being covered.

6. **I can usually provide thorough descriptive details** about the student knowledge and skills associated with each of my learning targets. For example, if the learning target is becoming a fluent reader, I can define what a fluent reader knows and is able to do and the stages of development in becoming one.

Learning = I know that it is important to be clear on student learning targets, and I am seeking more information. The following statements tend to describe me:

1. I can describe different kinds of learning targets, but **I'm unsure if my list is complete—** or—**I have some trouble finding examples.**
2. At any point in time **I can more or less describe my short- and long-term learning targets for students.**
3. I know that **some of my targets represent the best thinking in the field** but I'm not sure about others—or—I'm unsure how classroom level learning targets provide the building blocks for mastery of content standards, performance standards, and/or benchmarks.
4. **I can describe in general how my learning targets for students relate to those in previous and subsequent grades**, but I would have to look up the details.
5. **I plan instruction by identifying activities that would be engaging for students** and then I go back to identify which learning targets I am emphasizing.
6. **I can list features of a quality performance**, but I need some assistance to distinguish levels of performance. For example, I can state that a piece of writing needs to have voice, but I need help articulating what *strong* or *weak* voice looks like.

Ready to Learn = I am not sure what learning targets are. The following statements tend to describe me:

1. **I'm not sure I could define what a** learning target for students is—or—I'm not sure I could list various types of targets.
2. I think **it takes too much time** to identify learning targets for everything I teach.
3. **I'm not sure how my learning targets relate** to local content standards, performance standards, and/or benchmarks.
4. **Sometimes clear learning targets get in the way** of spontaneous teaching.
5. **I design instruction mostly by what engages students and what I like to teach**—or— **I count on the textbook**, or a series of prepackaged instructional materials, to define and sequence the important learning targets for students.
6. **I feel uncomfortable teaching certain subjects** because I don't completely understand them myself.

Developmental Continuum Key 3—Assess How?

Skilled = I use only assessments that I know to be accurate—correct methods, good sample, and no sources of bias and distortion. The following statements tend to describe me:

Assessment Design

1. **I can describe how each assessment I use is designed with the end user in mind.** For example, if assessment materials are used with students as instructional tools, they are "student friendly."

2. **My assessments are always focused on specific, important learning targets.** I always match learning targets to assessment methods (multiple choice, matching, short answer, essay, performance assessment, personal communication).

3. **I use test blueprints** that indicate how each learning target will be assessed and its relative importance.

4. **I use "prepackaged" assessments only when I'm sure** they cover the right learning tar gets in the right proportions, using the best methods.

Writing Quality Questions and Tasks

1. **I understand rules for** unambiguously **writing all types of assessment questions and tasks,** and I use them routinely when writing or selecting an assessment for use.

Sampling

1. **I plan my assessments to gather enough examples** of student performance to get a good sense of what a student knows and can do; **I sample well.**

Bias/Distortion

1. **In my assessments I consciously avoid doing things that might result in inaccurate results**; I consciously avoid potential sources of bias and distortion.

2. **I plan for multiple assessments of complex targets and use a variety of assessments** so that all of my students have opportunities to demonstrate their learning fully.

3. **I routinely discard from assessments questions that don't work** and I have good, consistent methods for identifying them.

4. **I do not use assessment information I know to be inaccurate.**

Practiced = I understand the range of assessment options and when to use each, the importance of sampling student performance well, and the importance of eliminating potential sources of bias and distortion in my assessments. I am in the process of applying what I know. The following statements tend to describe me:

Assessment Design
1. **I can describe various assessment methods** (multiple choice, matching, short answer, essay, performance assessment, personal communication) and show examples.
2. **I can describe when to use each assessment method**—how to match methods to targets and purposes (users and uses) and how to balance ideal choices with practical considerations.
3. **I'm practicing with test blueprints** to help me plan how each learning target will be assessed and its relative importance.
4. **I am trying never to use "prepackaged" assessments** without consciously looking at what they cover, the assessment methods used, and the proportion of content of each target.

Writing Quality Questions and Tasks
1. **I'm familiar with many rules for** unambiguously **writing good assessment questions and tasks**, and I am attempting to apply them routinely.

Sampling
1. **I can define sampling** and describe why it is important to consider when designing classroom assessments.
2. **I can find examples of assessments** that sample well and poorly.
3. **I am attempting to apply what I know about sampling.**

Bias/Distortion
1. I can **list potential sources of bias and distortion** in various assessment methods and describe why they are important to consider when designing classroom assessments.
2. **I can show examples of assessments with various problems, including linguistic and cultural barriers,** and can describe which problems can be fixed and which have to be lived with.
3. **I discard from assessments questions that don't work** when I discover them, but I'm not sure I catch them all.
4. **I am attempting to determine when assessment information is inaccurate,** so that I can avoid its use.

Learning= I am aware of the need to match assessment methods to learning targets and purposes, and I have the desire to be more intentional about selecting assessment methods, sampling, and avoiding potential sources of bias and distortion, but I'm not entirely sure what needs to be done or where to start. The following statements tend to describe me:

Assessment Design
1. **I use various assessment methods** but I sometimes have difficulty explaining why.
2. **I can list various assessment methods**, but sometimes I have trouble defining them or identifying examples.
3. **I sometimes feel afraid of using "traditional" assessment** methods because of the recent hype about performance assessment.
4. **I think there are some problems** in prepackaged assessments, but I'm not real sure what to do about it.

Writing Quality Questions and Tasks
1. **I am familiar with some rules** for writing unambiguous assessment questions and tasks, **but I'm not sure I understand them all.**

Sampling
1. **I have tried to sample student performance**, but I'm not sure I do it well.

Bias/Distortion
1. **I can identify some potential problems in real assessments and I have tried to fix them**, but I may not always know the best way.
2. **I'm experimenting with alternative ways to assess the learning of students** whose language, culture, or other characteristics differ from my own without losing vital information about the target, but I'm not sure if I'm doing it right.
3. **I have thought about discarding from assessments questions that don't work**, but I'm not sure how to do it.
4. **I don't want to use assessment results I know are inaccurate**, but I'm not sure what else to use.

Ready to Learn = I'm not sure what is meant by matching targets to methods. I know that such things as sampling and bias and distortion exist, but I don't quite see how it applies to me. The following statements tend to describe me:

Assessment Design

1. **I tend to use the same** assessment method all the time.
2. **I concentrate on using assessment methods that match our standardized test.**
3. **I mostly use the methods used by other teachers;** I'm not sure why.
4. **I use mostly prepackaged assessments** that come with instructional materials. I'm not sure what to look for to make sure these assessments match my learning targets for students or my purposes for assessment.

Writing Quality Questions and Tasks

1. **I'm not familiar with rules** for writing unambiguous assessment questions and tasks.

Sampling

1. **I'm not sure I can define "sampling"**—or—I don't know what to look for to determine if sampling is a problem.

Bias/Distortion

1. **I'm not sure I can define "bias and distortion."**
2. **I know that assessments can contain barriers** that mask some students' learning, **but I'm uncertain what to do about it.**
3. **I know that some assessment questions are better than others,** but I don't know what to do about it.
4. **I thought that sampling and bias and distortion are mainly problems with standardized tests.**

Developmental Continuum Key 4—Good Communication*

Skilled = I report student assessment results to a variety of audiences accurately and understandably. The following statements tend to describe me:

1. **My feedback/communication with students**
   - is based on learning targets they understand.
   - is frequent and describes strengths and next steps in learning. I avoid evaluative
   - feedback (e.g., grades) on practice work.
   - emphasizes what they already know how to do and limits corrective feedback to the amount they can absorb at any one time
2. **When I communicate with others I consciously**
   - use language and symbols they understand.
   - choose the reporting option that provides the right amount of detail for the audience—grades, narrative reports, rubric scores, developmental continuua, portfolios, student-led conferences, etc.
   - involve others in interpreting the results.
   - check to make sure the person understood what was communicated.
   - tailor the type of information for the audience. For example, if the audience is parents, I emphasize what students already know and the next steps in learning.
3. **I can explain various types of standardized test scores and displays** in ways others can understand: percentiles, standard scores, error intervals, mastery scores, etc.

Practiced = I understand the range of assessment reporting options and when to use each and the importance of frequent, descriptive feedback to students. I am in the process of learning how to apply what I know. The following statements tend to describe me:

1. **I understand that feedback to students needs to be based on learning targets they understand,** is frequent and descriptive, emphasizes what they already know and next steps in learning, and needs to be limited to the amount they can absorb at any one time; and, I am partially successful in doing these.
2. **I understand that feedback to others besides students needs to be consciously planned** and takes into account common understanding of symbols, the reporting option that provides the correct level of detail, their need to help interpret the results, their need to know what the student already knows and the next step in learning; and I am partially successful in doing these.

*Note: For recording and summarizing achievement, see the Rubric for Grading (Resource 6, p. 221); the Key 4 developmental continuum covers feedback/communication/reporting.

3. **I can mostly explain various types of standardized test scores and displays** in ways others can understand: percentiles, standard scores, error intervals, mastery scores, etc.

Learning = I understand that good communication of assessment results is important, but I don't know where to begin. The following statements tend to describe me:

1. **I know that feedback and communication with students is part of the learning,** but I'm not sure what type of feedback is best or how to deliver it.
2. **I would like to make reporting about achievement to parents and others more powerful,** but I'm not sure how to go about it.
3. **I know that explaining results of standardized tests to others is important,** but I only partially understand them myself.

Ready to Learn = I use standard, traditional ways of reporting assessment results to others. The following statements tend to describe me:

1. **My feedback/communication with students**
   - is based mostly on grades.
   - occurs on a "need to know" basis, as when a student is failing.
   - frequently involves comparing students to each other, e.g., grading on a curve.
   - consists mostly of going over a test and explaining the questions students got wrong.
2. **When I communicate with others I**
   - tend to use the same reporting option and symbols for all audiences, e.g., grades.
   - interpret results for them.
   - do it on a "need to know" basis, as when a student is failing.
3. **I don't understand various types of standardized test scores and displays,** or I don't feel such scores are important so I don't attend much to them.

Developmental Continuum Key 5—Involve Students How?

Skilled = I actively and consistently involve students in their own assessment, tracking progress, setting goals for learning, and communicating about their own progress. The following statements tend to describe me:

1. **Many of my students can accurately describe the learning targets they are to hit.** Vehicles include student-friendly language, rubrics, and samples of work that illustrate different levels of proficiency.
2. **Many of my students are accurate assessors.**
3. **My students regularly track their learning.**
4. **My students regularly self-assess,** set goals for learning, and develop a plan for achieving those goals.
5. **My students regularly communicate with others about their learning.** Vehicles include student-involved conferences, portfolio self-reflections, and letters to others.

Practiced = I can describe various student involvement activities and show examples. I am trying these out. The following statements tend to describe me:

1. **I consistently and frequently explain to students** the learning targets to be attained. Some of my students can accurately explain the targets in their own words.
2. **I regularly share performance criteria, samples of student work, and assessment questions with students** to help them understand the learning targets they are to hit and to help them be accurate assessors. Some students are accurate assessors.
3. **I regularly ask my students to self-assess, reflect on their learning, track their progress, set goals for learning, and/or communicate their learning to others.** I have used a variety of specific methods such as rubrics, self-reflection questions, portfolios, student writing, and answering practice test questions, But, my students are only partially successful.

Learning = I understand, in general, the types of things one might do to involve students in assessment, but I don't understand the precise steps involved. The following statements tend to describe me:

1. **I understand that students need to understand the learning targets,** but I am unsure how to do this.

2. **I understand that students need to be able to accurately self-assess** in order to take control of their learning and to realize associated achievement benefits, but I'm not sure how to begin.

3. **I know that student involvement in their own assessment, record keeping, and reporting is important**, but I don't know how to begin.

Ready to Learn = I don't understand what is meant by student involvement—or—I have tried it and it doesn't work—or—I don't believe it to be powerful. The following statements tend to describe me:

1. **I'm not always sure** if the target statements can be easily understood by all of my students.

2. My students exchange papers, mark questions right or wrong, and report total scores.

3. **My students have difficulty explaining why they get the grades they do**, self-assessing, and describing what quality works looks like.

4. **I'm not sure students have the ability to assess themselves**, and I'm not convinced that self-assessment is useful. I have not considered involving students in developing assessments.

5. I have students communicate progress to parents by sending work home and having parents sign off on it.

Competency 2

The leader understands the principles of assessment *for* learning and works with staff to integrate them into classroom instruction.

Over the years educators have been encouraged to think about assessment and instruction as hand-in-glove, to think about teaching as one seamless act melding curriculum, instruction, and assessment. This is easier said than done. Let's begin with a vision of what it means. We've created a list of nine principles that clarify instruction-embedded assessment, or assessment for learning. These nine principles are our best answer to teachers' frequently asked question, "Exactly how do I integrate assessment with instruction and truly make one an extension of the other?" The application of these principles achieves just that in the classroom, with assessment becoming another form of good teaching. Following are the nine Principles of Assessment *for* Learning:

1. Teachers understand and can articulate *in advance of teaching* the achievement targets students are to hit.
2. *Students are informed regularly* about those targets in terms they can understand, in part through the study of the criteria by which their work will be evaluated, and samples of high-quality work.
3. *Students can describe what targets they are to hit* and what comes next in their learning.
4. Classroom teachers can transform those targets into *dependable assessments* that yield accurate information.
5. Both the teacher and the student use classroom assessment information to *revise and guide* teaching and learning.
6. Feedback given to students is descriptive, constructive, frequent, and timely; *helping students identify their strengths and know how to plan and improve* their work.
7. *Students are actively,* consistently, and effectively *involved in assessment,* including learning to manage their own learning through the skills of self-assessment.
8. *Students* actively, consistently, and effectively *communicate with others* about their achievement status and improvement.

9. Teachers understand the relationship between assessment and student motivation and use *assessment to build student success* and confidence rather than failure and defeat.

Of the 10 leader competencies, Competency 2 is most clearly focused on your capacity to guide the development of an assessment-literate faculty. Each of the nine Principles of Assessment *for* Learning in Competency 2 has behind it a set of specific skills and teaching strategies. It is the consistent application of those skills and strategies throughout a school or district that produces significant gains in student achievement.

Here are some examples of what assessment-literate teachers do when applying the nine principles:

■ Translate learning targets into student-friendly terms, to clarify what students are expected to learn.

■ Gather accurate information about student achievement on a regular basis using high-quality formative assessments that adhere to standards of quality. In this process, teachers consider which assessment method will give the most accurate picture of student achievement on the specific learning targets.

    ■ Provide students descriptive feedback linked directly to the intended learning, giving them insight about current strengths and how to do better next time, rather than giving evaluative feedback consisting only of marks and letter grades. Students have an opportunity to practice, using this feedback, before a summative assessment.

■ Keep students connected to a vision of quality as the learning unfolds, continually defining for students what the learning expectations are for the lesson/unit (Chappuis & Stiggins, 2002).

■ Involve students in their own assessment in ways that require them to think about their own progress, communicate their own understanding of what they have learned, and set goals to close the gap between where they are now relative to the intended learning and where they need to be to meet standards. Assessment-literate teachers teach students the skills of self-assessment, and involve students in conferences, have students create practice test items, and evaluate anonymous classroom work for quality— all examples of students being involved in assessment.

■ Have students communicate the status of their own learning to interested adults through written journals, student-involved parent conferences, and portfolios that focus on growth toward the standards.

A school improvement strategy common today is the development of group assessments, administered every 4–6 weeks so as to get additional data to adjust instruction along the way. Although helpful, these assessments (*short-cycle, interim, common,* and *benchmark* are just some of the names that describe this practice) should not be confused with assessment *for* learning. They are in fact additional marks for the gradebook and summative scores to analyze, and in that description of use may not even be called formative. The fact that as summative tests they are being used in formative ways is beneficial, but it is not the same as assessment *for* learning, and these additional assessments, by themselves, are not sufficient. In fact, if they are not of high quality, adhering to the five Keys to Quality Assessment previously described, it will matter little if the results are used well, as the evidence will not be accurate.

Thinking About Assessment

Activity 7: Classroom Assessment *for* Learning

Purpose: Begin to identify examples of what the principles of assessment *for* learning look like when integrated into classroom instruction.

Time: 30 minutes

Directions: Read the following article, "Classroom Assessment *for* Learning" reprinted from ASCD's *Educational Leadership* and after reading, answer the following questions:

- Of the classroom practices listed in the article, which do you most commonly see in classrooms in your school/district?
- Which practices are least evident?
- What other teaching strategies do you see in your school/district that might support assessment *for* learning? Relate them to the nine principles of assessment *for* learning.
- How might you help teachers begin to incorporate some of these strategies into their classroom routine?

Closure: Many of the teaching strategies described in the article (and other strategies not included that also reflect assessment *for* learning practices) are present in many classrooms already. We can help teachers expand their repertoire of strategies and ensure they use them intentionally by beginning to see how their current practices relate to the nine principles and by providing the professional development opportunities needed to make the nine principles part of everyday teaching practice.

Classroom Assessment *for* Learning

Classroom assessment that involves students in the process and focuses on increasing learning can motivate rather than merely measure students.

STEPHEN CHAPPUIS AND RICHARD J. STIGGINS

IMAGINE a classroom assessment as a healthy part of effective teaching and successful learning. At a time when large-scale, external assessments of learning gain political favor and attention, many teachers are discovering how to engage and motivate students using day-to-day classroom assessment for purposes beyond measurement. By applying the principles of what is called *assessment for learning,* teachers have followed clear research findings of the effects that high-quality, formative assessment can have on student achievement.

We typically think of assessment as an index of school success rather than as the cause of that success. Unfortunately, largely absent from the traditional classroom assessment environment is the use of assessment as a tool to promote greater student achievement (Shepard, 2000). In general, the teacher teaches and then tests. The teacher and class move on, leaving unsuccessful students, those who might not learn at the established pace and within a fixed time frame, to finish low in the rank order. This assessment model is founded on two outdated beliefs: that to increase learning we should increase student anxiety and that comparison with more successful peers will motivate low performers to do better.

STEPHEN CHAPPUIS is Director of Professional Development and RICHARD STIGGINS is President and Founder of the Assessment Training Institute, Portland, OR.

By contrast, assessment for learning occurs during the teaching and learning process rather than after it and has as its primary focus the ongoing improvement of learning for all students (Assessment Reform Group, 1999; Crooks, 2001; Shepard, 2000). Teachers who assess for learning use day-to-day classroom assessment activities to involve students directly and deeply in their own learning, increasing their confidence and motivation to learn by emphasizing progress and achievement rather than failure and defeat (Stiggins, 1999; 2001). In the assessment for learning model, assessment is an instructional tool that promotes learning rather than an event designed solely for the purpose of evaluation and assigning grades. And when students become involved in the assessment process, assessment for learning begins to look more like teaching and less like testing (Davies, 2000).

STUDENT-INVOLVED ASSESSMENT

Research shows that classroom assessments that provide accurate, descriptive feedback to students and involve them in the assessment process can improve learning (Black and Wiliam, 1998). As a result, assessment for learning means more than just assessing students often, more than providing the teacher with assessment results to revise instruction. In assessment for learning, both teacher and student use classroom assessment information to modify teaching and learning activities. Teachers use assessment information formatively when they

---

- Pretest before a unit of study and adjust instruction for individuals or the entire group.
- Analyze which students need more practice.
- Continually revise instruction on the basis of results.
- Reflect on the effectiveness of their own teaching practices.
- Confer with students regarding their strengths and the areas that need improvement.
- Facilitate peer tutoring, matching students who demonstrate understanding with those who do not.

We tend to think of students as passive participants in assessment rather than engaged users of the information that assessment can produce. What we should be asking is, How can students use assessment to take responsibility for and improve their own learning?

Student involvement in assessment doesn't mean that students control decisions regarding what will or won't be learned or tested. It doesn't mean that they assign their own grades. Instead, student involvement means that students learn to use assessment information to manage their own learning so that they understand how they learn best, know exactly where they are in relation to the defined learning targets, and plan and take the next steps in their learning.

Student-involved assessment means that students learn to use assessment information to manage their own learning.

Students engage in the assessment for learning process when they use assessment information to set goals, make learning decisions related to their own improvement, develop an understanding of what quality work looks like, self-assess, and communicate their status and progress toward established learning goals. Students involved in their own assessment might

- Determine the attributes of good performance. Students look at teacher-supplied anonymous samples of strong student performances and list the qualities that make them strong, learning the language of quality and the concepts behind strong performance.
- Use scoring guides to evaluate real work samples. Students can start with just one criterion in the guide and expand to others as they become more proficient in scoring. As students engage in determining the characteristics of quality work and scoring actual work samples, they become better able to evaluate their own work. Using the language of the scoring guide, they can identify their areas of strength and set goals for improvement—in essence, planning the next steps in their learning.
- Revise anonymous work samples. Students go beyond evaluating work to using criteria to improve the quality of a work sample. They can develop a revision plan that outlines improvements, or write a letter to the creator of the original work offering advice on how to improve the sample. This activity also helps students know what to do before they revise their own work.
- Create practice tests or test items based on their understanding of the learning targets and the essential concepts in the class material. Students can work in pairs to identify what they think should be on the test and to generate sample test items and responses.
- Communicate with others about their growth and determine when they are nearing success. Students achieve a deeper understanding of themselves and the material that they are attempting to learn when they describe the quality of their own work. Letters to parents, written self-reflections, and conferences with teachers and parents in which students outline the process they used to create a product allow students to share what they know and describe their progress toward the learning target. By accumulating evidence of their own improvement in growth portfolios, students can refer to specific stages in their growth and celebrate their achievement with others.

EFFECTIVE TEACHER FEEDBACK

"You need to study harder." "Your handwriting is very nice." "Good job." Traditionally, teachers use such statements to register their approval or disapproval of student performance. But such evaluative feedback, long a classroom staple, is of limited value for improving student learning and can actually have negative effects on students' desire to learn. And grades, those traditional coded symbols and markings—B-, 71 percent, 4/10, Satisfactory, F—actually communicate even less about what students have done well or need to do to improve. By contrast, teacher comments that focus on student work and not on individual student characteristics can increase student's motivation and desire to learn.

Black and Wiliam (1998) point to the benefits of replacing judgmental feedback with specific, descriptive, and immediate feedback. When the goal is to increase student motivation and learning, productive feedback tells students what they are doing right, pinpointing strengths and helping learners develop those strengths even further. For some students, receiving this feedback in writing and having time to reflect on it is sufficient. Other students need face-to-face teacher feedback to reinforce what they have done well.

Effective teacher feedback describes why an answer is right or wrong in specific terms that students understand. Students can also generate their own descriptive feedback by comparing their work with teacher-provided examplars or posted examples. They can then compare their own feedback with that of their teacher.

Descriptive feedback should provide ways for students to improve in clear, constructive language. Instead of simply labeling student errors or omissions, effective feedback guides students to better performance throughout the learning process. Useful comments focus specifically on improving only one area at a time.

Finally, teacher feedback for learning draws an even bigger picture by telling students where they are now relative to the defined learning targets—and where teachers ultimately want them to be. By modeling for students a variety of suggestions designed to narrow the gap between where they are and where they should be headed, teachers can help students learn to generate their own strategies for improvement.

THE SKILLS OF SELF-ASSESSMENT

Eventually, we want students to be able to direct their own learning. Yet it often seems unclear just how students will achieve this goal. Assessment for learning helps students become self-directed learners by developing their self-assessment skills. The principles of assessment for learning are interrelated: Just as involving students in the assessment process helps make assessment more like instruction, students need to learn to self-assess so that they can use the descriptive feedback from the teacher to its best advantage. Sadler (1989) and Atkin, Black and Coffey (2001) describe a model of formative assessment in which learners continually ask themselves three questions as they self-assess.

Where Am I Trying To Go?

Students need clearly articulated, concise learning targets to be able to answer this first question. Learning is easier when learners understand what goal they are trying to achieve, the purpose of achieving the goal, and the specific attributes of success. Teachers should continually help students clarify the intended learning as the lessons unfold—not just at the beginning of a unit of study. Teachers share learning intentions with students when they

- Phase objectives in terms that begin with "We are learning to…" or "I can…"
- Ask students to read the objectives aloud and ask clarifying questions.
- Separate what they want students to do—the instructions for completing the task—from what they want students to learn. Otherwise, the directions might overshadow the intended learning.
- Inform students why they need to learn what comes next and how it connects to previous and future learning.
- Display the learning objectives in the classroom.

• Provide students with examples of outstanding work as well as samples of lesser quality so that they can see the differences.

• Ask students to rephrase the learning targets or describe what attainment of a target looks like (Arter & Busick, 2001; Clarke, 2001).

Where Am I Now?

Students can practice comparing their work to models of high-quality work and trying to identify the differences. They can use teacher feedback from formative assessments to gather evidence of what they know and can do relative to the defined learning target. They can use questions designed to prompt students to reflect on what they have learned individually relative to the intended learning. All of these strategies help students ascertain—and, even more important, learn *how* to ascertain—where they are and where they need to be, an awareness that is central to their ultimate success.

Teachers share learning intentions with students when they separate what they want students to do—the instructions for completing a task—from what they want students to learn.

How Do I Close The Gap?

Assessment for learning helps students know what to do to move from their current position to the final learning goal. To meet learning goals, students must participate fully in creating the goals, analyzing assessment data, and developing a plan of action to achieve the next goal (Clarke, 2001).

Students should learn question-and-answer strategies that they can use to close the gap: What do I need to change in my work to improve its quality? What specific help do I need to make these changes? From whom can I get help? What resources do I need?

Sadler (1989) notes that a steady flow of descriptive feedback to students encourages continual self-assessment around what constitutes quality.

Keeping students connected to a vision of quality as the unit of study progresses helps them close the gap by formulating their next steps in learning.

ALL STUDENTS LEARNING WELL

The habits and skills of self-assessment are within the grasp and capabilities of almost every student. Students take greater responsibility for their own learning when they regularly assess themselves (Shepard, 2001). In the hands of trained teachers, assessment for learning breeds confidence in learning. It provides students with opportunities for monitoring and communicating to others their own progress.

Educators open the door to using assessment in more productive ways when they acknowledge that students respond differently to the use of test scores as threats of punishment or promises of reward. Those who succeed keep striving; those who fail may give up. By contrast, most students respond positively to classroom assessment environments that promote success rather than simply measure it.

Students demonstrate unprecedented score gains on standardized assessments when their teachers apply the principles of assessment for learning in the classroom (Black and Wiliam, 1998). With appropriate training, teachers can improve the accuracy of their day-to-day assessments, make their feedback to students descriptive and informative, and increase the involvement of students in the entire assessment process. In this way, classroom assessment for learning becomes a school improvement tool that helps create responsible, engaged, and self-directed learners.

References

Arter, J. A., & Busick, K. U. (2001). *Practice with student-involved classroom assessment.* Portland, OR: Assessment Training Institute.

Assessment Reform Group. (1999). *Assessment for learning. Beyond the black box.* Cambridge, England: University of Cambridge.

Atkin, J. M., Black, P., & Coffey, J. (2001). *Classroom assessment and the National Science Education Standards.* Washington, DC: National Academy Press.

Black, P., & Wiliam, D. (1998). Inside the black box: Raising standards through classroom assessment. *Phi Delta Kappan*, *80*(2), 139–148.

Clarke, S. (2001). *Unlocking formative assessment.* London: Hodder and Stoughton.

Crooks, T. (2001). *The validity of formative assessments.* Leeds, England: British Educational Research Association.

Davies, A. (2000). *Making classroom assessment work.* Merville, British Columbia, Canada: Connections Publishing.

Sadler, R. (1989). Formative assessment and the design of instructional systems. *Instructional Science, 18,* 119–144.

Shepard, L. A. (2000). The role of assessment in a learning culture. *Educational Researcher, 29*(7), 4–14.

Shepard, L. A. (2001, July). *Using assessment to help students think about learning.* Keynote address at the Assessment Training Institute Summer Conference, Portland, OR.

Stiggins, R. J. (1999). Assessment, student confidence, and school success. *Phi Delta Kappan, 81*(3), 191–198.

Stiggins, R. J. (2001). *Student-involved classroom assessment* (3d ed.). Upper Saddle River, NJ: Merrill-Prentice Hall.

Thinking About Assessment

Activity 8: Principles of Assessment *for* Learning: A Self-Analysis

Purpose: This activity is helpful in charting next steps for learning and professional development by identifying which principles of assessment *for* learning are already in place and which principles need additional attention in order to be applied consistently in the school/classroom. This activity can be done individually by leadership team members and then summarized, or an entire faculty can get together and rate their school or district as a group. The point is to identify strengths and potential areas for growth among the nine principles.

Time: 30 minutes

Directions: Using the checklist provided in this activity, select the level of your educational organization (district, building, classroom) with which you are most familiar and analyze it. Each participant rates each principle on a scale of 1–5 using the following descriptors:

> 1 = doesn't happen
> 2 = infrequently happens
> 3 = sometimes
> 4 = frequently happens
> 5 = routinely done

Then tally the results.

- Which principles came out strongest? How do you account for that?
- Which principles appear like they need the most improvement or work?
- How could you go about organizing improvement in those areas?

Closure: When using this as a group activity, especially with teachers, participants need to have more than a passing familiarity with the nine principles before doing a self- or school analysis. Having discussions about each principle, reading about assessment *for* learning, and sharing ideas with each other help clarify each of the principles, making it easier to judge the current state of affairs regarding the level of school or district implementation. Further, allow people to rate anonymously to create a safe environment for those who may need a level of personal privacy. This will also help maximize the accuracy of the responses, and therefore, the profile of the group.

One engaging way to use this activity and to maintain anonymity is to have participants rate themselves low to high using a scale of 1–5 on a separate blank sheet of paper. No names are written on the paper. When participants are all finished, ask them to crumple up the paper into a snowball, give it a toss, and then pick one up, making sure it isn't their own.

At this point, have participants create a "human histogram." Tape big numbers 1 to 5 on the wall. Then ask participants to line up by the number that is shown on their sheet, starting with the first principle. When everyone is lined up, a bar graph emerges that represents the group's rating on that particular principle. Do this for each of the nine principles. This can lead to discussions about strengths and weaknesses, patterns, and professional development priorities.

Assessment Training Institute
Principles of Assessment *for* Learning

1. I understand and can articulate in advance of teaching the achievement targets students are to hit.
    Low 1_____ 2_____ 3_____ 4_____ 5_____ High

2. My students are informed regularly about those targets in terms they can understand, in part through the study of the criteria by which their work will be evaluated and samples of high-quality work.
    Low 1_____ 2_____ 3_____ 4_____ 5_____ High

3. My students can describe what targets they are to hit and what comes next in their learning.
    Low 1_____ 2_____ 3_____ 4_____ 5_____ High

4. I can transform those targets into dependable assessments that yield accurate information.
    Low 1_____ 2_____ 3_____ 4_____ 5_____ High

5. I use classroom assessment information to revise and guide teaching and student learning, and share this information with students.
    Low 1_____ 2_____ 3_____ 4_____ 5_____ High

6. The feedback I give to students is descriptive, constructive, frequent, and immediate, helping students know how to plan and improve.
    Low 1_____ 2_____ 3_____ 4_____ 5_____ High

7. My students are actively, consistently, and effectively involved in assessment, including learning to manage their own learning through the skills of self-assessment.
    Low 1_____ 2_____ 3_____ 4_____ 5_____ High

8. My students actively, consistently, and effectively communicate with others about their achievement status and improvement.
    Low 1_____ 2_____ 3_____ 4_____ 5_____ High

9. I understand the relationship between assessment and student motivation and use assessment to build student success and confidence rather than failure and defeat.
    Low 1_____ 2_____ 3_____ 4_____ 5_____ High

Thinking About Assessment

Activity 9: Converting Learning Targets to Student-Friendly Language

Purpose: One key principle of assessment *for* learning requires the development of student-friendly versions of achievement targets. This activity shows teachers how to think about that translation. It can be especially helpful to use reasoning learning targets for this activity.

Time: 30–45 minutes

Directions,
Part A: Gather a sample of two or three grade-level learning targets from your district or state and turn them into student-friendly "I can" statements like those in the Ohio example here. (You might want to use your reading content standards and find *predict, summarize,* and *infer* learning targets so you can use the wording here.) Share the examples with participants, showing how you first identify the terms to be defined, then define them, and then turn the learning target into one or more "I can" statements, using language our students will understand.

Ohio Sixth-Grade Reading Grade-Level Indicators

■ Predict from information in the text, substantiating with specific references to textual examples that may be in widely separated sections of text.

■ Summarize the information in texts, recognizing important ideas and supporting details, and noting gaps or contradictions.

■ Answer inferential questions to demonstrate comprehension.

Turning Grade Level Indicators into Student-Friendly Language
Predict from information in the text.
1. Word to be defined: *Predict*
   Predict: to make a statement saying that something will happen in the future.
2. Student-friendly language: I can predict from information in the text. This means I can use information from what I read to guess at what will happen next. (Or, to guess what the author will tell me next.)

Summarize the information in texts.

1. Word to be defined: *Summarize*

   Summarize: To give a brief statement of the main points, main events, or important ideas.

2. Student-friendly language: I can summarize the information in texts. This means I can make a short statement of the main points or the big ideas of what I read.

Answer inferential questions.

1. Word to be defined: *inferential*

   Inferential: Requiring a conclusion drawn using the information available and reasoning.

2. Student-friendly language: I can answer inferential questions. This means I can use information from what I read together with my own reasoning to draw a conclusion.

Directions, Part B: Using your own content standards, ask participants to identify one that would be unclear to most of their students. If it is a complex content standard, have them identify and define key elements. Last, have them turn the learning target into one or more "I can" statements.

The Process

1. Find important learning target.
2. Identify word(s) needing definition.
3. Define word(s).
4. Rewrite the learning target in student-friendly language.
5. Try it out on a partner or students; get feedback.
6. Refine as needed.

Closure: Participants may wonder about the amount of time it takes to clarify learning targets. Ask them to discuss how they might economize in this process, set priorities, or manage it effectively. If they do not come up with ideas, you might prime the pump by suggesting that (1) a good place to start is with a learning target that students generally do not do well on, and (2) you can have students share in this work on some learning targets as an introduction to the learning. Close with a discussion of the benefits to students. Bring the discussion back to the necessity of students' knowing where they are going.

Thinking About Assessment

Activity 10: Ways That Teachers and Students Use Formative
Assessment

Purpose: To introduce participants to the range of formative uses of assessment and to expand their awareness of what constitutes formative assessment

Time: 20–30 minutes

Directions: After providing a brief summary of the Black and Wiliam (1998) research on the effects of formative assessment on student learning, ask participants to think of the formative assessment strategies they are familiar with—methods they use in the classroom, or have seen, or have heard of.

Formative assessment strategies I'm familiar with:

Then ask participants to read through the accompanying three lists of assessment practices, marking those practices with which they are familiar.

Closure: Ask participants to reflect on and share any surprises or new ideas.

Formative Assessment Practices

Teacher

Just as we want a balance of assessment methods used in classrooms to reflect the different kinds of learning targets we hold for students, we also want a balance of summative (assessment *of* learning) and formative (assessment *for* learning) practices in the classroom. Many teachers are delighted to agree with this statement, but may not know just how to go about putting **formative** assessment—assessment *for* learning—into action. Or, they may be engaging in formative assessment without knowing it's what they're already doing. Here is a list of ways the **teacher** can function as a formative assessor:

- Use diagnostic assessments, designed to reflect the intended learning targets, to make preinstruction decisions.
- Share learning targets/objectives/goals in advance of teaching lessons, giving assignments, or doing activities. (Okay, if it's a pure discovery learning activity, you can hold off. But you need to know what you're aiming for, unless you regularly run out of things to teach before you run out of year. And eventually, they'll need to know too.) Use language students understand, and check to make sure they understand; e.g., ask "Why is it we are doing this activity? What is it we are learning?"
- Let students know the purpose of each assignment or activity. Is it for practice? What kind of feedback will they get on it? Informal? Formal? Where does it fit in the grading scheme?
- Provide descriptive feedback (oral or written) in place of summative grades during learning, including on homework, *especially if the homework is intended to reinforce concepts taught that day*. Everything that moves does not have to be graded.
- Focus feedback on learning targets/objectives/goals. Let students know what they *have* learned well before launching into what they need to work on. Consider how much corrective feedback the learner—especially the struggling learner—can reasonably be expected to act on at one time.

Student

Teacher feedback functions as a model for students—to teach them how to begin thinking about their own work. We provide descriptive feedback and encourage students to join us in that endeavor, gradually reducing our role as their own capabilities grow. Here is a list of ways **students** can learn to become formative assessors:

- Respond to the questions, "What did you do in Music today? What did you learn?" (oral or written response).
- Determine, with the teacher, attributes of a good performance or product.
- Use criteria to evaluate the quality of anonymous work and then to identify strengths and weaknesses in their own work.
- Before a discussion or conference with the teacher, identify their own perception of strengths and weaknesses on a specific piece of their work.
- Write letters home to parents explaining what they've learned that day/week/month.
- Write letters home to parents explaining how they can help them with a piece of work.
- Offer feedback to peers.
- Engage in self-assessment, self-reflection, and goal-setting
- Accumulate evidence of their improvement in growth portfolios. (This means **students** are able to identify samples that constitute evidence of improvement.)
- Participate in conferences with parents.
- Talk about their growth: identify their progress and explain what they need to do to improve.

Summative Assessment Practices

Preparing and administering **summative** assessments comes with the job. That does not doom them to necessary-evil status; summative assessments can be used formatively in service of increased student learning. For example, have **students** do the following:

- Develop practice test blueprints based on their understanding of the learning targets they are to hit and the essential concepts in material to be learned.
- Self-assess on learning targets or test blueprint a few days prior to the test, then create a study plan and/or study group based on what each student needs to learn. Remember, it is the student creating the plan. You can help with the grouping.
- Generate and answer questions they think might be on the test, based on their understanding of the content/processes/skills they were responsible for learning.
- Create practice tests, based on understanding of what was taught. This is a good small group activity—different groups can answer each others' test questions as a way to review.
- Use item formulas and a test blueprint or list of learning targets to construct 3–4 test items for a particular topic that will be on the test.
- Assign each cell of the test blueprint to a small group of students and have them write propositions for that cell. Then have another group write test questions for the cell. Have each group take another's "test."
- Before a test (a few days in advance is a good idea), practice "positive talk" by answering the following questions:
  - Why am I taking this test? Who will use the results? How?
  - What is it testing?
  - How do I think I will do?
  - What do I need to study?
  - With whom might I work?

To think about why using the summative assessment formatively might be a good idea, *just remember what happens to your own clarity about the intended learning* when **you** engage in activities such as the following:

- Creating a test plan
- Preparing a quiz to help students know what to study
- Writing propositions from which to develop test items

- Generating test questions
- Explaining to students what's going to be tested without giving away the exact contents of the test

Also, think about where the balance of work is in your classroom when it comes time to review for a summative assessment. Who does the majority of the reviewing work? Who needs to do it?

Thinking About Assessment

Activity 11: Using Feedback to Set Goals

Purpose: To help teachers learn more about providing descriptive feedback. For students to set meaningful goals for their work, they need to understand what they have accomplished as well as what, specifically, they need to work on. To prepare them to do this thinking, it is helpful if the teacher models it for them first by offering descriptive feedback on a sample of their work. In the activity, students think about their work sample's strengths and needed improvements. Then the teacher offers either written or verbal feedback on strengths and improvements. Last, the student makes a plan for what to work on and where to get feedback from next.

Time: 20–30 minutes

Directions: Start with a sample of typical student work that requires a performance rating, for example, a piece of writing. Have teachers score it using your building, district, or state scoring guide. Then have teachers pair up. One becomes "Partner A," the other is "Partner B." Activity directions for teachers:

1. Do this first item independently (about 5 minutes):
    Partner A: You are a student. You have just produced this sample of work. Take a few moments to prepare to confer with your teacher about your sample. Use the language of the scoring guide to identify your sample's strengths and problems, if any. Write the strengths and problem(s) on the form, "Using Feedback to Set Goals," page 145, under "My Opinion."

    Partner B: You are Partner A's teacher. She or he has just produced this sample of work. Take a few moments to prepare to confer with Partner A about her or his sample. Use the language of the scoring guide to identify the sample's strengths and problems, if any. Write the strengths and problems on the form "Using Feedback to Set Goals," page 145, under "My Teacher's Opinion."

2. Read the description of a three-minute conference on page 146.
3. Conduct a three-minute conference with your partner. Let the student be the writer on the form.

Closure: Ask teachers to discuss how this form could be used in their classrooms, and what problems it might solve.

Using Feedback to Set Goals

TRAIT(S): _____   NAME: _____

NAME OF PAPER: _____   DATE: _____

MY OPINION

My strengths:

_____

_____

What I think I need to work on:

_____

_____

MY TEACHER'S OPINION

Strengths:

_____

_____

Work on:

_____

_____

MY PLAN

What I will do now:

_____

_____

Next time I'll ask for feedback from:

_____

_____

Using Feedback to Set Goals

The Three-Minute Conference

If you confer with students as a way to offer feedback on their work, consider asking them to do some thinking prior to meeting with you. This causes the conference to take less time and your feedback to be more meaningful.

1. Identify a focus for the feedback—narrow it, if needed. Have them focus only on a few aspects of quality—either you choose the aspects of quality based on what you have been teaching them to do or let them choose, depending on their level of sophistication. (For example, in writing, a teacher may be focusing short lessons on how to include details that are interesting, important, and informative, which is part of the trait of "Ideas and Content" in her scoring guide. So she may ask students to think about the quality of their details.)

2. Before meeting with you (or submitting their work for your feedback) have students use the scoring guide (or whatever description of quality you have taught) to identify what aspects of quality are present in a particular piece of their work. Encourage them to use the language of the scoring guide.

3. Have them follow the same procedure to identify one or two aspects of quality they think need work.

4. Offer your feedback. If you agree, it's simple. If you can, point out a strength the student overlooked. Add to or modify what the student needs to work on, if needed.

5. Ask students to take their own and your opinions into account and decide what to do next. At first, students may set large, unmanageable, or non-specific goals. Help them, if needed, focus their plan on what is doable in the short term.

6. If your students have practiced giving formative feedback, encourage them to use each other as feedback providers.

Offering Written Feedback

You can also use the form, "Using Feedback to Set Goals," as a vehicle for offering written feedback. The student completes the top information and "My Opinion" before turning in the work. You fill out the teacher portion as you are reviewing the work, hand it back, and the student fills in the plan.

How does this activity benefit you and your students? Engaging in self-assessment prior to receiving feedback and in action planning afterwards shifts the primary responsibility for improving the work to the student, where it belongs. If you use this as part of your conferences, you will notice that gradually you will have fewer students to confer with and more students thinking about how the elements of quality you are teaching relate to their own work. In either written or verbal feedback situations, if you are spending time providing feedback, you want it to be used. Students are more likely to understand and act on your suggestions because you have asked them to think about quality in advance, which provides a mental "hook" for your feedback.

Applying the Skills

Resource 1: Using Test Results to Self-Assess and Set Goals

What this resource is:

A chart that students complete to analyze the results of a test they have already taken and determine areas for further study, along with a simulation to introduce it to staff. Students often take tests without knowing what the test measures beyond the most general level: "reading," "social studies," or "science." If called on to use test results to set goals, without more specific understanding of what learning the test represents, students write the most general of goals: "study more," "take my book home," or "try harder." Although noble, these goals do not focus on what students actually need to learn, and therefore are of limited use.

This activity requires that a teacher administering a test first make a numbered list of the learning targets to be assessed. Then the teacher transfers that information to the chart, "Identifying Your Strengths and Focusing Further Study," page 150, by filling out the "Learning Target #" column, which identifies the learning target addressed by each item. Last, the teacher copies the chart for each student and hands it out with the test.

As students take the test, they note on the chart whether they feel confident or unsure of the correct response to each item. The teacher corrects the tests as usual and hands them back to students, along with the numbered list of learning targets. The students are now ready to identify their own specific strengths and areas for further study by following the steps explained on the form, "Analyzing Your Results," page 151.

This activity addresses principles of assessment *for* learning 1, 3, 5, 7, and 9, with a primary emphasis on principles 3, 5 and 7.

Ideas for making it useful:

Preparation:

To introduce this resource to staff, plan an activity where they use it just as students would. First, obtain a corrected test. Next, identify which learning target each item addresses and create a numbered list of all of the targets tested. Then, fill out the two lefthand columns of the chart. In the first column, write the test item number (done for you in the example). In the second column, write the number corresponding to the learning target that item tests. Last, make copies of the corrected test, this chart, and the numbered list of learning targets to pass out to each participant.

The activity:

1. For purposes of this simulation, have participants pretend they are students, marking "Confident" or "Unsure" for each item on the chart, as though they had done so while taking the test.
2. Then have them complete the section entitled "Analyzing Your Results."
3. Last, ask participants to discuss when this would be useful for students to do and what it would accomplish.

Student chart, to be handed out as students take a test:

IDENTIFYING YOUR STRENGTHS AND FOCUSING FURTHER STUDY

As you answer each question on the test, decide whether you feel confident in your answer or are unsure about it, and mark the corresponding box.

Problem	Learning Target #	Confident	Unsure		Right	Wrong	Simple Mistake	Further Study
1								
2								
3								
4								
5								
6								
7								
8								
9								
10								
11								
12								
13								
14								
15								

Student analysis activity, to be completed using the same chart after receiving the correct test:

ANALYZING YOUR RESULTS

1. After your test has been corrected, identify which problems you got right and which you got wrong by putting *X*s in the "Right" and "Wrong" columns.
2. Of the problems you got wrong, decide which ones were due to simple mistakes and mark the "Simple Mistake" column.
3. For all of the remaining wrong answers, mark the "Further Study" column.
4. To identify your areas of strength, write down the learning target numbers corresponding to the problems you felt confident about *and* got right. Then write a short description of the target or problem.

MY STRENGTHS:

Learning Target #	Learning Target or Problem Description

5. To determine what you need to study most, write down the learning target numbers corresponding to the marks in the "Further Study" column (problems you got wrong *not* because of a simple mistake). Then write a short description of the target or problem.

MY HIGHEST PRIORITY FOR STUDYING:

Learning Target #	Learning Target or Problem Description

6. Do the same thing for the problems you were unsure of and for the problems on which you made simple mistakes.

WHAT I NEED TO REVIEW:

Learning Target #	Learning Target or Problem Description

Applying the Skills

Resource 2: Student Self-Assessment and Goal-Setting Activities

**What this
resource is:** A collection of ideas for what students can do to self-assess and set goals for further learning.

**Ideas for
making
it useful:** Handout of ideas for teachers to use with students (after a discussion about self-assessment and goal setting).

TRACKING THEIR OWN LEARNING*

Give students a blank sheet of paper (11″ x 17″) before you begin a new unit of study. Have students sketch, write, or diagram anything they think they already know on the topic. Collect these sheets. Partway through the unit, return the sheets to students and ask them to add information they now know on the topic using a different colour of ink. At the end of the unit, repeat the process.

What I know about fractions
April 17
April 26
May 5

*Source: From *Self-Assessment and Goal-Setting* (p. 25), by K. Gregory, C. Cameron, and A. Davies, 2000, Merville, BC: Connections. Reprinted with permission.

SELF-ASSESSMENT

"Traffic-Light Icons"

Students mark their work with a large dot—either a green, yellow, or red dot—to judge it. The colors, analogous to traffic lights, can represent variations on the basic meanings of "go," "exercise caution," and "stop" (Atkin, Black, & Coffey, 2001).

For example, when a student uses a rubric to evaluate her solution to a complex mathematics problem, she might use a key such as this:

Green dot = High-quality solution, "ready to go"

Yellow dot = Some difficulties present, "rework"

Red dot = Solution stopped dead in its tracks, "need help"

Or, students might use the colors to assess their understanding of a concept, in which case the key could look like this:

Green dot = My work shows strong understanding of _____ (concept).

Yellow dot = My work shows partial understanding of _____ (concept).

Red dot = I am struggling mightily with _____ (concept).

The teacher can then group students by colors. The "greens" and "yellows" pair up to sort through their problems together, while the teacher meets with the "reds" to reteach whatever is needed (Black, Harrison, Lee, Marshall, & Wiliam, 2002).

GOAL SETTING**

We model how to fill out planning frames so students can see how using a frame can help them set long-term goals. Then we help students complete their own individual frames.

> To get better at _____, I could…
> -
> -
> -
> One thing I am going to start doing is…
> -
> I'll start doing this on _____ and work on it until _____
>   date   date
> One way I'll know I'm getting better is …

**Source: From *Self-Assessment and Goal-Setting* (p. 45), by K. Gregory, C. Cameron, and A. Davies, 2000, Merville, BC: Connections. Reprinted with permission.

Goal	Steps	Evidence
What do I need to get better at?	How do I plan to do this?	What evidence will show I've achieved my goal?

Time Frame: Begin _____ End _____

Date _____ Signed _____

Competency 3

The leader understands the necessity of clear academic achievement standards, aligned classroom-level achievement targets, and their relationship to the development of accurate assessments.

Competency 3 asks leaders to ensure that classroom instruction aims directly at learning targets that are clear to all stakeholders: teachers, students, and parents. It's fair to assume that if the curriculum floor of the house is in disarray then the assessment floor is going to be equally messy. The fact that we might already have a written curriculum may not be good enough.

- To what extent is it implemented in each classroom?
- Is it intentionally aligned with state standards?
- Is there a match between what is taught and what is tested, between what is written and what is learned?
- Is it high-quality curriculum, written with clarity and at a level of specificity to support instruction?
- Is the curriculum balanced among the four different types of learning targets (knowledge, reasoning, skill, product), resulting in the use of a variety of assessment methods?

Students learn more when they know what they are expected to achieve. Many students come to school every day prepared to learn yet are not given a clear sense of what is being asked of them. Those who cannot clearly see the target will have difficulty hitting it. Even with state standards, supporting curriculum frameworks, grade-level and subject-area documents, and guides aligning standards to textbook material, many teachers are adrift in a sea of standards because they are not given the training, support, and time needed to transfer it all into everyday teaching (Schmoker, 2002). Leaders demonstrate Competency 3 when they support teachers in curriculum mapping (see Jacobs, 1997) or grade-level/subject-area articulation activities to further clarify what is taught and assessed, and when they provide structured time for teachers to work together to develop lessons geared toward the standards and aligned assessments.

[handwritten margin notes: — cur. mapping; — collaboration; — activities to clarify what is taught and assessed]

155

kid friendly
Parent friendly

It is also important to ensure the curriculum is available to parents and students in versions written specifically for them. Curriculum documents translated to everyday language and in a user-friendly format can be posted on the refrigerator at home, and help parents not only know what their children are learning but support them in that effort. In addition, as discussed behind Door 1 in Part 3 of this guide, it is essential for leaders to ensure that all teachers are masters of the content knowledge they are assigned to teach. Effective leaders arrange for subject-area professional development where needed and institute hiring practices that place a high priority on selecting candidates with strong backgrounds in curricular content.

Beyond verifying that content standards drive classroom instruction and that daily lessons deliver the scaffolding students need to attain mastery of those standards as reflected on assessments *of* learning, strong leaders can also break down group achievement data into standard-by-standard information, so they can report individual student progress based on those same content standards. And to the greatest extent possible, leaders can also ensure instruction is aimed at all targets in the written curriculum, not just those assessed by the state for accountability purposes.

↓ *science*
soc. St.
health
etc.

- staff development
- hire well-trained
teachers

Applying the Skills

Resource 3: Implementing the Written Curriculum

What this resource is: By making sure the written curriculum of the state/district/school is used to plan and deliver instruction, school leaders help ensure that students receive instruction that matches the written curriculum. To increase the probability that the learning expectations for students are consistent across schools and classrooms, the written curriculum must be uniformly implemented. This resource provides ideas on how different roles/positions in the organization can help achieve that goal.

Ideas for making it useful: Before this tool can be of any value, you will need to gather some information on the level of curriculum implementation in your school or district. There may be uniformity in certain schools and not others, in certain grade levels and departments and not others, or implementation issues may exist systemwide. It mat be that teachers already use the written curriculum for its intended purpose. But in schools and/or districts where that is not the case, the plan that follows can be used to solidify curriculum implementation. We suggest that you use these lists of responsibilities as the basis for self-study—to see if all roles are being fulfilled.

Teaching the Written Curriculum

Ensuring implementation and continued use of district-adopted curricula in every classroom of the school district is a responsibility best shared. The roles-based plan below defines responsibilities for each member of your district's education team.

Curriculum Office:

- Make the written curriculum readily available in multiple ways and easily read for all subjects, all grade levels, K–12.
- Provide ongoing inservice training for teachers in understanding and teaching all learning targets.
- Provide targeted ongoing training for teachers new to the district.
- Provide "at a glance" sheets to teachers and other public documents like parent handbooks to use with parents during back-to-school nights, conferences, etc.
- Provide skill continuum documents when appropriate.
- Over time, provide evidence that the new curriculum improves student learning.
- Provide sample classroom assessments linked to the written curriculum.
- Carefully review all instructional materials for clear alignment and support of the written curriculum.
- Ensure alignment of local curriculum with state standards.

Building Principal:

- Focus supervision and evaluation of classroom teaching on use of the curriculum in planning and delivering instruction and in assessing student progress.
- Frequently observe the curriculum in action in the classroom.
- Provide teachers common planning time to work together to plan lessons leading to the accomplishment of the standards.
- Act as conduit between Curriculum Office and school staff.
- Promote use of the written curriculum through personal knowledge of the specific objectives.
- Help connect and align adopted curriculum with classroom practice through staff development, faculty meetings, vertical teaming groups, etc.
- Help secure resources for teachers to help understand/teach the curriculum, as needed.
- Call on curriculum specialists or master teachers to assist as necessary.
- Encourage teachers to follow a process to "audit" classroom curriculum against the adopted curriculum, if necessary.
- Help ensure instructional materials support the written curriculum.

Classroom Teacher:
- Teach and assess the written curriculum.
- Use district documents as the basis for daily planning and formative and summative assessment.
- Communicate the learning expectations to students and parents, regularly and in understandable terms.
- Possess detailed knowledge of subject-area objectives and be able to classify the type of learning target.
- Monitor each student's progress toward the content standards.
- In summary: know it, teach it, and assess it.

School Board Policies:
- Develop curriculum implementation policy.
- Align district policies/curriculum to state goals.
- Ensure professional development policies support subject-specific training.

Others: (department heads, learning specialists, management team, etc.)
- Site-based teams support and problem-solve implementation issues.

In addition, the following functions have roles to play in implementing the written curriculum:

Staff Development:
- Clearly focus on curriculum implementation through a common training model for schools to follow.
- In instrumental strategies training, use essential learning as context/examples.
- Offer professional development in content areas, linked to identified standards/curriculum.
- Continue teacher involvement in curriculum revision/improvement.
- Provide school-based training on units of study based on the new curriculum.
- Develop enrichment units/lessons and distribute them.
- Continue training related to specific curricula.
- Offer teachers an audit of building/classroom materials to ensure curriculum alignment.

Teacher Evaluation:
- Continue to encourage staff to write professional growth goals related to curriculum implementation for formative evaluation.
- Summative evaluation criteria/indicators relate to planning lessons, teaching, and assessing the written curriculum.
- Pre/post conferences always focus in part on the intended learning.

Curriculum Documents:	Texts/Supplemental Materials:
■ Readily available, user friendly, similar formats for all subjects. ■ Curriculum at-a-glance documents provided. ■ Aligned to state standards. ■ Available electronically through district website as well as hard copy.	■ Must reflect and support standards and curriculum. ■ Selection requires support and alignment. ■ Requires appropriate level of introduction/training for teachers
Special Education, LAP, Title 1: ■ IEP's (academic portion) and LAP instructional plans need to be tied to district curriculum.	**Principal Evaluation:** ■ Accountability for curriculum implementation through the School Learning Plan.
Reporting Student Progress and Student Work: ■ Link report card phrases to the written curriculum.	

Thinking About Assessment

Activity 12: Deconstructing Standards into Classroom-Level Achievement Targets: Practice for School Leaders

Purpose: The goal of state standards is to set priorities on what students need to know and be able to do. Sometimes standards are broken down into *benchmarks* or *indicators* to further define these priorities. But, have you ever looked at content standards, benchmarks, or indicators and still been confused about what they meant?

- What am I going to teach here?
- How do I explain the target to students?
- Will my colleagues interpret this the same as I do?
- What do I *do* to enable students to do well on *this*?

No matter how carefully their creators list, describe, and break down content standards, many still must be translated into daily classroom teaching activities. We've found that it's helpful to "deconstruct," or break down, unclear standards to see what knowledge, reasoning proficiencies, skills, and/or products underpin student success. Classroom instruction and assessment is then built around these "deconstructed" learning targets. This Activity is designed to help educators do needed deconstructing.

Time: 1 hour

The Process: 1. Choose a standard, indicator, or benchmark that is unclear—where it isn't immediately clear what you might teach, or where teachers might have different interpretations of what the indicator might mean. For example, "Knows the binomial theorem" might mean
   a. Knowledge interpretations: (1) Knows it by sight—can pick it out of a list. (2) Can reproduce it when asked.
   b. Reasoning interpretations: (1) Can use it to solve a problem when instructed to do so. (2) Can choose the problems best solved using the binomial theorem. (3) Can write a problem that would require the binomial theorem to solve.

Each of these interpretations would have different implications for instruction. Which interpretation is correct?

161

2. For your chosen standard, identify whether it is, ultimately, a knowledge, reasoning, skills, or product learning target. Each of these is defined in the accompanying list, "Types of Achievement Targets."

3. To help determine the "ultimate" target type of a particular benchmark, look for key words. Key words are shown in Table 4-2, "Types of Achievement Targets—Key Words." For example, identify the "ultimate" type of each of the following standards:

   ■ Identify words that have similar meanings (synonyms).

   ■ Use clear diction, pitch, tempo, and tone, and adjust volume and tempo to stress important ideas.

   ■ Keep records of investigations and observations that are understandable weeks or months later.

   ■ Identify that hypotheses are valuable even when they are not supported.

   ■ Classify ideas from informational texts as main ideas or supporting details.

   ■ Model a problem situation using physical materials.

   ■ Write, simplify, and evaluate algebraic expressions (including formulas) to generalize situations and solve problems.

   ■ Evaluate policies that have been proposed as ways of dealing with social changes resulting from new technologies.

(Answers: knowledge, skill, product, knowledge, reasoning, product, knowledge or reasoning, knowledge or reasoning.)

Note: Key words won't always identify the "ultimate" target type of a standard, indicator, or benchmark. For example, what is the ultimate goal of "Knows the binomial theorem"? The word *knows* indicates that it's a knowledge target, but is it really ultimately a reasoning target? Since there may be ambiguity on "ultimate" type, the first job is to come to agreement on what the standard, benchmark, or indicator means.

4. Next, consider the knowledge, reasoning, and/or skills prerequisite to and underpinning competence of your selected standard, benchmark, or indicator. Ask yourself the following four questions. (Don't list every little piece of knowledge or minor skill, just the major ones.)

   ■ What does a student need to *know and understand* to attain mastery on this benchmark?

- What *patterns of reasoning*, if any, are required to attain mastery on this benchmark?
- On what specific *performance skills*, if any, must students attain proficiency to attain mastery on this benchmark?
- What *products*, if any, would students be proficient in creating if they were masters of this benchmark?

These form a hierarchy. If the ultimate type of target is "product," then it has all four types of underpinnings: knowledge, reasoning, skills, and products. However, if the standard is ultimately a skill, then there will be only knowledge, reasoning, and skill underpinnings. Likewise, if the standard is ultimately reasoning, there will be only knowledge and reasoning underpinnings. And, like the nursery rhyme, knowledge stands alone.

For example, you might decide that "Knows the binomial theorem" is a reasoning target. Therefore it has knowledge underpinnings—knows what the binomial theorem is and when to use it. It also has reasoning underpinnings that need to be practiced—use the binomial theorem to solve problems, identify problems best solved using it, and so on. All of these things should be incorporated into instruction.

Key Points to Remember

1. **Not all benchmarks embody all types of learning targets. There is a hierarchy.** Knowledge targets embody no reasoning, skill, or product underpinnings. Reasoning targets require knowledge but no skills or products. Skills targets require underlying knowledge and reasoning, but not products. Product targets might be underpinned by all four types of learning targets.

2. **You are looking at what the benchmark requires students to know and be able to do,** *not* **how you will assess it.** Because the import of this statement might not be immediately obvious, consider "Compare and contrast democracies with other forms of government." This is a reasoning target. It requires:
   - *Knowledge* of what a democracy is and knowledge of other types of government—purposes and how power is acquired, used, and justified; and how government can affect people.
   - It also requires practice in comparing and contrasting—a *reasoning* target—using the knowledge of different forms of government.

You might assess these knowledge and reasoning underpinnings through an oral presentation (a skill). If you unpack the *assessment,* you get the following underpinnings:

■ As above, the assessment requires knowledge of what a democracy is and knowledge of other types of government—purposes and how power is acquired, used, and justified; and how government can affect people.

■ The assessment also requires knowledge of oral presentations, for example, the need to use language that fits the audience, have eye contact, organize the presentation in a way that the audience will understand (and the various options for this), etc.

■ As above, the assessment also requires practice in comparing and contrasting— a *reasoning* target—using the knowledge of different forms of government.

■ But, other reasoning proficiencies are involved in the assessment that are not required by the original standard; for example, choosing one's particular presentation style, organization, and props from all those possible, to serve the needs of the current presentation.

■ There are also skills involved in the assessment that are not required by the standard itself: actually giving the oral presentation—modulating voice tone and speed, actually looking at the audience, actually manipulating props, etc.

The point??? An assessment developed to elicit the desired standards might require other knowledge, reasoning, skills, and/or products that are not actually part of the standard(s) being assessed. So, when you unpack a standard, you might be tempted to list all these. **But don't**. All of this extra information is not required for the benchmark, just for the assessment. Any knowledge, reasoning, skill, or product that is required for the assessment that is not required for the standard is a potential source of bias that can distort one's ability to determine student status on the learning target(s) under consideration. The effect of these "extras" needs to be minimized or you won't know how students perform on the actual benchmarks under consideration.

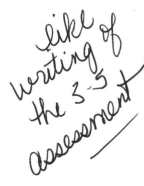
like writing of the 3-5 assessment

Types of Achievement Targets

Use this list to help you understand and identify the different kinds of classroom learning to be developed and assessed as students work toward achieving state standards:

Master Factual and Procedural *Knowledge*
Some to be learned outright
Some to be retrieved using reference materials

Use Knowledge to *Reason* and Solve Problems
Analytical or comparative reasoning
Synthesizing
Classifying
Induction and deduction
Critical/evaluative thinking

Demonstrate Mastery of Specific *Skills*
Speaking a second language
Giving an oral presentation
Working effectively on a team
Science process skills

Create Quality *Products*
Writing samples
Term projects
Artistic products
Research reports
Shop projects
Science exhibits

Acquire Positive *Affect/Dispositions*
Positive self-concept
Desire to learn/read/think critically
Positive attitude toward school
Good citizenship
Respect toward self and others
Flexibility
Perseverance

Table 4-2

Types of Achievement Targets—Key Words

Target Type	Explanation	Content Standards/Benchmark Key Words	Examples
Knowledge/ Understanding	Some knowledge/facts/ concepts to be learned outright; some to be retrieved using reference materials	Explain, understand, describe, identify, recognize, tell, name, list, identify, give examples, define, label, match, choose, recall, recognize, select	Vocabulary Measurement concepts U.S. government structure Patterns of growth and development
Reasoning	Thinking proficiencies; using one's knowledge to solve a problem, make a decision, plan, etc.	*Analyze:* components, parts, ingredients, logical sequence, steps, main idea, supporting details, determine, dissect, examine, order *Compare/contrast:* discriminate between/ among; alike and different, relate, distinguish between *Synthesize:* combine into, blend, formulate, organize, adapt, modify *Classify:* categorize, sort, group *Infer/deduce:* interpret, implications, predict draw conclusions *Evaluate:* justify, support opinion, think critically, debate, defend, dispute, evaluate, judge, prove	Think critically Analyze authors' use of language Solve problems Compare forms of government Self-evaluation Analyze health information
Skills	Behavioral demonstrations; where the doing is what is important; using one's knowledge and reasoning to perform skillfully	Observe, focus attention, listen, perform, do, question, conduct, work, read, speak, assemble, operate, use, demonstrate, measure, investigate, model, collect, dramatize	Read fluently Oral presentations Play an instrument Use laboratory equipment Conduct investigations
Products	Where the characteristics of the final product are important; using one's knowledge, reasoning, and skills to produce a final product	Design, produce, create, develop, make, write, draw, represent, display, model, construct	Writing Artistic products Research reports Make a map Personal fitness plan Make a model that represents a scientific principle

Source: Adapted from *Classroom Assessment for Student Learning: Doing It Right—Using It Well.* (p. 64), by R. J. Stiggins, J. Arter, J. Chappuis, & S. Chappuis, 2004, Portland, OR: Assessment Training Institute. Adapted by permission.

Examples

"Drive with skill." This is a skill level target. Therefore, it has only knowledge, reasoning, and skill underpinnings.

Learning to Drive a Car

Knowledge/ Understanding	Know the law Understand informal rules of the road, e.g., courtesy Understand what different parts of the car do Read signs and understand what they mean Understand what "creating a danger" means Understand what "creating a hazard" means
Reasoning	Analyze road conditions, vehicle performance, and other driver's actions, compare/contrast this information with knowledge and past experience, synthesize information, and evaluate options to make decisions on what to do next. Evaluate "am I safe" and synthesize information to take action if needed.
Skills	Steering, shifting, parallel parking, looking, signaling, backing up, etc. Fluidity/automaticity in performing driving actions
Products	None (undamaged car...?)

"Distinguish fact from judgment and opinion; recognize stereotypes; compare and contrast historical information" This is a reasoning level target. Therefore, it has only reasoning and knowledge underpinnings.

History Example

Knowledge/ Understanding	What facts are and how to identify them What opinions are and how to identify them What stereotypes are and how to identify them What it means to compare and contrast things The basis (bases) or criteria on which to compare and contrast (events, people, conditions, events, consequences?)
Reasoning	Distinguish facts from opinions in the context of news reporting. Recognize novel stereotypes. Find the correct information on which to compare and contrast. Compare and contrast the historical information specified on the bases specified.
Skills	None required
Products	None required

Examples from State Standards

"Students will evaluate different interpretations of historical events." This is a reasoning level target, therefore it has only knowledge and reasoning underpinnings.

Sample State Standard 1

Knowledge/ Understanding	Students must know and understand key features of each historical event, and must understand each of the alternative interpretations to be evaluated. The teacher must determine if students are to know those things outright or if they can use reference materials to retrieve the required knowledge.
Reasoning	Evaluative reasoning requires judgment about the quality of each interpretation. Thus students must demonstrate both an understanding of the criteria by which one judges the quality of an interpretation and the ability to apply these criteria.
Skills	None required
Products	None required

"Students will use styles appropriate for their audience and purpose, including proper use of voice, word choice, and sentence fluency." Writing is a product level target, therefore it will have all four types of target underpinnings.

Sample State Standard 2

Knowledge/ Understanding	Writers must possess appropriate understanding of the concept of style as evidenced in voice, word choice, and sentence fluency. They need to know what voice, word choice, and sentence fluency are, why they are important, and the ways they can vary. They need to understand various audiences and purposes for text and how these might influence style. In addition, students must possess knowledge of the topic they are to write about.
Reasoning	Writers must be able to reason through voice, word choice, and sentence fluency choices for novel audiences and purposes. They also must figure out how to make appropriate voice, word choice, and sentence construction decisions while composing original text for various audiences and purposes.
Skills	Students will either write longhand or will compose text on a keyboard. Each requires its own kind of skill competence.
Products	The final evidence of competence will be written products that present evidence of the ability to write effectively for different audiences and purposes.

Directions:

Listed here are several more state benchmarks. Pick one where it is not immediately clear what you would teach, or for which teachers might disagree. Determine the type of target each ultimately represents. Then analyze it for the knowledge/understanding, reasoning, skill, and/or product prerequisites (as appropriate; remember the hierarchy) needed to perform well on the benchmark. Ask yourself, "What would students need to know and understand to perform well? What reasoning, if any, does this standard require? What skills, if any, would the students need to practice? What products, if any, would students need practice producing?" Practice deconstructing as many as you need to understand the curriculum development task at hand.

1. **Reading, Comprehension Processes, Grades 2–3**—Relate critical facts and details in narrative or information text to comprehend text.
2. **Reading, Comprehension Processes, Grades 6–8**—Interpret text(s) from multiple perspectives (e.g., historical, cultural, gender, political).
3. **Writing, Rhetoric, Grades 4–5**—Convey meaning, provide important information, make a point, fulfill a purpose.
4. **Writing, Rhetoric, Grades 9–12**—Have an organizing structure that gives the writing coherence (e.g., weaves the threads of meaning into a whole).
5. **Social Studies, Political Science/Civics, Grades K–3**—Create and use surveys, interviews, polls, and/or tallies to find information to solve a real problem or make a decision, e.g., create tally sheets to monitor frequency and amount of littering.
6. **Social Studies, Political Science/Civics, Grades 6–8**—Explain and apply tools and methods drawn from political science to examine political issues and/or problems.
7. **Science, Domain I, Inquiry, Grades 4–5**—Design and conduct simple investigations to answer questions or to test ideas about the environment.
8. **Science, Domain I, Inquiry, Grades 9–12**—Communicate and defend scientific explanations and conclusions.
9. **Science, Domain II, Grades K–3**—Explain how sanitary practices, vaccinations, medicines, and other scientific treatments keep people healthy.
10. **Science, Domain II, Grades 6–8**—Describe and exemplify how information and communication technologies affect research and work done in the field of science.
11. **World Languages, Cultures, Grades 4–5**—Identify and use appropriate gestures and other forms of nonverbal communication.
12. **World Languages, Comparisons, Grades 9–12**—Use knowledge of contrasting structural patterns between the target language and the student's own language to communicate effectively.
13. **Music, Singing, Grades K–3**—Sing expressively with appropriate dynamics and phrasing.
14. **Music, Singing, Grades 6–8**—Sing expressively with appropriate dynamics, breath control, phrasing, and nuance, demonstrating understanding of text and style.

(Ultimate type of target: 1 = reasoning; 2 = reasoning; 3 = product; 4 = product; 5 = reasoning and product; 6 = knowledge and reasoning; 7 = reasoning and skill; 8 = reasoning and skill or product; 9 = knowledge; 10 = knowledge; 11 = knowledge and skill; 12 = knowledge and reasoning; 13 = skill; 14 = skill.)

Thinking About Assessment

Activity 13: Using Interviews to Hire Teachers with Content Knowledge and Assessment Competence

Purpose: Interviews of prospective teachers often leave out questions that check for competence in classroom assessment. Questions related to classroom management, instructional skill, and issues of student discipline are common; less common are questions about the teacher's assessment beliefs, grading practices, and knowledge of standards of assessment quality. Also sometimes overlooked is the candidate's mastery of the content knowledge necessary for the specific teaching assignment. Frequently, evidence of content mastery is gathered from college transcripts, previous teaching assignments, or candidate portfolios to help inform the hiring decision. This activity asks participants to think about what questions could be included in the interview that would help school leaders evaluate the assessment literacy of teacher applicants, as well as their academic preparation to teach the assigned subject(s).

Time: 1 hour

Directions: Think about and discuss the following questions:

- What should we reasonably expect the interview component of the overall hiring process to produce in terms of useful information about the candidate's subject matter knowledge and assessment competence?
- Given that, what questions could we design that would help inform us about the applicant's subject matter knowledge? What is the range of acceptable answers to those questions?
- What questions could we design that would inform us about the applicant's assessment competence? What answers would we consider acceptable for that set of questions?

Closure: Look at the questions on some of the interview forms currently in use in your school/district and see if they include questions related to assessment. If they do, are the questions related to assessment *of* learning, assessment *for* learning, or both? If your district has a comprehensive assessment plan, check it to see if it spells out classroom assessment competencies. Also, consider asking teachers whom you believe already understand the principles of quality assessment to tell you what questions they think should be included in the interview.

Important note: The stronger your foundation of understanding of the principles of sound assessment (Competency 1), the easier it will be to formulate your answer.

Finally, whatever questions you might ask about subject matter knowledge, and especially about assessment competence, consider the following points:

- Is there a link between what questions are asked in the interview and subsequent teacher evaluation? If not, should there be? Why or why not?
- Is there a link between those same questions, which in part act as our expectations of teacher skills and knowledge, and the staff development program of the school or district? If not, should there be? Why or why not?

Thinking About Assessment

Activity 14: Auditing Your Classroom Curriculum

Purpose: When introduced to a new standards-aligned curriculum, teachers swiftly and accurately identify the primary roadblock to implementation: "When am I going to find time to teach *all this*?" The following activity provides a process by which teachers can compare what they currently teach and assess to the content of a new curriculum, in order to determine the following:

- Where their instruction and assessment already align
- What parts of the new curriculum they need to insert
- Which instructional activities and assessments they can eliminate

Preparation: To complete the activity, teachers need to have created a personal curriculum map for the year or course, including the content and skills they will teach and assessments they will use for each. In addition, you will need to provide them with a numbered list of the new curriculum standards/grade-level learning targets for each subject to be addressed.

Directions: *Data Gathering*

1. *New and current curriculum—Where's the match?* Compare your curriculum map's list of content and skills to the numbered list of the new curriculum standards/grade-level learning targets. On your curriculum map, highlight those content and skill entries that show up on the list. Next, go back through the highlighted content and skill entries and write the number of the new curriculum standard(s)/grade-level learning target(s) next to each highlighted content and skill on your curriculum map to show the match.

2. *Instruction—How's the balance?* Working with the content and skill entries you highlighted on your curriculum map in Step 1, determine the amount of emphasis each new standard or grade-level learning target receives in your current teaching. Is it about right, given its relative importance to everything else students must learn, and its emphasis in state and district assessments? Is it overrepresented? Underrepresented? Not present at all? Mark the corresponding column on the chart, "Comparing the Classroom Curriculum to District/State Standards," page 174.

3. *Assessment—How's the balance?* Again working with the content and skill entries you highlighted in Step 1, refer to the assessments students take over the course of the year. Is each new standard or grade-level learning target sufficiently sampled, given its relative importance to everything else students must learn, and its emphasis in state and district assessments? Is it over-sampled? Undersampled? Or, not assessed at all? Mark the corresponding column on the chart, "Comparing the Classroom Curriculum to District/ State Standards."

Decision Making

4. *What to leave out?* Examine the content and skills you **didn't** highlight in Step 1 to determine which can and should be eliminated from your curriculum map. If you can address the new curriculum in less than the full year, consider which of these content and skills can and should remain in your teaching plan.

5. *What to adjust?* Use the information on the chart, "Comparing the Classroom Curriculum to District/State Standards" gathered in Steps 2 and 3, to rework your curriculum map.

Comparing the Classroom Curriculum to District/State Standards

Standard/Grade-Level Learning Target	Instruction and Activities				Assessment			
	Right amount of emphasis	Too much emphasis	Not enough emphasis	Not present	Sufficient sample	Over-sampled	Under-sampled	Not assessed
1.								
2.								
3.								
4.								
5.								
6.								
7.								

Competency 4

The leader knows and can evaluate teachers' classroom assessment competencies, and helps teachers learn to assess accurately and use the results productively.

Evaluating teachers' classroom assessment competencies is not yet a norm for many districts. Whether teacher evaluation is summative in nature, using the traditional observational checklists of criteria and indicators, or whether it is a formative model that relies on personal/professional growth goals as the structure for the evaluation, accountability for assessment competence is often absent. Whatever supervision and evaluation model is in place, if something is worth knowing and doing properly in the classroom, especially something that can either harm or help students, solid guidance is essential. Specifically, principals need to know how well teachers do the following:

1. Attend to the purpose of each assessment given, who will use the results, and in what way.
2. Address the learning targets being assessed and explain why they are important to assess.
3. Select proper assessment methods for the content.
4. Assure accuracy of the results with good design, proper sampling, and a minimum of bias.
5. Involve students in assessment.
6. Communicate assessment results to meet the needs of a variety of audiences.

Further, do students receive the evaluation criteria in advance, and are the criteria written in terms they understand? Do students receive descriptive feedback?

When evidence suggests that teachers do these things well a principal knows that high-quality assessment is a priority in the classroom, and that the teacher understands the use of assessment *for* learning to improve student learning. When the principal holds regular discussions with teachers about these practices and is capable of providing supportive, meaningful feedback to staff, regardless of the teacher evaluation model in place, conversations in the school begin to center on the importance of using assessment in ways that contribute to learning, beyond final report card grades.

Thinking About Assessment

Activity 15: Should Teachers Be Held Accountable for Assessment Competence Through Evaluation?

Purpose: Teacher evaluation criteria and instruments vary greatly and may or may not contain indicators of classroom assessment competence. This leadership team activity asks you as school leaders to think about whether teachers should be evaluated for assessment competence and if so, what the criteria for that evaluation should include.

Time: 45–60 minutes

Directions: Collect copies of the forms used for teacher evaluation in your school/district. Using the forms, make a separate list of the criteria that relate to assessment competence that are currently included.

In your group, discuss the following question:

- Should teachers be held accountable for assessment competence through evaluation?
  1. If your answer is "Yes," begin to list criteria, in addition to what may already be included, that you believe should be part of the evaluation document. The criteria would describe the specific knowledge and/or skills that you would want teachers to be able to demonstrate routinely in assessment. Several resources and activities in this guide can be used as references.
  2. If your answer is "No," explain why you do not believe assessment competence should be part of teacher evaluation.

Closure: This issue, and therefore the activity itself, may be complicated by the fact that many schools and districts no longer use a summative form or process for teacher evaluation. The traditional classroom observation by the principal and checklist with criteria/indicators used for pre-/post-evaluation conferences about individual strengths and areas for improvement has been replaced in some schools. In many cases, new evaluation systems rely more on formative processes, where the teacher selects a few, focused professional-growth goals or instructional goals, sometimes in partnership with the supervisor. Indicators of assessment competence would not necessarily be part of that model or others similar to it. If that is the case in your system, what other ways can schools and districts ensure each teacher is a competent assessor of student learning?

To assist those who wish to add assessment competence to their summative evaluation, the main question to be addressed is, "What are the indicators of competence we want to see demonstrated?" You can compare answers generated in this activity to indicators in several of the other activities in this guide, as well as to the list of principles of assessment *for* learning.

Competency 5

The leader can plan, present, or secure professional development activities that contribute to the use of sound assessment practices.

This competency links the school or district's staff development program with the leader's goal of every instructional staff member becoming assessment literate. If, for example, a principal wants to establish common quality standards for all end-of-course tests in every subject area, then he or she must secure the professional development necessary to ensure teachers have the ability to create tests that meet those standards.

To be effective, leaders should attend to both the content and form of professional development. Professional development needs to offer teachers opportunities for continuous learning focused on school/district goals, about what we want students to know and do and how to assess it. Teachers need to learn about and practice developing and using formative classroom assessments, individually and with peers. The learning team model combines research-based assessment content with an adult learning process that honors teacher professionalism, fosters collaboration, and takes place over time, allowing for focus and concentrated effort.

Professional development in classroom assessment often connects to professional development in other school/district initiatives and priorities. Finding and establishing those connections and helping teachers see the relationships among them brings coherence to a professional development program that often appears as isolated events entirely disconnected from each other. (See Activity 25.) For example, when teachers become assessment literate they learn to begin assessment planning with the established learning targets. As a result, training in classroom assessment can also be a strategy to assist in implementing the written curriculum. And as we help teachers understand and teach the content standards of a given discipline, helping them understand the Principles of Assessment *for* Learning at the same time introduces assessment not just as a vehicle to collect reliable evidence of student learning but also as a form of good instruction.

We all want our professional development programs to, in the end, demonstrably raise student achievement. Evaluating our programs for their effectiveness becomes a leader's responsibility, and we'll address that in more detail in Part 5.

Thinking About Assessment

Activity 16: Analyzing Your Professional Development Program

Purpose: This activity helps you profile your school's or district's professional development program by using a set of guidelines for sound, effective programs. Having conducted the analysis, leaders can take whatever next steps they deem necessary to improve the quality of the program and its impact on student learning.

Time: 1 hour

Directions: Using the "Guidelines for Effective Professional Development," page 182, profile your own staff development program. There are several ways you can do this:

1. For each of the eight guidelines, rate the overall professional development program in your school/district using a scale of 1–5 for each guideline, with 1 being low and 5 being high.

   1 = We have not considered this or it is never present
   2 = We rarely see this characteristic
   3 = We see or apply this guideline some of the time
   4 = We see this frequently but not always
   5 = This is built into our professional development program

2. Make a list of those staff development models used most in your school or district. A sample has been started for you in Table 4-3, which includes such models as early release/late arrival days, summer institutes, local workshops/conferences, etc. You will need to add other models used in your school/district. Rank each of those models against the eight guidelines. When using the guidelines as evaluative criteria, which of your local models appear to be effective? Which forms of professional development in use appear to be less effective?

3. Discuss with teachers the eight guidelines. Ask them to identify which ones they value most and which ones have contributed most to their learning.

Closure: Certainly there are other considerations that go into thinking about and improving professional development. As financial resources become increasingly stretched, what are the most cost effective models? What does current research tell us about model effectiveness?

Guidelines For Effective Professional Development

Productive programs of teacher and administrator professional development do the following:

1. Focus on improving student learning by enabling teachers to reflect on and improve their classroom practice in ways that lead to higher student achievement.

    1_____   2_____   3_____   4_____   5_____

2. Arise from an analysis of discrepancies between current student achievement and desired achievement as reflected in standards.

    1_____   2_____   3_____   4_____   5_____

3. Are ongoing, promoting continuous improvement over time.

    1_____   2_____   3_____   4_____   5_____

4. Include examination of new perspectives and strategies, collaborative interaction, study of the research, and hands-on practice.

    1_____   2_____   3_____   4_____   5_____

5. Merge comfortably into what all consider to be the normal work of teachers.

    1_____   2_____   3_____   4_____   5_____

6. Are flexible, accommodating differences in teachers' knowledge bases as well as rate of learning.

    1_____   2_____   3_____   4_____   5_____

7. Are supported with sufficient resources and are economical in that they provide maximum impact for resources invested.

    1_____   2_____   3_____   4_____   5_____

8. Are evaluated for effectiveness.

    1_____   2_____   3_____   4_____   5_____

Table 4-3

	Professional Development Days	Early Release Days for Common Planning	Summer Institute	Local Workshop	Conference	Learning Teams	Other
Focus on improving student learning by enabling teachers to reflect on and improve their classroom practice in ways that lead to higher student achievement.							
Arise from an analysis of discrepancies between current student achievement and desired achievement as reflected in standards.							
Are ongoing, promoting continuous improvement over time.							
Include examination of sound new perspectives and strategies, collaborative interaction, study of the research, and hands-on practice.							
Merge comfortably into what all consider to be the normal work of teachers.							
Are flexible, accommodating differences in teachers' knowledge bases as well as rate of learning.							
Are supported with sufficient resources and are economical in that they provide maximum impact for resources invested.							
Are evaluated for effectiveness.							

Thinking About Assessment

Activity 17: Learning Teams for Assessment Literacy

Purpose: Leadership teams or school faculties may use the accompanying passage from *Classroom Assessment for Student Learning: Doing it Right—Using it Well* as a foundation for staff development programs relating to assessment literacy.

Time: 45 minutes

Directions: The accompanying passage explains the need for staff development in the area of classroom assessment and the range of development options available, and describes why learning teams are an effective and efficient vehicle for developing an assessment-literate faculty.

Take 20 minutes to read the passage. Then work together as a team to address the following questions:

1. Does the idea of learning team–based professional development make sense in our context?
2. Has anyone had experience with this process? What was the result?
3. What resources would we need to allocate to implement learning teams for assessment literacy?

To Get the Most from Professional Development, Form a Learning Team

Although you can certainly learn what you need to know about sound classroom assessment on your own, your learning experience will be deeper if you gather together a few colleagues for periodic discussion of what you've been trying in the classroom. The field of staff development has long been concerned with how to optimize learning for teachers, and much research has focused on answering the question, "What kind of learning environments and experiences are most conducive to adult learning?" The results of numerous studies converge on these key ingredients: access to effective new ideas and strategies, opportunities to try ideas and strategies in the classroom, ability to exercise control over your own learning, and collaboration. As Putnam & Borko (2000, p. 10) state, "For teachers to be successful in constructing new roles, they need opportunities to participate in a professional community that discusses new teacher materials and strategies and that supports the risk-taking and struggle entailed in transforming practice." DuFour (2001, p. 15) amplifies this thought: "Professional development moves from the workshop to the workplace. Emphasis shifts from finding the right speaker to creating opportunities for staff to work together, engage in collective inquiry, and learn from one another. . . . The single most effective way in which principals can function as professional development leaders is in providing a school context that fosters job-embedded professional development."

WHY WORKSHOPS ARE NOT ENOUGH

Attending workshops, reading journals and books, and observing in others' classrooms all provide access to new ideas and strategies. However, if

our professional development actions stop there, research and experience tell us the new information has little chance of changing our classroom practice. We also need opportunities and support for experimentation in the classroom, coupled with the time to reflect on the results of what we tried. At this point, the workshop model of staff development falls short—all responsibility for figuring out how to apply new information to our classrooms, all experimentation, critiquing, and revision—are left up to the individual, with no time or support for implementation provided. This is where a collaborative learning model of professional development weighs in strongly. Individual teachers are still responsible for trying new ideas out in the classroom, but the model provides time for small groups of teachers to help each other refine implementation.

This collaborative learning is most effective in a model we call a learning team approach. In this model, selected texts and resources furnish new ideas and strategies. Specific activities offer step-by-step guidance and resources for strategies to try in the classroom. Regular meetings with a group of colleagues provide a forum for discussion and problem solving. In addition, participants in learning teams have opportunity to control which aspects of study they will focus on, the pace of study, and the meeting schedule.

WHAT IS A LEARNING TEAM?

Through our experiences with effective adult learning, we have come to the following definition of a learning team: "a group of three to six individuals who have committed to meet regularly for an agreed amount of time guided by a common purpose." Because learning along with others who bring different areas of expertise to the table is a

*Adapted from R. J. Stiggins, J. Arter, J. Chappuis, & S. Chappuis, *Classroom Assessment for Student Learning: Doing It Right—Using It Well*, (pp. 19–22), Portland, OR. Assessment Training Institute, 2004. Adapted by permission.

central feature of learning teams, we recommend having three to six participants on a given team. This structure provides diversity of experience, interpretation, and viewpoint while still allowing time for each member to participate actively in meetings.

The second phrase of our definition, "who have committed to meeting regularly for an agreed amount of time," reflects the promise team members make to each other: "You can count on me to be there, because we together create the environment and the expertise necessary for peak learning." If any team member is not committed and present, the team loses the richness of that person's perspective, arguments, and insights.

The last phrase, "guided by a common purpose," is the reason team members make the commitment: "Our common purpose in this study is to make classroom assessment work better for our students and ourselves. We know that we won't contribute as productively toward that end if we don't do the agreed reading, viewing, or experimentation between team meetings." Thus, the learning team's goal is to help all members become assessment literate through collaboration during team meetings and individual study and action between meetings. To be assessment literate means to be skilled both in gathering accurate information about students learning and in using it effectively to promote further learning.

A learning team is not a book group. As pleasant an experience as book groups are, they do not share our goals. While we hope you will find at least portions of this book a pleasure to read, we are fairly certain you are not reading purely for enjoyment and to engage in lively conversation. "What is happening differently in our classrooms as a result of what we are doing and learning in our study teams?" Carlene Murphy (Murphy & Lick, 2001, p. 12), a leader in the field of learning teams, raises this question when she helps others establish study teams, and it puts the emphasis where, in our opinion, it belongs. The discussion that occurs during team meetings is a means to the end, and not the end itself. If we don't commit to trying things

out between team meetings, nothing different will be happening in our classrooms, and if that's the case, what's the purpose of our study?

THE LEARNING TEAM PROCESS

The learning team process consists of the following steps:

- Thinking about classroom assessment
- Reading and reflecting on new classroom assessment strategies
- Shaping the strategies into applications
- Trying out applications, observing, and drawing inferences about what does and doesn't work
- Reflecting on and summarizing learning and conclusions from that experience
- Sharing and problem solving with team members

You will notice that the bulk of time is spent in activities between team meetings—acquiring new ideas and applying them in the classroom. Team meetings themselves constitute a small but powerful portion of your learning time.

FINDING TIME

The problem of time is always with us, yet when learning is a priority, school districts, buildings, and groups of teachers have found ways to secure the time needed, both for the individual work required and for team meetings. Options commonly employed include paying a stipend for a set number of hours, offering college and salary-advancement credit, and setting aside contract time.

Applying the Skills

Resource 4: How Principals Can Support Learning Teams

What this resource is: This resource assumes that teachers will join learning teams to study the ATI program built around the text, *Classroom Assessment for Student Learning: Doing It Right—Using It Well* (Stiggins et al., 2004). It offers an explanation of the content that teachers will be studying, along with suggested actions principals can take to support implementation of the content and of the learning team.

Ideas for making it useful: Read through the two lists of suggestions, "What Principals Can Do to Support the Content of the Program" and "What Principals Can Do to Help Teams Succeed." Select actions that suit your context.

WHAT PRINCIPALS CAN DO TO SUPPORT THE CONTENT OF THE PROGRAM

- First, make sure you can articulate the big ideas of what the teams are studying:
  1. *Quality*—How to select and create high-quality (accurate and efficient) assessments for classroom use.
  2. *Balancing Assessments* of *and* for *Learning*—How to meet parents', teachers', and students' information needs.
  3. *Student Involvement*—How to use student-involvement strategies to increase student motivation and achievement.
- Get a schedule of your teams' meeting dates and assigned readings. Ask questions about the specific chapters they are reading. (See "Content Highlights to Discuss/Reinforce.")
- Identify a "concept of the week (or month)." Highlight it at a staff meeting, such as through examples, an activity, testimonials, or student work. Consider co-planning the meetings with the team facilitator or the whole team.
- Be quick to notice success. If someone tells you, "I tried this out, and it really worked!" do something with that information. Email a response. Recognize small successes; make those small but important changes visible in some way. Get them into faculty meetings—plan a short (5 minute), regular "Successful Assessment Ideas Sharing Time" to help people realize that huge successes build on small ones, and that we/they are learning one step at a time. Celebrate the steps!
- Ask members of the team to invite you into the classroom the next time they try a new idea. Get in there to watch student involvement in action. "I'm intrigued by... and wondered if you would let me know the next time you..." Write a short note commenting on one positive aspect of what you saw.
- Release teachers to watch each other. Sub for them if need be. Schedule joint planning time for team members to create and/or critique an assessment together. Apply all the tactics you already have in your bag of tricks for making sure an important initiative gets off the ground (and stays aloft...).

WHAT PRINCIPALS CAN DO TO HELP TEAMS SUCCEED

- First, make sure you understand the "why" and the "what" of learning teams—the rationale for this model of professional development and what process learning teams will be following. Then follow these suggestions for actions you can take to support the process.

- The most effective step you can take to support learning teams in your school is to *join a learning team yourself.* More than any words you can put together, this act telegraphs that you believe assessment quality—accuracy and effective use—to be a high priority, a skill set worthy of your own time.

- Your team(s) will have regularly scheduled meeting times. Hold that time sacred for them. Avoid asking individuals to do something else during their meeting time.

- Members of the learning teams have committed a great deal of their own time, as well as team time, to become assessment literate. They may also be willing to assist you on other committees/teams, but consider not asking them for additional time commitments this year.

- They are acting on intrinsic motivation. The greatest reward for them will be seeing the changes in their students. Help them track those changes by asking about them. Encourage members to document students' changes for their own personal growth portfolios. If this seems overwhelming, ask them to select three students—one strong learner, a midrange learner, and a struggling learner—and look for changes in them.

- If you are a member of a team, consciously adopt a "learner stance." In team or committee settings, some people watch the principal to see how she or he responds and then pattern their actions after the principal's. You want your team members to feel safe enough to admit that something doesn't work well and to try new ideas. Model this: "I always did _____ when I was teaching, and now I see why it wasn't the best choice. If I had it to do over again, I think I'd try _____." In a learning team setting, it can work to your advantage to be a learner along with your staff, and it can work against you if they see you as the "expert," because you are not there to teach the class, you are there to learn along with them.

CLASSROOM ASSESSMENT FOR STUDENT LEARNING: DOING IT RIGHT—USING IT WELL

Content Highlights to Discuss/Reinforce

Part 1   Principles of Assessment for Learning and Assessment Quality
   Chapter 1   Classroom Assessment—Every Student a Winner!

- The five Keys to Quality Classroom Assessment are defined. Were any a surprise?
- The definition of *assessment quality* goes beyond accuracy; it also requires that the assessment results be used to support learning.
- What do you find to be the most effective staff development model for your own learning?

Chapter 2   Assessment for *and* of Learning

- The first key to assessment quality is to attend to the purpose of the assessment.
- How would you define assessment *for* learning? Assessment *of* learning? How would you explain the differences between the two?
- Think about the purpose of assessment more broadly, not just as a vehicle for getting a grade for the report card.
- Think beyond teachers as the main users of assessment information.
- Consider the student as the most important user of assessment information, whose information needs must be met. What are those information needs?
- We often equate assessment *for* learning with formative assessment, but for many people, formative assessment is limited to teachers' diagnostic actions. What does assessment *for* learning look like in the classroom? How does it differ from how we currently understand formative assessment?

Chapter 3   Assess What? Clear Targets

- Thinking about assessment begins in the planning stages of a unit, when teachers identify the targets they'll be teaching to. Being a standards-based teacher involves also being a standards-based assessor.
- It's important to know what kinds of learning targets we hold for students, and to understand them, in order to teach and assess them well.
- It's important to communicate those targets clearly to students, in advance of teaching.
- Are district curriculum documents adequate to the task of guiding instruction and assessment effectively?

Part 2   Assessment Methods

Chapter 4   Assess How? Designing Assessments to Do What You Want

■   How teachers select an assessment method depends on the kind of target they want to assess and the purpose for the assessment.

■   When choosing an assessment method, aim for accuracy and efficiency (keeping purpose in mind).

■   Teachers need to be comfortable with using all four methods. Creating a test plan is one of the crucial first steps in assessment development; even when planning to use an already-developed assessment, teachers still need to ensure that it matches the teaching content and represents a fair sample of the expected learning.

Chapter 5   Selected Response Assessment

■   Creating a test plan, in advance of teaching (or along the way), is a good thing.

■   Teachers don't need to become full-time item writers, but they do need to know how to audit a test for quality, which includes its match to what was taught (and the learning targets), and how to revise a selected response test so that it adheres to standards of quality.

■   Student-involvement strategies can be used with selected response testing, but only if teachers and students know the learning targets tested by each item on the test. This takes time—how can teachers make this time? What happens if they don't?

■   How much summative assessment information about student achievement is enough for grading purposes? How much is too much? Could some summative assessment events be converted to formative assessment events?

Chapter 6   Extended Written Response Assessment

■   Teachers need to pay attention to guidelines for writing essay test questions (extended response items), because a poorly worded, or poorly thought out question can cause students to write a poor-quality answer.

■   Teachers need to have in place a scoring mechanism (points or rubrics) for essay questions that they communicate to students prior to giving the test.

■   Teachers need to know how to involve students productively in essay assessment, which takes time. How can teachers make this time? What happens if they don't?

■   How much summative assessment information about student achievement is enough for grading purposes? How much is too much? Too little? Could some summative assessment events be converted to formative assessment events?

Chapter 7   Performance Assessment

- Performance assessment cannot do everything, but it does provide teachers with the opportunity to engage students in "life beyond school" applications of subject-matter knowledge.

- Adhering to guidelines for creating the task is as important as adhering to guidelines when devising or selecting criteria.

- Teachers need to know how to involve students productively in performance assessment, which takes time. How can teachers make this time? What happens if they don't?

- How much summative assessment information about student achievement is enough for grading purposes? How much is too much? Too little? Could some summative assessment events be converted to formative assessment events?

Chapter 8   Personal Communication as Assessment

- Assessing with personal communication provides a great opportunity to assess formatively—and especially to diagnose strengths and weaknesses in reasoning proficiencies.

- Journals and logs can offer windows into students' thinking and need not be evaluated summatively to further learning.

Part 3   Communicating Assessment Results

Chapter 9   Communicating About Student Learning

- There are a number of ways to plan for balance of assessments *for* and *of* learning.

- One of the first problems teachers encounter with assessments *for* learning is some students' resistance to doing work that will not count toward a grade. Teachers must adopt strategies that will motivate practice without requiring it to be graded.

- Both assessment *for* learning and standards-based teaching and assessing dictate some changes in record-keeping procedures.

Chapter 10   Assessment of Learning: Report Cards

- Sound grading practices can be sorted out by adhering to three grading principles, summarized in the following statement: Report card grades communicate about level of achievement at a point in time. The next three conclusions follow from that statement:

- Level of achievement on the subject learning targets is the only factor that belongs in a subject-area report card grade.

- Practice activities should not be figured into the report card grade.

- Factoring in a zero for late or missing work misrepresents achievement.

- How do district grading policies and procedures stack up against the rubric for grading practices?

Chapter 11   Portfolios

■ It needs to be clear at the outset what the purpose for a particular portfolio is—all other decisions flow from this first decision.

■ The learning targets the portfolio represents need to be stated clearly.

■ The purpose for the portfolio and the learning targets to be represented guide decisions about the artifacts to be included.

■ Portfolios provide a meaningful vehicle for student self-assessment, goal setting, and reflection.

■ Having a portfolio without student involvement, such as student self-reflection, is of extremely limited instructional use.

Chapter 12   Conferences About and with Students

■ The purpose of a conference can be to offer feedback, assist with goal setting, plan an intervention, demonstrate growth, or to communicate about level of achievement.

■ Student involvement in conferences benefits all ages and all levels of students.

■ Students can participate in and lead conferences with proper preparation throughout the year.

■ Student-involved conferences can be time-consuming if teachers think they must participate in each one. Many student-involved conference options do not require the teacher's presence.

Chapter 13   Practical Help with Standardized Tests

■ Some of our problems with standardized testing come from misuse of the information— it's not the test, it's what we try to make the results do that confounds us.

■ Classroom teachers and building-level administrators are the first line of defense against misuse of standardized test information.

■ Anyone giving *or taking* a standardized test must understand what it measures and how the results are to be used (refer back to the first Key to Quality, "Clear and Appropriate Purposes").

■ Teachers must be able to differentiate between ethical and unethical test preparation practices.

Competency 6

The leader analyzes student assessment information accurately, uses the information to improve curriculum and instruction, and assists teachers in doing the same.

We have already established the need for balance between large-scale standardized tests and classroom assessments, while emphasizing the power of classroom assessment and the principles of assessment *for* learning. That does not mean that standardized testing doesn't have an important role to play in a balanced assessment system. It absolutely does; decisions about program effectiveness and professional development needs, among others, require this kind of information. Large-scale assessment results also offer evidence of system success, indicators that schools and districts can use to show the fruit of their efforts, solid proof that students are learning.

State and local testing systems together combine to create large amounts of student test data, and all school leaders must be prepared to interpret, manage, and use that data to improve student learning. (We'll examine how to coordinate local and state assessment systems in Activity 22.) Now more than ever, leaders have a responsibility for conducting meaningful data analyses and providing clear, accurate reports of student assessment results. At the school level, principals need to work with the building instructional staff to use test results to identify patterns in group achievement strengths and weaknesses. Principals need to be able to produce annual learning improvement goals and identify the specific instructional strategies and professional development teachers need to reach those goals, based on the analyzed data. The use of data for these purposes supplants the use of hunches and intuition about what to do next to improve student learning, and places the data in the center of decision making. While teachers should receive appropriate training in data analysis and review, more importantly they need structured, collaborative time to review disaggregated test data and consider answers to the questions it raises, under the leadership of the building principal.

The leader's first step in achieving Competency 6 is to conduct an audit of all standardized assessments used in the school/district to ensure the information needs of all users are being met. The audit, also described in Door 2 in Part 3 of this guide, provides information about each test, including the purposes for giving the test, the standards assessed by the test, and how the results will be used. The audit can be used to ensure that standardized assessments will function as a system, rather than as isolated, unconnected measurement events (Office of the Superintendent of Public Instruction [OSPI], 1996).

As a part of the audit, each test must be analyzed to determine the content standards and curriculum objectives assessed. This analysis creates the foundation for accurate data interpretation, reveals information gaps and overlaps (which standards are going unassessed and which standards appear to be over-assessed), and focuses attention on which assessments yield the most useful information. Test specifications, which identify the objectives tested, are frequently available from test publishers. Such information, often underutilized, is crucial to our ability to do anything meaningful with test scores. We protect student well-being when we identify the match between standardized test content and what students are learning through our local curriculum, and ensure that every educator in the school knows what specific standards each score represents, enabling them to use the test information appropriately.

To analyze data and to communicate the information to all who need it, many principals form school data teams. These teams, comprised of representatives of the building's instructional staff (and sometimes parents as well), are given the responsibility for collecting useful data and asking questions about what test results and other data tell the staff about the student' performance. Here is a sample of the questions that a data team might ask about assessment *of* learning data:

- How do the results for our school compare with other groups: schools, district, state?
- Are there some groups in the school that outperformed others? Which subgroups need further data analysis?
- In what areas is student performance improving? Not improving?
- What learning targets do students struggle with most?
- Is there a particular assessment method that appears to cause students difficulty?
- What does the data from our feeder school(s) suggest?
- How do students who have been in our school the longest perform relative to students who have been in the school only a short time?

- Are the test results from one test consistent with other tests given in the school? Are they consistent with report card grades/GPAs?
- What needs for improvement can we infer from the data?
- What is currently in place that addresses those needs?
- What else do we need to know, and what data do we need to get the answers?

Software programs are now readily available to help analyze and present data in multiple ways. Many are user friendly and can help compare test scores by sub-group (gender, ethnicity, etc.), examine data at the individual test-item level, and assist in conducting program evaluations or gauging the effectiveness of one instructional model over another. And when the test results are linked to individual student identification numbers, longitudinal analysis becomes possible. If your state or district doesn't offer training on data analysis, there are multiple print and media resources available to help you through the process, including the following:

- *Getting Excited About Data*, by Edie Holcomb (Thousand Oaks, CA: Corwin, 1999)
- *Data Analysis for Comprehensive Schoolwide Improvement,* by Victoria L. Bernhardt (Larchmont, NY: Eye on Education, 1998)
- *The School Portfolio Toolkit*, by Victoria L. Bernhardt (Larchmont, NY: Eye on Education, 2002)
- *The Handbook for SMART School Teams*, by Anne Conzemius and Jan O'Neill (Bloomington, IN: National Educational Services, 2002)
- *Using Data to Close the Achievement Gap*, by Ruth S. Johnson (Thousand Oaks, CA: Corwin, 2002)
- *Using Data to Improve Student Achievement: A Handbook for Collecting, Organizing, Analyzing and Using Data*, by Deborah Wahlstrom (Suffolk, VA: Successline, 1999)

Standardized testing information is less useful, however, when it comes to informing the continuous instructional decisions that help each student attain state standards. For that we need classroom assessment information, based directly on the content standards and curriculum objectives taught. Common grade-level or department assessments, diagnostic assessments, classroom formative assessments, collaborative examination of student work, and data from teachers' observations can all be used to make decisions about curriculum and instruction and reveal why some students are learning better than others. It is the principal's role here to provide teachers time to meet to interpret the information they have and make instructional decisions on its basis, in both job-alike teams and in articulation teams with groups of teachers from adjoining grade levels.

The following resources also may be of value:

- *Professional Learning Communities at Work: Best Practices for Enhancing Student Achievement*, by Rick DuFour (Bloomington, IN: National Educational Service, 1998)
- *Results: The Key to Continuous School Improvement*, 2d ed., by Mike Schmoker (Alexandria, VA: Association for Supervision and Curriculum Development, 1999)

Applying the Skills

Resource 5: Conducting an Assessment Audit

What this resource is: Schools and districts need to map the "big picture" of the tests administered in local assessment systems to ensure that the information needs of all stakeholders are being met. The audit will capture such information as what learning expectations are being measured in each assessment, when assessments are given, how often, how much time each one takes, and the purpose of each assessment. When completed with the relevant information, the templates provided with this resource act as such an assessment inventory. Administrators can then use it to manage the local assessment system, analyze its contents, and find the testing gaps and redundancies relative to academic standards (OSPI, 1996; Stiggins, 2005).

You can create other grids, depending on your local program, to help gather and catalogue the information that will paint a picture of the total testing program in the school/district. We include here three templates (pp. 199–201) that will help you begin to analyze your assessment program.

Ideas for making it useful: The results of an assessment audit can also be a valuable tool to use when communicating with parents about standardized test administration and results. Once each test is catalogued, the information about that test (time, purpose, standards assessed, methods used, scoring procedures, etc.) is all in one place and can all be transferred into a letter home to parents to provide the necessary information. (See Resource 7.)

If you're trying to merge a local and state assessment system and ensure they work together and don't overlap (see Activity 22) the information collected through the audit is essential.

A Model for Identifying Gaps in Your Assessment Plan

Name/form of each standardized test or other assessment administered (list by content area or test battery separately)	Grade level(s) tested	Time of year given	Total testing time	Specific state standards assessed by this instrument	Assessment method(s) used	Connection to the district curriculum	Intended uses and users of test results	Communication plans

Record of Required State, District, and School Assessments*

	Math	Language	Reading	Science	Social Studies	Other	Total State Required	Total District Required	Total School Required	Total
Grade 2										
Grade 3										
Grade 4										
Grade 5										

* Developed with Dr. Linda Elman, Central Kitsap School District, WA.

Assessments in <u>Math</u> (or other content area)*

Test Name	Test Uses: Purpose	Test Users	School Level	District Level	Classroom Level	Methods Used	Time Needed	K	1	2	3	4	5	6	7	8	9	10	11	12

* Adapted from OSPI, 1996.

Competency 7

The leader develops and implements sound assessment and assessment-related policies.

Many policies at both the school and the district level have the potential to either support or hinder the effective use of assessment *for* learning. Further, policies can either support each other, acting in concert as a system of beliefs and practices, or they can act in opposition to each other, creating inconsistency and even conflict. It is part of the school leader's assessment responsibilities to revise policies so they provide a framework for sound assessment practice and act in unison with each other. In fact, without policy support, assessment reform initiatives may flounder. Leaders are more likely to succeed at this task if they approach it with three perspectives in mind:

1. How we view the role of the policy manual is critical. School and district policy needs to be seen as more than the regulatory compliance arm of the organization. Beyond fulfilling the legal requirements of the state and federal governments, policy can serve as an implementation tool for strategic planning efforts and can be used as one of many strategies to help the vision become reality. It provides an opportunity to set and communicate standards, expectations, and the priorities most relevant to student achievement, and can help educate the local community. The integration of district planning and priorities with policy making is especially necessary in a standards-based assessment system (California School Boards Association, 1999).

2. Assessment systems need to be planned as just that: *systems* with connected parts all working toward a common goal. District policy manuals and faculty handbooks should be approached from the same perspective. The elements all need to fit together, which requires thinking about policies beyond revising one at a time or revising each only in response to some district crisis or legislative enactment.

3. A written comprehensive assessment plan clarifies the purpose of assessment and how it fits into effective teaching and learning. We will say more about this in Part 5, but essential for assessment reform is a document that states assessment beliefs and provides guiding principles and policies for both large-scale testing and classroom practice based on that set of beliefs.

Policies that have a strong connection with student assessment and that should be reviewed for appropriateness and congruence include the following:

Grading	Attendance
Homework	Student placement
Lesson planning	Graduation requirements
Hiring	Promotion and retention

Following are three global guidelines to follow when formulating assessment policy:

- In a standards-based educational environment, what grades mean should be unambiguous. If the grading policy allows effort, attitude, tardies, absences, or other variables having nothing to do with achievement of content standards to be factored into the grade, many students' achievement will be inaccurately reported.

- If grading policies dictate the practice of averaging the marks in the gradebook to calculate the final grade, if formative homework counts in the grade the same way summative quizzes or tests do, or if marks early in the grading period always carry the same weight as marks in the latter part of the grading period, the same risk of, if not certainty of, inaccurate reporting of student achievement will result (O'Connor, 2002).

- Basing a promotion/retention decision (or any other high-stakes decision, for that matter) on a single test score or other measure of student learning may lead to an ill-informed decision. Any single test is limited in its capability to show what students know and are able to do. The use of multiple measures is always preferred in order to increase the dependability of the evidence.

Thinking About Assessment

Activity 18: Using School/District Policies to Support Quality Assessment

Purpose: This activity requests that your team review a series of school/district policies, all of which have a connection in some way to assessment. Some are more complete than others; some are more current and better written than others. All are examples of policies at the district level, although school-level administrators can also make use of this activity simply by shifting the emphasis to school-level policies contained in a faculty handbook. By reviewing the policies with an eye toward how they could be rewritten or improved to be more supportive of quality assessment, your team and other school leaders practice building the framework for a productive assessment environment through the use of sound school/district policies.

One of the objectives of this activity and in working with policy in general is to see policies as a systemic whole, where the elements (in this case the policies themselves) hang together, all working toward a common purpose. Without approaching the policy manual in that way we risk having policies in opposition to each other: an attendance policy may contradict a grading policy, or a promotion/retention policy may conflict with a policy on student assessment that is grounded in a specific set of belief statements.

Lastly, the district-level policies in this activity are just that; without the implementation procedures that usually accompany policies and provide the specifics of how the policy is to be applied, we lack some context. However, the underlying concepts and ideas are apparent in each example. The intention of the activity is not to perfect each policy, but rather to get some practice in reviewing policies with quality assessment as the filter.

Time: 90 minutes

Directions: Before starting this activity, it will be helpful for your team to list a set of criteria to use when reviewing these policies (and any other policies you may choose to use from your local school/district). What is the group looking to achieve in assessment through school or district policies? What would constitute a strong policy? For example, your team might generate policy review criteria in the form of questions. The list that follows is a start, but other considerations may be important to your team.

Does this policy

■ Support the vision of assessment in the school/district?

■ Have a direct impact on student learning?

■ Have an impact on or connection to other policies that need to be considered?

■ Encourage the use of multiple measures of student learning, creating judgments made about students with combinations of data sources?

■ Require clear, meaningful, and frequent communication about learning?

■ Link standards, instruction, and assessment?

■ Require any specialized professional development?

Recognize that each of these criteria or those your team may generate might not be relevant or apply to each policy under review. After finalizing your list of criteria, read the first policy in this activity. Then pause and consider the following three questions with your team. Do this with the remainder of the sample policies in this activity. Use the criteria developed by your team to help answer the questions for each policy review.

1. What are the strong points of the policy the way it is currently written?
2. What are the weak areas of the policy?
3. What language could be omitted, and what language might be added to make it more supportive of sound assessment?

Closure: Completing this activity gives team members some experience in reviewing policies with assessment in mind. Your next step can be to undertake a similar activity using current policies from your school/district. Remember, if you find policies in need of reworking, improving them as a set of connected policies is more likely to result in policies that work in concert, whereas dealing with each in isolation can bring about conflicts in language and ideas.

POLICY 2101 – STUDENT RETENTION/PROMOTION

As the ability to read proficiently is the basic foundation for success in school, as it is indeed throughout life, it is the goal of the primary school, the first three (3) grades, to teach each child to read independently with understanding by the time he/she finishes the third grade. It is within this period when retention of a youngster in a grade can be most valuable. Teachers, taking into account factors such as achievement, mental age, chronological age, emotional stability, social and physical maturity may find it advisable in the case of some students to retain a child once or twice during this period. By following this policy, the District will find some children completing the first three grades in four (4) years and some in five (5) as well as the majority who will finish in the regular three (3) year period.

With the above as a basic policy, retention after the third grade should only be a problem in those cases where a student is not achieving and meeting the grade standards of which he is capable. In cases where it is contemplated holding a student in the same grade for an extra year, the teacher should notify the parents as early in the year as possible, but not later than the end of the third quarter.

No student shall be retained for more than two (2) years in the same grade.

Since it is the responsibility of the school to adjust the work in each grade to the child's individual needs and ability to provide an equal educational opportunity for all children, no arbitrary policy of promotion is suggested. Promotion should be made for grade to grade, based upon a consideration of the best interest of the student concerned.

The following factors shall be taken into consideration: achievement, mental age, chronological age, emotional stability, social and physical maturity. The curriculum should be so broad on each grade level that the needs of bright students are met, as well as the needs of average and slow students. Therefore, when accepting pupils who are new to District schools, the principal should make the best placement possible on the basis of the information he/she can obtain.

POLICY 2102– LESSON PLANS

To ensure proper planning and continuity of instruction, the Board requires that each teacher prepare lesson plans for daily instruction. To facilitate more effective instruction, lesson plans must be prepared in advance of the actual class presentation. The format for the lesson plan will be specified by the building principal and shall be reviewed on a regular basis. The plan book must be readily available when a substitute teacher is needed.

POLICY 2103– CLASS RANK

The Board acknowledges the usefulness of a system of computing grade point averages and class ranking for secondary school graduates to inform students, parents, and others of their relative academic placement among their peers.

The Board authorizes a system of class ranking, by grade point average, for student in grades 9–12. Class rank shall be computed by the final grade except that non-numerical marks/grades shall be excluded from the calculation of the grade point average.

A student's grade point average shall be reported on his/her term grade report. Such calculations may also be used for recognizing individual students for their achievement.

POLICY 2104—HOMEWORK

The Board believes that homework is a constructive tool in the teaching/learning process when geared to the age, health, abilities, and needs of students. Purposeful assignments not only enhance student achievement but also develop self-discipline and associated good working habits. As an extension of the classroom, homework must be planned and organized; must be viewed as purposeful to the students; and must be evaluated and returned to the student in a timely manner.

The purposes of homework assignments, the basis for evaluating the work performed and the guidelines and/or rules should be made clear to the student at the time of the assignment.

The school principal shall establish guidelines that clarify the nature and use of homework assignments to improve school achievement.

Make-up work, due to illness, is not to be considered as homework. Students shall be given the opportunity to make-up assignments missed during excused absences.

POLICY 2106—GRADING AND PROGRESS REPORTS

The Board believes that the cooperation of school and home is a vital ingredient in the growth and education of the student and recognizes the responsibility to keep parents informed of student personal development/work habits, as well as academic progress in school.

The issuance of grades and progress reports on a regular basis serves as the basis for continuous evaluation of the student's performance and determining changes that should be made to effect improvement. These reports shall be designed to provide information that will be helpful to the student, teacher, counselor, and parent.

For grades 9–12, the district shall comply with the marking/grading system incorporated into the statewide standardized high school transcript. The superintendent may consider alternative grading/progress reports. A student's grade point shall be reported for each term, individually and cumulatively.

The Board directs the superintendent to establish a system of reporting student progress and shall require all staff members to comply with such a system as a part of their teaching responsibility.

If classroom participation is used as the basis of mastery of an objective, a student's grades may be adversely affected by an absence, provided that on the day of the excused absence, there was a graded participation activity. If the teacher does not so advise students in writing, the teacher may not use attendance and participation in the grading process. Teachers shall consider circumstances pertaining to the student's inability to attend school. No student grade shall be reduced or credit denied for disciplinary reasons only, rather than for academic reasons, unless due process of law is provided. Individual students, who feel that an unjust application of attendance or tardiness factors has been made, may follow the appeal process for resolving the differences. Academic appeals have no further step for appeal.

POLICY 2107—INSTRUCTION

Effective Communication about Student Achievement

_____ School District is a standards driven district with the goal of communicating effectively about student achievement. It is the intent of the District to provide timely, understandable, and meaningful information about student progress towards clearly articulated achievement standards to students, parents, educational professionals and third parties with interest. Grading and reporting practices represent one of a variety of ways to communicate student progress towards standards and may serve the following purpose(s).

- Communication of the achievement status of students to parents/guardians in ways that describe progress toward district standards and provide an accurate focus on learning.
- Information students can use for self-evaluation and improvement.
- Data for the selection, identification, or grouping of students for certain educational paths or programs.
- Information for evaluation of the effectiveness of instructional programs.

Grading and reporting provide important information about student progress, but there is no single best way of communicating about student achievement. The District will use a variety of ways to deliver information about student achievement to intended users. All information users are important and are entitled to timely and accurate achievement data: some may require greater detail about achievement than can be provided by grades and test scores to make informed decisions. The following illustrate different types of communication about student achievement:

- Checklists of standards
- Narrative descriptions
- Portfolios of various kinds
- Report card grades
- Student conferences

All practices related to communication about student achievement should be carried out according to the best current understanding and application of the research. The District will provide staff members on-going professional development needed to gain that understanding.

Grading and Reporting

The District's policy and procedures on communication about student achievement, specifically grading and reporting practices, are based upon the principles that

- Individual achievement of clearly stated learning targets should be the only basis for grades, providing an accurate reflection of what each student knows and can do; the effectiveness of the communication is determined by the accuracy of the information about student achievement.
- Other characteristics (effort, behavior, attendance, attitude, etc.) should not be included in grades but should be reported separately.
- Different users and decision makers of achievement data need information in different forms at different times in order to make their decisions.
- Grading and reporting should always be done in reference to specified achievement targets, comparing students' performance against a standard rather than against other students in the class (on a curve).
- Grades should be calculated to ensure that the grade each student receives is a fair reflection of what he/she knows and can do, emphasizing the most recent summative assessment information.
- Consideration shall be given to the use of appropriate grade calculation procedures to ensure that assigned grades reflect the intended importance of each leaning goal.
- Grades have some value as incentives but no value as punishments.

During the first week of classes, teachers shall provide students and parents with a written syllabus of learning expectations and grading criteria in clear, easily understandable language, indicating how summative assessment throughout the grading period will be calculated into course grades. Teachers shall discuss classroom assessment practices with students, in an age appropriate manner, at the beginning of instruction.

The Superintendent shall develop written procedures that support the District policy on Communicating Effectively about Student Achievement.

Competency 8

The leader creates the conditions necessary for the appropriate use and reporting of student achievement information, and can communicate effectively with all members of the school community about student assessment results and their relationship to improving curriculum and instruction.

Because test scores and report card grades do not communicate sufficiently about how well students are learning in an era of standards-based instruction, educational leaders need to understand the variety of communication options available, including using students as communicators of their own progress toward standards (Stiggins, 2005).

Helping parents and community members understand what is underneath the grades and test scores they receive is an important practice in this competency. (See ATI's parent and community guide to assessment, *Understanding School Assessment* [Chappuis & Chappuis, 2002].) Parents learn about the results of their children's assessments *of* learning taken at school in a variety of ways, including through the local media. School leaders need to help parents understand assessment in ways that go beyond the scoreboard presented in the newspapers. Each time a standardized test is administered at school, whether at the department, school, district, or state level, these leaders need to communicate with parents/guardians about the purpose of the assessment. To help parents put assessment in context, teachers can send a letter home (see Resource 7) explaining what is being assessed and why, how the results will be used and by whom, and the relationship between the assessment and the improvement of the instructional program at the school.

We recommend the following components be included in communication with parents:

■ Explanation of what the test items measure
■ How long the test takes, if it is timed (and why or why not)
■ What assessment methods are used
■ How items are scored
■ Sample test items showing what the test looks like

- Written tutorials on how to interpret the results
- Sample interpretations of the results
- How the results are intended to be used, and how you will use them (linking the uses you will make of the information to the kinds of uses for which the test is designed)

Schools also can hold parent meetings to review these topics, as well as where each test fits into the total assessment program and what the results mean for individual students as they progress through the system. This helps create a foundation for common understanding and effective communication between the school and home. Teachers also can help parents use the test information wisely by cautioning them about how too much attention given to any one indicator of student achievement can skew the picture of individual or group progress. When educators clearly communicate the results of standardized testing in relation to state standards, and use report cards that communicate progress toward those same standards, parents get a more complete picture from the school about what students know and can do relative to a predetermined standard (Chappuis & Chappuis, 2002).

The report card grading issues raised in the policies reviewed in Activity 18 also extend to the quality of school-to-home communication. If grades are to reflect something meaningful and serve a useful communications function they must be based on accurate assessments. But beyond this, grading practices themselves also present many difficult and potentially contentious issues. Unless resolved, these issues can result in faulty communication about student learning. Some software grading programs, while on the surface appearing fair and precise, can use computerized routines to generate grades that are neither fair nor precise (Guskey, 2002). When the report card grade obscures more than it reveals about achievement, school leaders must take action to create the conditions needed to institute clarity and accuracy in both grading (see Activity 19) and communication about achievement that goes beyond grades (see Activity 22).

Schools and districts that have moved or are moving to new reporting systems based on student attainment of content standards can take steps to ensure both students and parents understand how student progress will now be reported.

That understanding can be built by comparing and contrasting for parents a traditional report card based on A–F letter grades with a new standards-based model, describing the characteristics of and the philosophical foundation for each type of system. Informing students and parents of what is factored into the report card grade and what isn't also is important in building a common understanding. And we can also ensure our systems use as few coded messages as possible (B-, 79%, satisfactory, emerging), and always provide clear definitions of what those coded symbols mean.

Thinking About Assessment

Activity 19: Grading Scenarios

Purpose: Communication about student achievement often relies on grades and report cards. The grading scenarios in this activity help leaders understand grading issues to help teachers use grades to accurately reflect student learning. This activity is intended as a tool for you, but if you use it with staff, don't use the results for formal teacher evaluation. Rather, use the results to plan professional development.

Time: Each scenario takes about 15 minutes.

Directions: Users can work through scenarios one by one or they can be divided up among groups in a staff meeting or workshop setting.

For each scenario choose the course of action one should take when assigning an overall grade for a grading period, and explain why. Use the "ATI Grading Guidelines," page 217.

Closure: Discuss both the "Grading Guidelines" and your responses to each scenario. Discuss how your local grading policies reflect guidelines for grading in a standards-based system. Are any changes needed?

Grading Scenarios*

Each of the following scenarios describes a decision a teacher has to make about assigning the report card grade. The teacher is unsure of what to do and has asked you for some advice. What issues does the teacher's situation raise? What questions ought the teacher consider before making a decision? What might be missing in the teacher's grading schemes?

Use the "ATI Grading Guidelines," page 217, to help make decisions. Our responses are included after each scenario to help facilitate the discussion.

Guideline 8—Relating grading procedures to learning goals (e.g., standards) rather than to sources of information (e.g., quizzes, exams, projects, homework) is a consideration for all scenarios. It is more difficult to decide what to do if one doesn't know what learning targets each source of information is addressing.

Scenario 1

In her 7th grade social studies class Ms. Nguyen's report card grades are based on quizzes, tests, and an out-of-class project that counted as 25% of the grade. Terry obtained an A average on his quizzes and tests, but has not turned in the project despite frequent reminders. In this situation, should Ms. Nguyen
a. Exclude the missing project and give Terry an A?
b. Assign Terry a 0 for the project and D on his report card because his average would be 68%?
c. Assign Terry a lower grade than A, counting off some for not turning in the project?
d. Something else . . .

Scenario 1: Not b because of Guideline 6. Zeros distort true level of achievement. Not c because of Guideline 2—Only count achievement. Answer c would count a behavior—not turning in work—as part of the grade. We would choose d—assign an incomplete because there is not enough information to make a true estimate of student learning.

Scenario 2

Mr. Marlowe's 9th grade English class has students of varying abilities. During this grading period, the students' grades are based on quizzes, tests, and homework assignments that involve practice exercises. Kelly has not turned in any homework assignments despite frequent reminders. His grades on the quizzes have ranged from 65% to 75%, and he received a D on each of the tests. In this situation, should Mr. Marlowe
a. Assign Kelly a 0 for the homework assignments and include this in the grade, thus giving him an average of F for the grading period?

*Scenarios adapted from *Grading* (pp. 188–191), by S. Brookhart, 2004, Upper Saddle River, NJ: Pearson Education. Scenarios based on unpublished survey instruments, B. H. Loyd, 1991. Reprinted with permission.

b. Ignore the missing homework assignments and assign Kelly a D?

c. Ignore the missing homework assignments and give Kelly a C?

d. Something else...

Scenario 2: Not a because of Guideline 6. Zeros distort true level of achievement. We would choose b or c because of Guideline 3—do not include all scores in grades, especially scores on practice work. Base grades on summative assessments. We don't know whether a grade of C or D is more appropriate because we don't know the grading scale. The only caveat is if the homework would provide additional information about student achievement; then we might assign an incomplete.

Scenario 3

Mr. Paderewski is the teacher in a 6th grade heterogeneously grouped class. Chris, one of his students, has strong academic abilities as shown by her previous work, tests results, reports of other teachers, and his own observation. As he looks over her work for the grading period he realizes that the quality of her work is above average for the class, but it doesn't represent the best that she can do. The effort shown has been minimal, but, because of her ability, the work is reasonably good. In this situation, should Mr. Paderewski

a. Grade Chris on the quality of her work in comparison to the class, without being concerned about the quality of work she could have done?

b. Lower Chris's grade because she did not make a serious effort in this class; she could have done better?

c. Give Chris a lower grade to encourage her to work harder?

d. Something else...

Scenario 3: Not a because of Guideline 1—don't grade on a curve, (norm referenced) use criterion-referenced grades. Not b or c because of Guideline 3—include only achievement in the grade. We would choose d—grade on a preset criterion-referenced standard.

Scenario 4

Ms. Quantum has a heterogeneously grouped 7th grade science class. Barbara is one of her lower performing students, as measured by her previous performance and the observation of her previous teachers. Throughout this grading period Barbara has worked very hard. She has turned in her assignments on time and has often come to Ms. Quantum for extra help before tests. Her average for this grading period is two points below what she would need to get a D on Ms. Quantum's grading scale. In this situation, should Ms. Quantum

a. Give Barbara a D for the effort she has shown?

b. Grade Barbara according to the grading scale and give her an F?

c. Something else...

Scenario 4: Not b because of Guideline 2—only include achievement in grades. We would choose c because we would want to make sure we have the best available evidence of achievement before failing a student. So, we would check for Guideline 4—use quality assessments and properly recorded evidence of achievement. Was there something in the assessment procedure that made test results inaccurate? We might also collect more information, perhaps from an oral exam (Guideline 5—use the most current information).

Scenario 5

Ms. Exponent is teaching high school algebra. In her class she gives two tests each grading period. David received an F on the first test and a low B on the second. In this situation, should Ms. Exponent

a. Assign David an overall grade of D based on the average of his performance on the two exams?

b. Assign David an overall grade of C because he showed improvement on his performance?

c. Assign David an overall grade of B because that was his level of performance at the end of the term?

d. Something else...

Scenario 5: The answer to this one depends on whether the second test covered material also covered on the first test. If the student really did use the F on the first test to learn the material, then Guideline 5 holds—use the most current information; so we'd choose c. If the tests covered different material then we'd choose a or b depending on the relative weight of the two tests.

Scenario 6

Ms. Phylum is teaching a heterogeneously grouped introductory biology class. In this class she gives two exams each term. In calculating Bernie's grade for this term, she notices that on the first exam he obtained a score equivalent to an A and on the second exam he received a low C. In this situation, should Ms. Phylum

a. Assign Bernie an overall grade of B, which is the average of his scores on the two exams?

b. Assign Bernie an overall grade of C, noting that there was a definite decline in his performance?

c. Assign Bernie an overall grade of A giving him the benefit of the doubt— perhaps he had personal problems during the term.

d. Something else...

Scenario 6: Not c because of Guideline 2—only include achievement in the grade. We might choose a, b, or d for the same reason as Scenario 5—we don't know how great the overlap in content is between the two tests.

ATI Grading Guidelines*

1. **Organizing the gradebook**
   - Arrange gradebook entries according to achievement target.

2. **Including factors in the final grade**
   - Report and summarize achievement evidence separately from other student characteristics.
   - Use extra credit work only if it supplies additional evidence of achievement.
   - Record a score of zero only if that is the score on the work.
   - Handle borderline cases by collecting additional evidence of student learning.

3. **Considering assessment purpose**
   - Use assessments *for* learning as the basis for providing students with descriptive feed back they can use to see how to improve; do not factor them into report card grades without compelling rationale.

4. **Considering most recent information**
   - Base grades on the most current evidence of the student's level of achievement.

5. **Summarizing information and determining final grade**
   - Make final grades criterion referenced.
   - Convert, weight, and combine information with care.
   - Convert rubric scores to grades using a decision rule.
   - Select the best measure of central tendency to use in combining assessment information into a final grade.

6. **Verifying assessment quality**
   - Base all grades on verifiably accurate assessments of student achievement.

7. **Involving students**
   - Keep students apprised of their current level of achievement.

---

* For background on these guidelines, refer to R. J. Stiggins et al., *Classroom Assessment* for *Student Learning—Doing It Right, Using It Well* (Chapter 10, "Assessment *of* Learning: Report Cards"), the ATI interactive training video, *Report Card Grades: Strategies and Solutions*, and Ken O'Connor, *How to Grade for Learning* (Skylight, 2002).

Thinking About Assessment

Activity 20: ATI Interactive Video, *Report Card Grading: Strategies and Solutions*

Purpose: The Assessment Training Institute interactive training video series for use with school faculties includes one presentation that provides a commonsense overview of a practical set of classroom assessment quality standards. These are the same five Keys to Quality Classroom Assessment addressed behind Door 3 in Part 3 of this guide and in all ATI professional development materials.

In this video and its associated trainer's guide, we provide a workshop for a faculty interested in an overview of how these standards lead to gathering accurate information about student achievement day to day in the classroom.

Important Note: While this program provides an easy to understand overview of sound classroom assessment practices, it cannot teach teachers to how to make those practices operational by itself. That requires further study of the principles of high-quality assessment.

Time: About 2 hours

Directions: Obtain a copy of the video and user's guide and follow directions provided in the guide.

Thinking About Assessment

Activity 21: When Grades Don't Match the State Assessment Results

Purpose: The case, "When Grades Don't Match the State Assessment Results," presents a phenomenon that is occurring with increasing frequency across the country—what happens when students consistently get high grades but fail to meet competency on a state test? This activity explores the reasons there might be a disconnect between report card grades and state test scores.

Time: 10–20 minutes

Directions: Read the case and think about or discuss the following questions:

Why might the situation be occurring? Consider the extent to which conditions for sound communication are violated. Are other standards of quality assessment being violated?

Possible reasons: (1) The state assessment only includes achievement, while grades might include factors other than achievement, such as absences. (2) Class work may cover more than the priorities in the state assessment, so classroom assessments might measure different things than the state assessment. (3) The classroom assessments underpinning the grades aren't accurate. (4) It is unclear how the state performance standard cutoff relates to teachers' grading cutoffs. (5) They were given at different times and might not match with respect to the content students have encountered.

Closure: Discuss what you can do in your school/district to deal with this situation.

Possible solutions: (1) Clarify state assessment and classroom learning targets. Do they match? If not, should they? Is instruction aligned? (2) Check classroom assessments for accuracy—do they meet the five Keys to Quality? (3) Calibrate classroom assessments to the state assessment so that teachers and students know the level needed to perform on classroom assessments to meet state standards.

When Grades Don't Match the State Assessment Results—Case Study

"It seems important to let you know of a phenomenon I'm experiencing in my school as we deal with the data about students who do and do not meet standards on the state assessment in relationship to the grades they earn. While it remains true that most of the kids who are meeting standards are those who also get As, we are discovering a significant number of students who do get As who don't meet standards and a similar number who get rather poor grades who do meet the standards. What should we do?" (Personal communication to authors, 1997).

Applying the Skills

Resource 6: Rubric for Grading

What this resource is: This resource is a rubric that adds detail to the guidelines for grading presented earlier. The rubric represents our best thinking at the current time on what constitutes sound grading practice—i.e., grading practices that best support assessment *for* learning. It includes several dimensions that cover sound grading processes and defines levels of quality for each.

Ideas for making it useful: To understand this rubric fully and use it well, both leaders and teachers need to engage in comprehensive study of sound classroom assessment practices. The rubric (shown in Table 4-4) is included here to help leaders understand the complete "grading target" at which they are aiming.

Please use the rubric as a discussion starter for policy and practice rather than as a mechanism to rate teacher performance formally. For example, principals could use it to analyze their school grading policies and/or staff practices to see how nearly they approach the ATI grading guidelines.

Table 4-4

Rubric for Evaluating Grading Practices*

Criterion	Beginning	Developing	Fluent
1. Organizing the gradebook	The evidence of learning (e.g., a gradebook) is entirely organized by sources of information (tests, quizzes, homework, labs, etc.).	The evidence of learning (e.g., a gradebook) is organized by sources of information mixed with specific content standards.	The evidence of learning (e.g., a gradebook) is completely organized by student learning outcomes (content standards, benchmarks, grade level indicators, curriculum expectations,
2. Including factors in the grade	Overall summary grades are based on a mix of achievement and nonachievement factors (e.g., timeliness of work, attitude, effort, cheating). Nonachievement factors have a major impact on grades. Extra credit points are given for extra work completed; without connection to extra learning. Cheating, late work, and missing work result in a zero (or a radically lower score) in the gradebook. There is no opportunity to make up such work, except in a few cases. Borderline-grade cases are handled by considering nonachievement factors.	Overall summary grades are based on a mix of achievement and nonachievement factors, but achievement counts a lot more. Some extra credit points are given for extra work completed; some extra credit work is used to provide extra evidence of student learning. Cheating, late work, and missing work result in a zero (or lower score) in the gradebook. But, there is an opportunity to make up work and replace the zero or raise the lower score. Borderline cases are handled by considering a combination of nonachievement factors and collecting evidence of student learning.	Overall summary grades are based on achievement only. Extra credit work is evaluated for quality and is only used to provide extra evidence of learning. Credit is not awarded merely for completion of work. Cheating, late work, & missing work is recorded as "incomplete" or "not enough information" rather than "0." There is an opportunity to replace an 'incomplete' with a score without penalty. Borderline grade cases are handled by collecting additional evidence of student achievement, not by counting nonachievement factors.
3. Considering assessment purpose	Everything each student does is given a score and every score goes into the final grade. There is no distinction between "scores" on practice work (formative assessment or many types of homework) and scores on work to demonstrate level of achievement (summative assessment).	Some distinctions are made between formative (practice such as homework) and summative assessment, but practice work still constitutes a significant part of the grade.	Student work is assessed frequently (formative assessment) and graded occasionally (summative assessment). "Scores" on formative assessments and other practice work (e.g., homework) are used descriptively to inform teachers and students of what has been learned and the next steps in learning. Grades are based only on summative assessments.

* Based on suggestions from Ken O'Connor, personal communication, 2003. Copyright 2005, ATI and Ken O'Conner.

Criterion	Beginning	Developing	Fluent
4. Considering most recent information	All assessment data is cumulative and used in calculating a final summative grade. No consideration is given to identifying or using the most current information.	More current evidence is given consideration at times but does not entirely replace out-of-date evidence.	Most recent evidence completely replaces out-of-date evidence when it is reasonable to do so. For example, how well students write at the end of the grading period is more important than how well they write at the beginning, and later evidence of improved content understanding is more important than early evidence.
5. Summarizing information and determing final grade	The gradebook has a mixture of ABC, precentages, +✓-, and/or rubric scores, etc. with no explanation of how they are to be combined into a final summary grade. Rubric scores are converted to percentages when averaged with other scores—or—there is no provision for combining rubric & percentage scores. Final summary grades are based on a curve—a student's place in the rank order of student achievement. Final grades for special needs students are not based on learning targets as specified in the IEP. Final summary grades are based on caluclation of mean (average) only.	The gradebook may or may not have a mixture of symbols, but there is some attempt, even if incomplete, to explain how to combine them. Rubric scores are not directly converted to percentages; some type of decision rule is used, the final grade many times does not best depict level of student achievement. Final grades are criterion referenced, not norm referenced. They are based on preset standards such as A = 90–100% and B = 80–89%. But, there is no indication of the necessity to ensure shared meaning of symbols—i.e., there is no definition of each standard. There is an attempt to base final grades for special needs students on learning targets in the IEP, but the attempt is not always successful—or—it is not clear to all parties that modified learning targets are used to assign a grade. The teacher understands various measures of central tendency, but may not always choose the best one to accurately describe student achievement.	The gradebook may or may not have a mix of symbol types, but there is a sound explanation of how to combine them. Rubric scores are converted to a final grade using a decision rule that results in an accurate depiction of the level of student attainment of the learning targets. Final grades are criterion referenced, not norm referenced. They are based on preset standards with clear descriptions of what each symbol means. These descriptions go beyond A = 90–100% and B = 80–89%; they describe what A, B, etc. performance looks like. Final grades for special needs students are criterion referenced, and indicate level of attainment of the learning goals as specified in the IEP. The targets on which grades are based are clear to all parties. The teacher understands various measures of central tendency (average, median, mode) and understands when each is the most appropriate one to use to accurately describe student learning.

Criterion	Beginning	Developing	Fluent
6. **Verifying Assessment Quality**	There is little evidence of consideration of the accuracy/quality of the individual assessments on which grades are based. Quality standards for classroom assessment are not considered and the teacher has trouble articulating standards for quality. Assessments are rarely modified for special needs students when such modifications would provide much more accurate information about student learning.	The teacher tries to base grades on accurate assessment results only, but may not consciously understand all the features of a sound assessment. Some standards of quality are adhered to in judging the accuracy of the assessment results on which grades are based. The teacher can articulate some of these standards—or—uses standards for quality assessment intuitively, but has trouble articulating why an assessment is sound. Assessments are modified for special needs students, but the procedures used may not result in accurate information and/or match provisions in the IEP.	Grades are based only on accurate assessment results. Questionable results are not included. The teacher can articulate standards of quality, and can show evidence of consideration of these standards in his/her classroom assessments: ■ clear and appropriate learning targets ■ clear and appropriate users and uses ■ choosing the best assessment method ■ writing clear, unambiguous questions ■ good sampling ■ avoiding potential sources of bias and mismeasurement). Assessments are modified for special needs instructional modifications described in IEPs. Such modifications result in generating accurate information on student achievement.
7. **Student Involvement**	Grades are a surprise to students because (a) students don't understand the bases on which grades are determined; (b) students have not been involved in their own assessment (learning targets are not clear to them, and/or they do not self-assess and track progress toward the targets); or (c) teacher feedback is only evaluative (a judgment of level of quality) and includes no descriptive component.	Grades are somewhat of a surprise to students because student-involvement practices and descriptive feedback are too limited to give them insights into the nature of the learning targets being pursued and their own performance.	Grades are not a surprise to students because (a) students understand the basis for the grades received; (b) students have been involved in their own assessment throughout the process (they understand the learning targets they are to hit, self-assess in relation to the targets, track their own progress toward the targets, and/or talk about their progress); and/or (c) teacher communication to students is frequent, descriptive, and focuses on what they have learned as well as the next steps in learning. Descriptive feedback is related directly to specific and clear learning targets.

Applying the Skills

Resource 7: A Standard Cover Letter to Parents

What this resource is:

Parents report they appreciate proactive efforts on the part of the school to communicate with them about important matters, including school testing. Whenever possible, communicating with parents preceding test administration helps put the test in context and build support for the school assessment program. When not possible or practical, a letter home from the school after the test has been taken is essential.

The sample letter that follows is for a norm-referenced test and provides information from the following list. The letter can be adapted for a standards-based assessment or a diagnostic assessment, and can also be adapted to include other information specific to that assessment or based on the local interests of parents:

- A brief explanation of the test, including the purpose of the assessment, the grade levels to be taking the test, the amount of time the test will take, etc.
- What learning targets are assessed, and how those targets relate to the total district curriculum
- How the test items are scored
- What assessment methods are used
- How the results will be reported and used
- What strategies parents can use to help students improve
- And for more information, contact . . .

Ideas for making it useful:

Refer back to the assessment audit conducted in Resource 5 in Competency 6. The grids created in that activity could act as the information foundation for any communication that goes home to parents about tests being given at school.

Date

Dear Parent,

Last May your tenth-grade student took the _____ Test of High School Skills along with all other tenth graders at other high schools in ABC School District. This combination of tests is designed to measure your student's general progress in fundamental high school skills as compared to that of a national comparison group called the "norm" group. It is administered by the district for the purpose of identifying students who are low in skill levels and therefore perhaps not on track to pass the state test administered in the senior year. As you may know, a passing score on that test is required for graduation, and our intent is to identify those students who need additional help in preparing for that test.

The test taken in May had three sections: reading, language use, and mathematics. The items are drawn from a general national curriculum, and are not specifically designed to match the curriculum in either ABC School District or the state of _____. They are traditional multiple-choice tests, and students mark their response to each question on a separate answer document. The answer sheets are then machine scored by _____, the leading test publisher in the country. The results arrived in the summer and we are providing them to you now.

Tests of this kind come with many different score reports. But the score to examine most closely is the NPR. It stands for National Percentile Rank and tells you the percent of students in the norm group who scored below that score. So, if your student is at the 50th NPR, it means that 50 percent of the students in the norm group had fewer items correct than your child. The 50th percentile is the score that would be earned by a *typical tenth grader*. Because test scores of this type are not always exact indicators of a student's skill level, the district will consider other information, including other test scores, student GPAs, and individual teacher comments and observations before determining which students will be offered additional assistance.

Additionally, these test results will be used to examine strengths and weaknesses in our district curriculum and instructional practices. If you have any questions, please contact the _____ at _____.

Sincerely,

Principal
or
Assistant Superintendent
for Curriculum

Competency 9

The leader understands the attributes of a sound and balanced assessment system.

Assessment-literate school leaders know what needs to be balanced in a local assessment system. First, they attend to the balance of assessments *of* learning that check achievement status at a given point in time, including both classroom status checks and those conducted using standardized tests, with classroom assessments *for* learning, specifically designed to involve students and to inform them about their own progress. Each requires its own support resources, professional development, and integration into school improvement. Second, they look for a balance of achievement targets. If the grade level or course curriculum derived from state standards predominantly reflects *knowledge* targets at the expense of *reasoning, skill, and product* targets, an imbalance in what students learn results (Stiggins, 2005). Third, they monitor balance of assessment methods (selected response, essay, performance assessment, and personal communication), which is in part achieved through a proper balance of learning targets in the written curriculum. And fourth, they ensure a balance of communication methods, which allows students, parents, and other stakeholders to gain access to timely and understandable information about student achievement.

School leaders also need to examine the balance between what is assessed at the state level and what is assessed at the local level. The state testing program may seem so comprehensive that the need for a local assessment system may not be apparent. However, just as classroom assessment is not likely to meet all information needs regarding attainment of state and district standards, by the same token, the state's assessment system may not provide all the information district decision makers need about student achievement. Especially in a time of heavy focus on accountability testing, we need to ensure our state and local systems are working in concert to afford useful information about state and local achievement priorities.

Thinking About Assessment

Activity 22: Merging Local and State Assessment Systems

Purpose: We've advocated that a local assessment program function as a system, with each component sharing a common purpose, working toward the same goal of improved student learning. Assessments that do not contribute to that end or act in harmony with the system as a whole should be eliminated. This activity extends the systems-thinking approach to assessment by asking team members to consider what is necessary to achieve a level of balance and synergy between state and local assessment systems.

Time: 1 hour

Directions: First, gather the grids your team used to conduct an assessment audit in Resource 5. That activity helped map the "big picture" of assessment in your school or district. In addition, gather information about the state assessment system, including test and item specifications if available, examples of the various assessments and methods used, and sample reports from state assessments to the various levels: district, school, teacher, and student. Then consider the following:

Remember that it is difficult for any single test to deliver accurate, reliable, and meaningful information if the test is spread too thinly among multiple purposes. With that in mind, answer the following questions:

■ What is the purpose(s) of the state test?
   Is it to satisfy accountability legislation?
   To serve as indicators of system quality?
   To ascertain attainment of state standards by large groups of students?
   To improve curriculum and instruction?
   To certify individual student mastery?
   To function as a gatekeeper for student placement or promotion/ graduation decisions?
   Other?

- Given the purpose(s), what information is provided by the state system?
- What (and whose) information needs are being met by that information?
- What information does it not provide? Whose needs are going unmet in the state system?
- Is the information provided deemed adequate for the purpose(s)?

Now go back to the "big picture" of assessment in your school/district and compare it to the answer to the last question. If information needs are unmet by the state tests, are they being met currently by a district or school assessment? Are there subjects that seem over-tested while others are not tested at all? Is there redundancy between the information yielded by state tests and information from district assessments?

What information should your local assessment system provide? To whom? For what purposes? Answers to these questions can guide your choices of what to test locally and how to test it.

Ideas for making it useful:

No doubt there are many other questions your study team could pose in thinking about how to get the most from a system that integrates state and local assessment. Our purpose in this activity is to illustrate the opportunity local leaders have to improve balance and quality, even when the state system drives the majority of public focus and attention.

Competency 10

The leader understands the issues related to unethical and inappropriate use of student assessment and protects students and staff from such misuse.

School leaders are responsible for protecting the well-being of students whose achievement is assessed either by means of standardized tests or through classroom assessment. This standard of ethical practice underpins all of the previous nine competencies, and is accomplished when leaders promote interpretation, use, and communication of results that leads to appropriate inferences about student learning and proper action on behalf of student success. Leaders are obliged in all contexts to help avoid and discourage misinterpretation, misuse, and miscommunication of assessment results.

School leaders also have a responsibility to protect the confidentiality of individual student assessment results, obtain parental consent for certain assessments prior to the assessment being given, and follow procedures that protect test security. They also need to ensure that students with special needs be provided with assessment accommodations appropriate for their circumstance and consistent with their own IEP (OSPI, 1996; Stiggins, 2005). Allowing the widest range of students possible to participate in school testing programs provides the most accurate picture of system performance, and gives as many students as possible the opportunity to show what they know.

Monitoring test preparation practices is another important part of the leader's ethical responsibilities. Although we know that the best test preparation comes from a high-quality curriculum and good teaching, there is a great deal of pressure today to raise test scores, and so it becomes paramount that educators understand the differences between ethical and unethical practices. Ethical practices are aimed at raising student achievement; some unethical practices bypass increasing achievement and go directly to raising test scores.

Some state tests measure a narrow slice of their state content standards; by assessing only what is easily measured, the tests do not address many important content standards (CISA, 2001). In such cases, school leaders need to guard against the practice of narrowing the curriculum to teach only to those standards easily tested at the state level. This can skew the curriculum balance in favor of learning at the knowledge level, at the expense of how to reason, perform skillfully with that knowledge, and create quality products (Chappuis & Chappuis, 2002).

Listed here are standards of responsible practice* that should guide professional actions. Effective school leaders follow these guidelines and provide assistance to teachers to ensure that they do the same:

1. Interpret, use, and communicate results in a fair manner that is consistent with the assessment's limitations and with full awareness of the implications of the decisions to be made for students and their academic success.
2. Inform all assessment users of the reasons for the assessment (including all decisions to be made), as well as its limitations and dangers of potential misinterpretation.
3. Provide understandable score reports that include guidelines for proper interpretation and caution against potential misinterpretations.
4. Communicate all information needed to ensure proper interpretation and use of results. If a norm-referenced test is used, the norms used to compare student results must be clearly and completely described. If a standards-referenced test is used, standards must be clearly and completely described as well. In all high-stakes assessment contexts, standard error of measurement should be reported and explained along with scores.
5. Use assessment results in ways that maintain student confidence in themselves as learners and that motivate them to keep striving to succeed academically; that is, use assessments in ways that prevent students from giving up in hopelessness.
6. Accommodate the special needs of students with academic gifts and challenges in test administration, interpretation, and use.
7. Encourage decision makers to tap multiple sources of information about student achievement to inform instructional decisions; as the potential impact of the decision increases in importance, so does the need to tap multiple sources.

*Adapted from the "Code of Professional Responsibilities in Educational Measurement" of the National Council on Measurement in Education (Washington, DC: NCME, 1995).

8. Avoid making, and actively discourage others from making, inaccurate reports, unsubstantiated claims, inappropriate interpretations, or other false or misleading statements about assessment results.

9. Inform users of procedures for appealing results, requesting review of scores or rescoring, and rights of access to assessment results.

10. Address improprieties in assessment development, administration, scoring, reporting, or use in a forthright manner, to prevent misinterpretations or misuse.

11. Protect the privacy rights of individuals and institutions involved in assessment.

12. Discourage unethical, dishonest, or inappropriate preparation of students for tests, such as reliance on practices that inflate test scores without promoting greater learning. (Guidelines for principals and teachers for proper test preparation are included with the Activities for this competence.)

13. Promote public understanding of standards of sound assessment practice to develop community support for proper assessment and communication of results.

Thinking About Assessment

Activity 23: "Is This Responsible?"

Purpose: This activity is for use with a building staff to stimulate thinking and discussion about responsible practices before, during, and after standardized testing. We recommend that you use this list as a springboard for your own needs; consider modifying it so that it reflects the kinds of tests your teachers administer and includes those practices you want to discuss with them.

Time: 30–60 minutes

Directions: Have participants read each practice on the chart, "Is This Responsible?" pages 234–236, and then mark each as "Responsible," "Irresponsible," or "It Depends." Let participants discuss the reasons for their answers with partners or in small groups. Then conduct a large-group discussion. Identify practices on which the whole group has consensus, and then discuss those practices on which there is more than one opinion. Or, you could hand out your answers and have discussion center on clarifying why each practice is either responsible or irresponsible, or conditions that are required to be in place for the practice to be one or the other.

Closure: Hand out a list of appropriate practices developed for your building or district testing situations.

Is This Responsible?

PRACTICE	RESPONSIBLE	IRRESPONSIBLE	IT DEPENDS
Tell students what the test results will be used for.			
Use locally developed tests that parallel the content of an upcoming standardized test to help students get ready.			
Define on the test form words students don't understand.			
Discuss with students how the test will be administered, in advance of the test.			
Incorporate into the curriculum all subject-area objectives measured by an upcoming test.			
Teach test-taking skills.			
Use published test preparation material that promises to raise scores on a specific standardized test.			

PRACTICE	RESPONSIBLE	IRRESPONSIBLE	IT DEPENDS
During the test, pronounce words used in the test.			
Review skills, strategies, and concepts previously taught just before administering a standardized test.			
Limit curriculum and instruction to the skills, strategies, and concepts included on a standardized test.			
Review standardized test question answers after the test.			
Give help to those students who are confused during the standardized test.			
Exclude eligible students from taking the standardized test.			
Reproduce part of the test to help students understand it after they've taken the test.			
Comment on the quality of student work during the test.			
Hint that a student should change an answer.			

PRACTICE	RESPONSIBLE	IRRESPONSIBLE	IT DEPENDS
Read a part of the standardized test to a student to help him or her understand it better.			
Keep students focused and on task during the test.			
Teach directly to the state standards that are represented on a standardized test.			
Teach students to apply a performance assessment scoring rubric before a high-stakes assessment.			
Change a student's grade based on recent test evidence revealing a higher level of achievement.			
Report invasions of student test score privacy issues.			
Hand score a sample of student standardized test papers to evaluate the accuracy of electronic scoring services.			

Applying the Skills

Resource 8: Guidelines for Test Preparation and Administration

What this resource is: Two lists of actions principals and teachers can take to enhance the testing atmosphere in the school. The lists are taken by permission from "Ethical Standards on Testing: Test Preparation and Administration," developed by members of the Washington Educational Research Association (WERA) in 1999 and revised in 2001.

Ideas for making it useful: Read through each list and determine which practices are already in place in your building or district. Decide which to implement. Additionally, you may want to find similar documents produced by national organizations and by organizations within your state:

American Educational Research Association, American Psychological Association, National Council of Measurement in Education. (1985). *Standards for educational and psychological testing*. Washington, DC: APA.

American Educational Research Association. (1992). *Ethical standards of the American Educational Research Association*. Washington, DC: Author.

American Federation of Teachers, National Council on Measurement in Education, National Education Association. (1990). *Standards for teacher competence in educational assessment of students*. Washington, DC: Author.

National Council of Measurement in Education, Ad hoc Committee on the Development of a Code of Ethics. (1995). *Code of professional responsibilities in educational measurement*. Washington, DC: Author.

Guidelines for Test Preparation and Administration

The Principal's Role

There are a number of things the principal can do to enhance the testing atmosphere in the school:

1. Inform both students and parents about what each test does and does not do, when and how it will be administered, and how the results will be used. Indicate the importance of tests for students, staff, and the school. Stress the importance of school attendance on the scheduled testing dates.

2. Encourage the implementation of appropriate test-wiseness teaching and review. Teaching test-wiseness skills should be independent of subject matter being tested and should include an understanding of test books, use of answer sheets, item response strategies, time management, listening, and following directions.

3. Let parents know about upcoming tests and what they can do to encourage their children's performance.

4. Work with teachers to develop a building testing schedule. Attempt to maximize the efficiency of the building's physical layout and staff resources.

5. Pay careful attention to building schedules during the testing period. Avoid planning assemblies, fire drills, maintenance, etc., during the testing period.

6. Develop a plan to keep tests and answer sheets secure before and after administration, and ensure that all are returned properly.

7. Arrange, where possible, for teachers to have proctoring help in administering tests. Ensure that tests are carried out according to ethical and legal practice.

8. Provide a policy statement or handbook to all involved with test administration spelling out proper and improper testing procedures.

9. Create a process to check out any suspicions or allegations of cheating.

10. Require a detailed written explanation about why a student was not tested or the reason a score was not figured into a school's average.

11. Encourage teachers' participation in district inservice sessions on assessment.

12. Ensure that all students are tested. Review all test accommodations, including exclusion as a last resort, made for students with special needs. Ensure that accommodations and exclusions are consistent with specific testing program guidelines.

13. Ensure that there are no interruptions in classrooms during the testing period, including custodial tasks, intercom calls, delivery of messages, etc.

14. Work with the test coordinator and classroom teachers to schedule and staff makeup days for students who miss parts of the test. This might include bringing in a substitute or finding other ways to use building staff creatively to administer makeup test in an appropriate setting.

15. Share test results with staff. Neither the testing program nor the results are "owned" by any particular grade. The results are an indication of how well things are going in the school generally. Staff members need to work together to ensure that the testing process is a smooth one. School improvement is a team effort.

Guidelines for Test Preparation and Administration

The Teacher's Role

Students will do their best on tests if they find an encouraging and supportive atmosphere, if they know that they are well prepared, and if they know that they will do well with hard work. To create a situation that will encourage students to do their best, teachers should:

1. Attend inservice workshops on test administration.

2. Develop an assessment calendar and schedule.

3. Prepare students well in advance for assessment by teaching test-wiseness skills. Independent of subject matter being tested, teach and review test-taking skills that include an understanding of test books and use of answer sheets, item response strategies, time management, listening, and following directions.

4. Develop a list of which and how many students will be tested, and when they will be tested. Determine students for whom special-needs accommodations may be necessary.

5. Develop a list of students who will be exempted from testing and the reason for the exemption. The list must be reviewed and approved by the principal or test administration committee. Parents must be notified and alternative assessments identified.

6. Develop plans for the administration of makeup tests for students absent from the scheduled testing period.

7. Prepare and motivate students just before the test.

8. Prepare to administer the test, with sufficient materials available for all students to be tested.

9. Prepare classrooms for the test. Arrange for comfortable seating where students will not be able to see each others' test materials, but will be able to hear test directions. Eliminate posters or other materials that may be distracting or contain information that could be used with the test.

10. Alert neighboring teachers to the testing schedule and ask their help in keeping noise levels to a minimum.

11. Arrange a separate, supervised area for those students who finish early and may cause a distraction for other students.

12. Read the test administration manual carefully, in advance. Administer the test according to the directions.

13. Meet with proctors to discuss their duties and responsibilities. Carefully and actively proctor the test.

14. Arrange for appropriate breaks and student stress-relievers.

15. Follow the rules for test security and return all test material to the test administrator.

Thinking About Assessment

Activity 24: A Self-Analysis for School Leaders

Purpose: Up to this point you have largely worked with your leadership study team members. This activity asks you to reflect individually on the 10 competencies using the following three questions:

1. Each of the 10 competencies for educational leaders offers many ways for principals to demonstrate proficiency. With the list of competencies in front of you, examine each one in relation to your knowledge and actions as a school leader. Try to attach specific examples to each competency that you carry out as the assessment leader in the school.

2. Using the worksheet, "Assessment Competencies for Educational Leaders," page 243, rate yourself on the 10 competencies. What areas stand out as your strengths? Which one(s) could you target for improvement?

3. Look at your areas of strength and areas in which you'd like to improve, and compare those rankings with the school/district self-analysis profile you created at the end of Part 3 of this guide. You can use for reference Table 4-5, which cross-references the doors with the 10 competencies. What similarities do you see between the systems analysis and your own individual analysis? What major differences are there? How could these two ratings be combined to further clarify the assessment priorities of your school/district?

Assessment Competencies for Educational Leaders

1. The leader understands the standards of quality for student assessments and how to ensure that these standards are met in all assessments.
   Low 1_____ 2_____ 3_____ 4_____ 5_____ High

2. The leader understands the principles of assessment *for* learning and works with staff to integrate them into classroom instruction.
   Low 1_____ 2_____ 3_____ 4_____ 5_____ High

3. The leader understands the necessity of clear academic achievement targets, aligned classroom-level achievement targets, and their relationship to the development of accurate assessments.
   Low 1_____ 2_____ 3_____ 4_____ 5_____ High

4. The leader knows and can evaluate teachers' classroom assessment competencies and helps teachers learn to assess accurately and use the results productively.
   Low 1_____ 2_____ 3_____ 4_____ 5_____ High

5. The leader can plan, present, or secure professional development activities that contribute to the use of sound practices.
   Low 1_____ 2_____ 3_____ 4_____ 5_____ High

6. The leader accurately analyzes assessment information, uses the information to improve curriculum and instruction, and assists teachers in doing the same.
   Low 1_____ 2_____ 3_____ 4_____ 5_____ High

7. The leader can develop and implement sound assessment and assessment-related policies.
   Low 1_____ 2_____ 3_____ 4_____ 5_____ High

8. The leader creates the conditions necessary for the appropriate use and reporting of student achievement information, and can communicate effectively with all members of the school community about student assessment results and their relationship to improving curriculum and instruction.
   Low 1_____ 2_____ 3_____ 4_____ 5_____ High

9. The leader understands the attributes of a sound and balanced student assessment system.
   Low 1_____ 2_____ 3_____ 4_____ 5_____ High

10. The leader understands the issues related to the unethical and inappropriate use of student assessment and protects students and staff from such misuse.
    Low 1_____ 2_____ 3_____ 4_____ 5_____ High

Table 4-5

Competency	Relates to Door	Activities	Resources
1. The leader understands the standards of quality for student assessments and how to ensure that these standards are met in all assessments.	3. Assessment Literacy	4. ATI Interactive Video *Evaluating Assessment Quality: Hands-on Practice,* pg. 104 5. Analyze Assessments for Clear Targets, pg. 105 6. Developmental Continua for Teachers, pg. 109	
2. The leader understands the principles of assessment *for* learning and works with staff to integrate them into classroom instruction.	1. Clear targets 2. Users/Uses 3. Assessment Literacy 4. Communication	1. Building the Foundation, pg. 8 2. "Emily's Story," pg. 42 7. Classroom Assessment *for* Learning, pg. 127 8. Principles of Assessment *for* Learning, pg. 133 9. Converting Learning Targets, pg. 136 10. Ways That Teachers and Students Use Formative Assessment, pg. 138 11. Using Feedback to Set Goals, pg. 143	1. Using Test Results, pg. 148 2. Student Self-Assessment and Goal-Setting, pg. 152 6. Rubric for Grading, pg. 221
3. The leader understands the necessity of clear academic achievement standards, aligned classroom-level achievement targets, and their relationship to the development of accurate assessments.	1. Clear targets 3. Assessment Literacy	12. Deconstructing Standards, pg. 161 13. Using Interviews to Hire, pg. 170 14. Auditing Your Classroom Curriculum, pg. 172	3. Implementing the Written Curriculum, pg. 157
4. The leader knows and can evaluate teachers' classroom assessment competencies, and helps teachers learn to assess accurately and use the results productively.	3. Assessment Literacy	15. Should Teachers Be Held Accountable for Assessment Competence, pg. 176	

Competency	Relates to Door	Activities	Resources
5. The leader can plan, present, or secure professional development activities that contribute to the use of sound assessment practices.	3. Assessment Literacy	16. Analyzing Your Professional Development Program, pg. 180 17. Learning Teams for Assessment Literacy, pg. 184	4. How Principals Can Support Learning Teams, pg. 187
6. The leader analyzes student assessment information accurately, uses the information to improve curriculum and instruction, and assists teachers in doing the same.	2. Users/Uses 3. Assessment Literacy 4. Communication		5. Conducting an Assessment Audit, pg. 198
7. The leader develops and implements sound assessment and assessment-related policies.	5. Policies	18. Using School/District Policies to Support Quality Assessment, pg. 204	
8. The leader creates the conditions necessary for the appropriate use and reporting of student achievement information, and can communicate effectively with all members of the school community about student assessment results and their relationship to improving curriculum and instruction.	2. Users/Uses 3. Assessment 4. Communication	19. Grading Scenarios, pg. 213 20. ATI Interactive Video *Report Card Grading*, pg. 218 21. When Grades Don't Match the State Assessment Results, pg. 219	7. Standard Cover Letter to Parents, pg. 225
9. The leader understands the attributes of a sound and balanced assessment system.	All 5 Doors	3. Creating An Assessment Profile, pg. 85 22. Merging Local and State Assessment Systems, pg. 228	
10. The leader understands the issues related to unethical and inappropriate use of student assessment and protects students and staff from such misuse.	2. Users/Uses 3. Assessment Literacy	23. Is This Responsible?, pg. 233	8. Guidelines for Test Preparation and Administration, pg. 237
Competencies 1–10		24. Self-Analysis for School Leaders, pg. 242 25. Connecting Assessment	

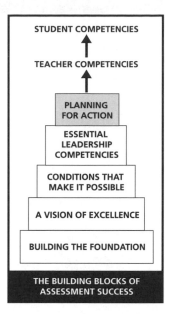

5

*A system that is in balance will ensure that the right kind of assessment is used for the right purpose, and that assessment will be used to continually improve student learning. Through the use of high-quality assessments **of** and **for** learning, linked to the targets of instruction, all students will be able to show what they know and can do.*

Part Five

PLANNING
FOR
ACTION

The final part of this guide helps you synthesize the thinking and work of your leadership study team from Parts 1 through 4. That synthesis will produce a plan of action that moves your vision of quality assessment closer to reality. At this point, you have developed some ideas about the current status of your assessment system. You also may have formed opinions about the level of your own assessment knowledge and skills, and about the professional development needs of your leadership team and teaching staff. Before acting on those conclusions, there is one final activity to complete.

Throughout this guide we've encouraged you to think systemically, to see the whole picture when planning for improvement in your assessment system. This is especially helpful when looking at the many school/district policies related to assessment, when thinking about the teacher hiring, evaluation, and staff development functions in your district and their relationship to sound assessment, and in looking at the total assessment program. The mission and purpose of assessment, what you believe assessment should accomplish, the grading and reporting systems, and the information needs of all stakeholders are just some of the system components. The final Activity, pages 250–253, asks that you consider the current goals of your school/district from a systems perspective by examining the connections between those goals and activities and an initiative that promotes assessment balance and quality through planning and professional development. How does creating a balanced assessment system and developing assessment-literate staff fit into the current scope of work and priorities of your school and/or district? How will one affect the other? How can you best communicate with staff about the relationship between existing and new priorities?

Thinking About Assessment

Activity 25: Connecting Assessment *for* Learning to Other School Improvement Initiatives

Purpose: Planning for assessment balance and quality, including professional development in assessment literacy, can be seen as "just one more thing we should do, in addition to differentiated instruction, curriculum mapping, improving teaching in the content areas, aligning to standards . . . ," or whatever the current school improvement goal happens to be. We need to be able to connect assessment *for* learning to these other initiatives in ways that help others understand the relationships among them.

This activity helps your leadership study team identify the logic that links assessment literacy with common initiatives:

- Developing local standards-based assessment systems, aligned with state standards
- Aligning instruction with standards
- Differentiating instruction
- Curriculum mapping
- Closing the achievement gap
- Improving instruction in the content areas
- Improving teacher quality
- Developing standards-based report cards

We've taken two of these—"Aligning Instruction with Standards" and "Closing the Achievement Gap"—and have provided examples of the possible connections between these initiatives and developing assessment literacy (pp. 252–253).

Time: 30–60 minutes, depending on the number of initiatives you choose to analyze.

Directions: **Step 1.**   Working individually and then as a team, make a list of the school improvement initiatives that are priorities in your school or district. Set this list aside for later use.

Step 2. Choose either "Aligning Instruction with Standards," or "Closing the Achievement Gap." Working alone or as a team, brainstorm your answers to the following question: *What role would/could a foundation of assessment literacy and the effective use of quality classroom assessment play in the success of this initiative?* If you needed to explain how assessment underpins the initiative's effectiveness, what point(s) would you make?

Step 3. Compare your points to the points in the sample initiatives. It doesn't matter if they match; it only matters that you've thought it through and begin to see concrete connections. Reflect on and discuss the similarities and differences between the two lists.

Step 4. Work with the other school improvement initiative from Step 2 and repeat Steps 2 and 3.

Step 5. Compare the lists of talking points that you generated for both initiatives. What similarities do you see? Aside from a few initial entries unique to each initiative, do you find commonalties between them? This activity helps make it clear that many school improvement initiatives can reach their potential only when accompanied by sound classroom assessment.

Step 6. Select one of your own school improvement initiatives from the list you made in Step 1. Brainstorm reasons why sound classroom assessment is essential for that effort as well. The goal is to state the connection between your local initiative and assessment literacy in such a clear manner that others can also see and understand how assessment literacy is vital to any foundation of success.

Aligning Instruction with Standards

For use in Step 3

Make the following points to connect a foundation of assessment literacy to this school improvement priority:

- Clearly articulated content standards and benchmarks state what is most important for students to know and be able to do. A grade-by-grade curriculum aligned to state standards focuses the instruction.

- In the standards-aligned classroom, teachers do not teach by proceeding page by page though the textbook, but rather select what to teach based on the curriculum. As students progress, teachers need to select, modify, or develop classroom assessments based on the curriculum. They must know which specific learning target each item on every test they give is intended to measure. If they don't, their standards-aligned teaching will not be accompanied by standards-aligned assessment. They will not be working with accurate information about student learning for summative or formative purposes—assessments *of* learning and assessments *for* learning will lead to inaccurate decisions on the part of teachers, students, and parents.

- Therefore, every teacher needs to understand how to build accurate assessments using the five Keys to Quality: how to develop clear and appropriate purposes for every classroom assessment; how to properly design sound classroom assessments that reflect clear learning targets; how to build assessments that yield accurate results and that avoid potential sources of bias and distortion; how to communicate clearly about student achievement and manage assessment results accurately (this includes, at the classroom level, how to provide descriptive feedback to students); and how to involve students in their own assessment to maximize student achievement and motivation.

- The most effective and efficient way to deliver professional development in classroom assessment is through establishing learning communities in which adults can learn new strategies and apply them in the classroom.

Closing the Achievement Gap

For use in Step 3

To help others understand how a foundation of assessment literacy underpins attempts to close achievement gaps, the following points apply:

- Black and Wiliam's (1998) research shows that one of the best ways to close the achievement gap is to improve classroom assessment. Their three recommendations are to improve the quality and accuracy of classroom assessment, increase descriptive feedback, and increase student involvement in assessment. They state that teachers and students must be able to answer three questions about student learning: "Where am I going? (standards-aligned instruction, with the standards clearly communicated to students); "Where am I now?" (descriptive feedback to students about the quality of their work and student self-assessment of that quality); and "How can I get there?" (teaching strategies designed to act on information about where students are in their learning relative to the standards, and student mastery of strategies to improve their own learning). These are foundations of assessment literacy.

- For reform efforts in closing the achievement gap to succeed, professional development needs to be focused on topics required to implement standards-based classrooms—understanding standards, being skillful with instructional methodologies that best promote learning, and using both assessment *of* and *for* learning to accurately assess and effectively promote learning. Accurate classroom assessment is an essential part of the mix.

  a. Every teacher needs to understand how to build accurate assessments using the five Keys to Quality: how to develop clear and appropriate purposes for every classroom assessment; how to properly design sound classroom assessments that reflect clear learning targets; how to build assessments that yield accurate results and that avoid potential sources of bias and distortion; how to communicate clearly about student achievement and manage assessment results accurately (this includes, at the classroom level, how to provide descriptive feedback to students); and how to involve students in their own assessment to maximize student achievement and motivation.

- The most effective and efficient way to deliver professional development on assessment is through establishing learning communities in which adults can learn new strategies and apply them in the classroom.

Action Planning for Assessment Balance and Quality

Now that your team has created a vision of quality assessment, considered the conditions that are necessary to make it possible, analyzed the leadership skills needed to implement and support the vision, and thought about the connections among assessment literacy and current school improvement priorities, it is time to plan the next steps.

Start by considering the following three questions, which you probably recognize from Part 4 of this guide:

- Where are you trying to go?
- Where are you now?
- What will you do to close the gap?

These questions help students learn to self-assess and set goals for their own improvement. To answer the first question, the learning expectations have to be clearly defined and communicated so students know where they are trying to go. The second question is a summative question, seeking a point-in-time summary about where students are right now relative to the intended learning. The third question prompts action. It relies on a repertoire of strategies students can call on to close the gap between where they are and where they need to be. In short, this series of questions relies on clear expectations, a vision of what quality and success look like, and a sense of control and responsibility by students for the personal actions they will take to help them hit the target.

The same three questions can serve as a planning framework for schools and districts as they strive to raise student achievement and build better assessment systems in service of that goal. Now you can use your leadership study team experiences to answer them.

Consider the first question, "Where are you trying to go?" The answer to this question is found in your thinking and discussions in Parts 1 and 2 of this guide regarding your vision of a perfect assessment system, about the essential ingredients in such a system, and particularly about your beliefs regarding balanced and quality assessment. The answer to this question describes where you want your school/district to be in the future relative to student assessment.

The second question, concerning the current status of your system—where you are now—was addressed in Part 3. When you rated your school/district using the Five Doors to Excellence self-analysis at the end of Part 3, you drew a picture of the current status of your assessment system. You identified what work has already been done, in what areas, what work is underway, and what work remains. Other indicators of work yet to be done may also have emerged along the way through team discussions or from other sections of this guide. The analysis of your own professional knowledge and skills relative to the 10 competencies in Part 4 may also influence how you regard the current status of your local assessment system and of the vision your team has created. Your team's profile may point to the need for professional development, or it may point to the need for a clearer, well-written curriculum, or to the need to communicate more accurately and efficiently about student achievement. Each leadership team will be in a different place, with perhaps multiple priorities. Now what you need are specific answers to the third and final question: "What will you do to close the gap?"

Closing the Gap

Now you must transfer your team's analysis of your current system and priorities for a new system to a written plan of action. Throughout this guide we have presented ideas and strategies for helping you close the gap between the reality of your current assessment system and one that is grounded in balance, quality, and student involvement. The work you must do now will vary based on the profile you created. Some leadership teams will be able to take action on their own; others may want to bring into the process a larger group of district or school stakeholders. Still others may first need to educate their peers or the instructional staff about the need for and promise of assessment balance and quality.

But whatever the content, completed action plans have the potential to languish on a shelf, unimplemented. There could be a lack of shared ownership that causes the plan to be abandoned, a lack of funding or committed leadership, or simply too many plans for one organization to follow. Like the district curriculum guide that can collect dust on top of the file cabinet, there is no guarantee that ensures action plans will fulfill their promise. But just as you can raise the probability that the written district curriculum is also the taught, tested, and learned curriculum, you also can increase the likelihood that your action plans for assessment will succeed. Here's how:

- Ensure your plan is grounded in the clear vision your team refined over the course of its study, using well-articulated beliefs about assessment as the foundation for that vision.

- Use the Five Door profile analysis to focus on results by identifying long-term goals and specific, achievable milestones to chart the progress of your plan.

- Develop clear strategies aimed at reaching the goals and milestones with the required resources identified and allocated.

- Identify the staff development required for teachers and administrators and plan for it to be readily available.

- Recognize and communicate to others that the plan's sole purpose is to improve student learning, making it even more difficult to leave on a shelf.

Most school leaders are familiar with strategic planning with well-defined procedures that result in plans of improvement. If your school or district has a preferred planning process used successfully in the past, or has a series of planning templates for documenting the goals and objectives, or follows a policy that guides the make-up of a planning team, we encourage your leadership team to put those tools to use here. Success of the plan is paramount; flexibility in its content, creation, and documentation is important to that success. If you have no preferred process, let us propose one for you.

Our goal has been to keep the planning as straightforward as possible, relying in large part on the school/district self-analysis in Part 3. In documenting the current status of your assessment system relative to your vision of the future, your team has completed much of the needed information gathering, and it is now time to begin to draft a plan of action. You may base your draft action plan on any or all of the following:

- The team's final written assessment vision that has been refined over time
- The school/district profile created through the analysis of the Five Doors
- Any of the self-analysis tools (The 9 Principles of Assessment *for* Learning, The 10 Assessment Competencies for School Leaders, etc.)
- Any information produced through the "Thinking About Assessment" activities or "Applying the Skills" resources from this guide.

If you made notes in the margins of this guide during discussion or activities, now would be a good time to compile them into a usable summary. District policies and Table 4-5, which cross-references the Five Doors with the 10 Assessment Competencies for School Leaders and the activities and resources in this guide, also will be helpful tools. The final section of your self-analysis from Part 3, titled "Leadership for Assessment Reform," will also help you plan your next steps. This set of nine items takes a "big picture" view of the status of your assessment system from a leadership perspective, and profiles items such as the existence of a written, comprehensive assessment plan, coordinated local/state testing schedules, stakeholder involvement in planning, and the assessment literacy of local leaders. Your final action plan will not be complete without a consideration of these issues.

Action Planning Templates

To complete your action plan we have provided planning templates for each of the Five Doors described in Part 3. Remember, these are some of the questions asked behind each door. Each implies its own action plan if the answer is NO.

1—Clear Targets

- Do we have well-defined achievement goals for students?
- Are they connected across grade levels and within subjects?
- Are they taught by teachers who have themselves mastered the learning targets they are to teach their students?

2—Uses and Users

- What are our current sources of achievement information about students?
- What information do we need and not have?
- Are we meeting the information needs of all users?
- Have we balanced classroom assessment and standardized testing?
- Have we considered and defined the purposes for all of our assessments?
- Do we know how to avoid the misuse of assessment information?

3—Assessment Literacy

- Have we analyzed the level of assessment literacy in our instructional staff, administrators, and local community?
- Are classroom assessments aligned with state and district standards?
- Are we assessment literate? If not, what is our plan for developing assessment literacy where it is needed?

4—Communication

- Are we communicating effectively about student achievement?
- Do our grading practices help or hinder in that regard?
- Are we using a systems approach in reporting student progress that adheres to the principles of effective communication, including multiple methods of communicating?

5—Policies

- What policies guide practices that have the greatest impact on student learning?
- Do we have policies that support quality assessment, including fair and ethical practice?
- Do our policies work as a system to drive good practice relative to student assessment?

The top section of each of the five templates that follow (pp. 259–263) crosses the various roles and levels in the organization of a school system. It is designed to help your team think about all of the different levels and positions in the organization that could be called on to contribute to the plan's success. The intent is to foster thinking that reaches from the classroom to the boardroom in the design of the action plan. As an example: think about the work you need to do around achievement targets behind Door 1. Within each cell of the table, enter what responsibilities fall to each player at each level. What is the school board's job relative to achievement standards, if any? The superintendent's? Determine who in the system needs to do what to accomplish work related to Door 1.

The bottom half of each template is the action planning tool where you specify exactly what is to be done to create assessment balance and quality. Your team may have one goal for each of the Five Doors, or several goals for each, depending entirely on your school/district self-analysis profile. The activities supporting each goal for each of the Five Doors can be captured here, describing the intended outcome, the specific tasks required to achieve the outcome, the person(s) responsible, the resources required, and the timeline for accomplishment. Copy as many pages as needed per Door to accommodate the scope of work.

ASSESSMENT OF AND FOR LEARNING
Door 1 – Clear Targets

Roles and Responsibilities

Position	District Level	School Level	Classroom Level
School Board			
Superintendent			
Curriculum Director			
Principals			
C & I/Prof. Dev. Support Staff			
Teachers			

Action Plan Goal

Proposed Action(s)	Intended Outcome	Specific Task(s)	Evidence of Accomplishment	Person(s) Resp.	Resources Required	Due Date

ASSESSMENT OF AND FOR LEARNING
Door 2 – Uses/Users

Roles and Responsibilities

Position	District Level	School Level	Classroom Level
School Board			
Superintendent			
Curriculum Director			
Principals			
C & I/Prof. Dev. Support Staff			
Teachers			

Action Plan Goal

Proposed Action(s)	Intended Outcome	Specific Task(s)	Evidence of Accomplishment	Person(s) Resp.	Resources Required	Due Date

ASSESSMENT OF AND *FOR* LEARNING
Door 3 – Assessment Literacy

Roles and Responsibilities

Position	District Level	School Level	Classroom Level
School Board			
Superintendent			
Curriculum Director			
Principals			
C & I/Prof. Dev. Support Staff			
Teachers			

Action Plan Goal

Proposed Action(s)	Intended Outcome	Specific Task(s)	Evidence of Accomplishment	Person(s) Resp.	Resources Required	Due Date

ASSESSMENT OF AND *FOR* LEARNING
Door 4 – Communication

Roles and Responsibilities

Position	District Level	School Level	Classroom Level
School Board			
Superintendent			
Curriculum Director			
Principals			
C & I/Prof. Dev. Support Staff			
Teachers			

Action Plan Goal

Proposed Action(s)	Intended Outcome	Specific Task(s)	Evidence of Accomplishment	Person(s) Resp.	Resources Required	Due Date

ASSESSMENT OF AND FOR LEARNING
Door 5 – Policies

Roles and Responsibilities

Position	District Level	School Level	Classroom Level
School Board			
Superintendent			
Curriculum Director			
Principals			
C & I/Prof. Dev. Support Staff			
Teachers			

Action Plan Goal

Proposed Action(s)	Intended Outcome	Specific Task(s)	Evidence of Accomplishment	Person(s) Resp.	Resources Required	Due Date

Additional Planning Considerations

The five action planning templates linked to the Five Doors provide a framework that you may broaden to include assessment issues not directly raised or covered in detail in this guide. Following are other issues your team may want to consider either while developing your action plan or in future review and planning.

The Comprehensive Assessment Plan

The action planning process and templates in this guide will help your team focus on improving assessment balance and quality while emphasizing the role assessment *for* learning can and should play in the total system. Although similar in some respects, it is not the same as developing a school/district comprehensive assessment plan. A comprehensive assessment plan helps manage the assessment business of the school or district and acts as a guide for all issues related to testing, assessment, and monitoring the progress of all students. Issues such as appropriate student placement in special programs, testing accommodations for special populations, total system costs, test materials maintenance and security, technical and legal issues, student promotion and retention, and the information needs, sources, and models for program evaluation are examples of topics addressed in a comprehensive assessment plan. Those types of issues may or may not find their way into your assessment *for* learning action plan; if they do not, remember that they can and should be addressed and communicated to staff in some way.

Helping Policy Makers Understand Balance and Quality

We've worked in this guide at the school/district policy levels, trying to make sure policies drive sound practice and support quality assessment at those levels. But there are other levels of policy you might also want to consider trying to influence in the same way. Policy makers, not just at the local school board level but also at the state and federal level, need a deep understanding of assessment issues if they are to assist schools and districts achieve balance and quality. Knowing the limitations of standardized testing, and also knowing the quality information and data that assessment-literate teachers can produce about individual students is an important start for policy makers at these levels. Further, they need to understand the role of professional development in improving schools and in achieving standards-based systems. Without that, educators will continue to be left without opportunity to learn and apply in the classroom what we know works when assessment is used as part of instruction. You may find the ATI parent/community guide, *Understanding School Assessment* (Chappuis & Chappuis, 2002), a valuable resource in helping policy makers understand these issues.

Communicating and Monitoring the Plan

The success of many reform efforts is due as much to the collaboration used to develop the strategic plan and the effective communication of the plan to all stakeholders as it is to the plan's actual goals and content. Your leadership team should consider strategies for generating support for improvement plans both small and large by asking the following questions:

- Who needs to be either involved in the planning effort or informed along the way?
- Should there be different levels of involvement, from direct decision making to advisory in nature?
- Whose advice do we want/need relative to our plan?
- Once written, is it clear that a leadership plan is in place that is across levels: district, school, and classroom?
- Is there a communications component of the plan that will be uniformly applied to reach all stakeholders? Will those stakeholders, including the school board, be regularly updated on the plan's progress?

Reconciling Current and Future Systems

Some action plans may seek both to improve present conditions in the current assessment system and to create and plan for future conditions in a new system. Some advocate differentiating these purposes into one set of plans that focuses on present-day operations, maintaining a short-term view of improvement, and a second set of plans with an emphasis on the long term, concentrating on creating the new system as described in the team's vision (Blanchard & Waghorn, 1998). The two sets can then be intentionally merged into one comprehensive plan by a team familiar with both.

Evaluating the Action Plan

The assessment system itself, when functioning properly, provides data for program evaluation, continuous improvement, and school/district accountability, while also providing teachers, students, and parents the information they need on a daily basis to positively affect learning. Your own action plan is a statement about what parts of that system need to get better. You may have sequenced it in stages, stepping out the activities so that progress can be more easily monitored and reported. As part of the plan, it is important to document what data you can collect as evidence of accomplishment along the way.

It is likely that in many plans there will be goals and objectives related to staff acquiring the knowledge and skills necessary for the vision to become reality. Professional development in classroom assessment will be at the center of many plans. Even though there is much research evidence that student involvement in classroom assessment can increase student learning, we strongly recommend that all who implement assessment literacy professional development programs design and conduct their own local program evaluations. These evaluations can be both formative and summative. Formative evaluations help program directors monitor and adjust their professional development efforts as they go. The purpose of evaluation in this case is program improvement. Summative evaluations provide evidence of effectiveness to those who fund the professional development efforts or who are responsible for their success. These evaluations inform judgments of overall program effectiveness. Evaluators can conduct meaningful evaluations by focusing evidence gathering at any of a variety of levels. Here are some examples.

Case Study of an Individual Teacher or a Few Teachers

Evaluation results can be derived from the in-depth study of a single teacher or just a few teachers. Precisely what did these teachers experience and what effect did it have on their classroom assessment practices? A clear portrait of individual teachers' experiences can provide information on what worked and what did not. Because evaluation resources are being invested in understanding a few specific experiences, one can examine in detail how and why the professional development effort worked or didn't. In this case, generalizability of results is sacrificed for depth of understanding.

However, generalizability of results can be enhanced by including teachers from a range of contexts (grade levels and content areas). This kind of evaluation can be conducted by following teachers as they develop their assessment literacy. Or, it can center on the teachers' design and implementation of action research studies focused on student-involved classroom assessment (described in the next subsection).

The Study of a Learning Team

A slight variation on this plan focuses the evaluation on all members of a single local learning team. Here again, the power of the investigation resides in the depth of insight that it can yield, not the breadth. The objective is to generate a composite picture of the learning, experimentation, growth, and impact of a group of teachers working together. The strength of this approach is the lessons it can teach about the power of collaborative learning. How did the group define success? What procedures did they follow? What were their norms for interaction? What went on at team meetings? What evidence of greater assessment literacy emerged? What kinds of experimentation resulted? What was the extent of success and challenges? What were the joys and disappointments?

The Study of a School District

Information might be pooled on the collective experience of a sample of students, teachers, administrators, and teams across a school district. Why did professional development begin? Was there a leadership commitment? What did it take to secure a district commitment? Who was involved in the program and why? What events took place? What did they cost? What was their impact on classroom assessment quality? Efficiency? Student, teacher, or community dispositions? Student achievement? In this case, assuming that resources are limited, depth of information is sacrificed for the sake of results that generalize across individuals, classrooms, and schools.

Classroom Action Research—The Study of Impacts on Students

It can also be instructive from a program evaluation perspective to understand the impact of an assessment literacy development program by studying its effects on the classroom learning experience of the students whose teachers implement a student-involved classroom assessment environment. Precisely what happened to those students and what impact did that experience have on their achievement and dispositions? This kind of action research evaluation invests its resources in obtaining rich and deep understanding of program effects by using a high-resolution microscope. But again, those results may not generalize beyond those students studied.

Two Evaluation Focal Points

At any of these levels, program evaluations can be designed to document the nature of the professional development *processes*, or events as they unfold, and/or document the *effects* or *impacts* of those events on teachers or students. While evaluations can focus on either, we believe that the most powerful evaluations cover both.

Process Evaluation

Process evaluation documents the nature of the professional development intervention that actually was implemented. Who did what, when, and where? Did actual interventions align with what was supposed to occur? If the program "worked," precisely what worked? Without this information, you will be unable to replicate the same effective program in the future. If the professional development intervention did not work, then the results of a process evaluation provide an information base from which to make procedural adjustments.

In the case of assessment literacy development programs, the process evaluator seeks to answer procedural questions such as these:

- What procedures were used to introduce the ideas of balanced assessment systems, student-involved assessment, and the use of learning teams as the professional development process?
- How many learning teams were formed?
- What was their composition?
- What materials were available for use, were actually used, and to what extent?
- What were the teams' schedules of events?
- What happened at team meetings?
- What kinds of ongoing facilitation did teams need?

- How many learning teams were completed?
- What proportion of participants actually experimented with student-involved assessment in their classrooms?
- What student-involved classroom assessment procedures did teachers actually experiment with in their classrooms?
- What was the cost of program implementation?

To generate answers to these and similar process questions, program evaluators must maintain open lines of communication with those working to manage the learning team process and with the learning teams themselves. This may require developing a simple reporting system, with specific procedural information flowing to the program director for summary across teams. Evidence might come from team meeting minutes, training logs or diaries, or direct participation in or observations of team meetings.

Evaluation of Impact

Program effects typically unfold over time, as the professional development experience under study provides participants with new insights, ideas, and experiences. So program evaluations are likely to be most helpful in shaping program improvement and making summative judgments if they collect, summarize, and interpret evidence at the beginning, during, and at the end of a learning experience. For this reason, we urge program evaluators to plan to document progress along the way to be sure that things proceed as intended. They then must gather evidence verifying that the intervention delivered what it promised—higher levels of assessment literacy and confidence.

Program evaluators have a variety of potential sources of impact information:

- Increased assessment literacy
- Increased teacher confidence
- Increased assessment efficiency
- Increased assessment quality
- Increased student confidence
- Impact on student achievement
- Learning teams as professional development

In Closing

Through the use of high-quality assessments *of* and *for* learning, linked to the targets of instruction, all students will be able to show what they know and can do. A system that is in balance will ensure that the right kind of assessment is used for the right purpose, and that assessment will be used to continually improve student learning. We have focused the contents of this guide on our belief that strong classroom assessment is the heart of any assessment system. But it is through a combination of assessments, working in a coordinated fashion, that students can truly prosper and where all information needs can be met. Your work and the work of your colleagues in pursuit of assessment balance and quality will benefit teachers, schools, and communities, but will benefit most especially the students we all serve.

References

Amrein, A., & Berliner, D. (2003). The effects of high-stakes testing on student motivation and learning. *Educational Leadership, 60*(5), 32–38.

Arter, J. A., & Busick, K. U. (2001). *Practice with student-involved classroom assessment.* Portland, OR: Assessment Training Institute.

Arter, J., Stiggins, R., Duke, D., & Sagor, R. (1993). Promoting assessment literacy among principals. *NASSP Bulletin, 77*(556), 1–7.

Assessment Reform Group. (1999). *Assessment for learning: Beyond the black box.* Cambridge, UK: University of Cambridge.

Atkin, J. M., Black, P., & Coffey, J. (2001). *Classroom assessment and the National Science Standards.* Washington, DC: National Academy Press.

Barth, R. (1990). *Improving schools from within: Teachers, parents and principals can make a difference.* San Francisco: Jossey-Bass

Black, P., Harrison, C., Lee, C., Marshall, B., & Wiliam, D. (2002). *Working inside the black box: Assessment for learning in the classroom.* London: King's College.

Black, P., & Wiliam, D. (1998). Inside the black box: Raising standards through classroom assessment. *Phi Delta Kappan, 80*(2), 139–148.

Blanchard, K., & Johnson, S. (1982). *The one-minute manager.* New York: Morrow.

Blanchard, K., & Waghorn, T. (1998). *Mission possible.* Columbus, OH: McGraw Hill.

Bloom, B. (1984). The search for methods of group instruction as effective as one-to-one tutoring. *Educational Leadership, 41*(8), 4–17.

California School Boards Association. (1999). *Targeting student learning: The school board's role as policymaker.* Springfield, IL: Illinois Association of School Boards.

Center on Education Policy. (2003). *From the capital to the classroom: State and federal efforts to implement the No Child Left Behind Act.* Washington, DC: CEP.

Chappuis, J., & Chappuis, S. (2002). *Understanding school assessment: A parent and community guide to helping students learn.* Portland, OR: Assessment Training Institute.

Chappuis, S., & Stiggins, R. J. (2002). Classroom assessment for learning. *Educational Leadership, 60*(1), 40–43.

Commission on Instructionally Supportive Assessment. (2001). *Building tests to support instruction and accountability.* Arlington, VA: American Association of School Administrators.

Collins, J. (2001). *Good to great.* New York: Harper Collins.

Covey, S. (1989). *The seven habits of highly effective people.* New York: Simon & Schuster.

DuFour, R. (2001). In the right context. *Journal of Staff Development, 22*(1), 14–17.

DuFour, R., DuFour, R., Eaker, R., & Karhanek, G. (2004). *Whatever it takes: How professional learning communities respond when kids don't learn.* Bloomington, IN: National Educational Service.

Fullan, M. (2004, July). Leadership and sustainability. Presentation given at the Assessment Training Institute: Portland, OR.

Gladwell, M. (2000). *The tipping point.* Boston: Little, Brown & Co.

Goleman, D., Boyatzis, R., & McKee, A. (2002). *Primal leadership: Realizing the power of emotional intelligence.* Boston, MA: Harvard Business School.

Guskey, T. R. (2002). Computerized gradebooks and the myth of objectivity. *Phi Delta Kappan, 83*(10), 775–780.

Jacobs, H. H. (1997). *Mapping the big picture: Integrating curriculum and assessment K–12.* Alexandria, VA: Association for Supervision and Curriculum Development.

Murphy, C. U., & Lick, D. W. (2001). *Whole-faculty study groups: Creating student-based professional development,* 2nd ed. Thousand Oaks, CA: Corwin.

O'Connor, K. (2002). *How to grade for learning.* Arlington Heights, IL: Skylight.

Office of Superintendent of Public Instruction. (1996). *Designing a district assessment system.* Olympia, WA: OSPI.

Peters, T., & Waterman, R. (1982). *In search of excellence: Lessons from America's best run companies.* New York: Harper and Row.

Popham, W. J. (2005). F for assessment. *Edutopia News* (an online newsletter from the George Lucas Educational Foundation). Retrieved 6 April 2005 from http://www.edutopia.org/

Putnam, R. T., & Borko, H. (2000). What do new views of knowledge and thinking have to say about research on teacher learning? *Educational Researcher, 29*(1), 4–15.

Schmoker, M. (2002). The real causes of higher achievement. *SEDLetter, 14*(2). Retrieved July 2002 from http://www.sedl.org/pubs/sedletter/v14n02/1.html

Schmoker, M. (2004). Tipping point: From reckless reform to substantive instructional improvement. *Phi Delta Kappan, 85*(6), 424–432.

Senge, P. (1990). *The fifth discipline.* New York: Doubleday.

Stiggins, R. J. (2002). Assessment crisis! The absence of assessment for learning. *Phi Delta Kappan, 83*(10), 758–765.

Stiggins, R. J. (2005). *Student-involved assessment FOR learning*, 4th ed. Upper Saddle River, NJ: Merrill/Prentice Hall; distributed by Assessment Training Institute, Portland, OR.

Stiggins, R.J., Arter, J., Chappuis, J., & Chappuis, S. (2004). *Classroom assessment for student learning: Doing it right—Using it well.* Portland, OR: Assessment Training Institute.

Washington Educational Research Association. (2001). *Ethical standards in testing: Test preparation and administration.* White paper. University Place, WA: WERA.

Waters, J., Marzano, R., & McNulty, B. (2003). *Balanced leadership: what 30 years of q research tells us about the effects of leadership on student achievement.* Aurora, CO: Mid-continent Regional Educational Laboratory.

About the Authors

Steve Chappuis has been a teacher, counselor, and school and district administrator. His leadership experiences include serving as a junior high principal, a senior high principal, and executive director responsible for supervision of schools and principals. As an Assistant Superintendent for Curriculum and Instruction he implemented a standards-based instructional program that included comprehensive assessment plans and policies and professional development in classroom assessment. Steve is also the coauthor of *Understanding School Assessment: A Parent and Community Guide to Helping Students Learn* (ATI, 2002).

Rick Stiggins created the Assessment Training Institute in 1992 for the purpose of supporting educators as they face the challenges of day-to-day classroom assessment. He is committed to helping teachers learn to gather accurate information about student achievement and use that information to benefit (not just grade and sort) their students. He encourages teachers to involve students deeply in classroom assessment, record keeping, and communication to build their confidence and academic success. His two most recent books, *Student-Involved Assessment FOR Learning* (Pearson/Prentice Hall, 2005) and *Classroom Assessment* for *Student Learning: Doing it Right—Using it Well* (ATI, 2004), coauthored by Judy Arter, Jan Chappuis, and Steve Chappuis, are the latest descriptions of what assessment *for* learning looks like in the classroom.

Judy Arter is a recognized expert in performance assessment. Her background includes the development of statewide writing assessments, large-scale and classroom-based items and performance assessments, and interactive training videos. Prior to joining Assessment Training Institute, Judy directed Northwest Regional Educational Laboratory's (NWREL) assessment unit. She coauthored with Jay McTighe *Scoring Rubrics in the Classroom: Using Performance Criteria for Assessing and Improving Student Performance* (Corwin, 2001).

Jan Chappuis has been a teacher, curriculum and assessment specialist, and independent assessment trainer and consultant. She has more than a decade of experience in providing dynamic and hands-on staff development in classroom assessment. Jan leads ATI professional development efforts in writing assessment and student-involved assessment strategies. She is coauthor of *Understanding School Assessment: A Parent and Community Guide to Helping Students Learn* (2002), and a presenter and codeveloper of the training video, *Student-Involved Performance Assessment*.

CD-ROM/DVD Contents
Activities, Resources, and PowerPoint Presentations on the CD-ROM

Thinking About Assessment: Activities

Activity 1: Building the Foundation for Understanding Quality Assessment
Activity 2: "Emily's Story"
Activity 3: Creating an Assessment Profile for Your School/District
Activity 4: ATI Interactive Video: *Evaluating Assessment Quality: Hands-On Practice*
Activity 5: Analyze Assessments for Clear Targets
Activity 6: Developmental Continua for Teachers
Activity 7: Classroom Assessment *for* Learning
Activity 8: Principles of Assessment *for* Learning: A Self-Analysis
Activity 9: Converting Learning Targets to Student-Friendly Language
Activity 10: Ways That Teachers and Students Use Formative Assessment
Activity 11: Using Feedback to Set Goals
Activity 12: Deconstructing Standards into Classroom-Level Achievement
Targets: Practice for School Leaders
Activity 13: Using Interviews to Hire Teachers with Content Knowledge and
Assessment Competence
Activity 14: Auditing Your Classroom Curriculum
Activity 15: Should Teachers Be Held Accountable for Assessment Competence
Through Evaluation?
Activity 16: Analyzing Your Professional Development Program
Activity 17: Learning Teams for Assessment Literacy
Activity 18: Using School/District Policies to Support Quality Assessment
Activity 19: Grading Scenarios
Activity 20: ATI Interactive Video: *Report Card Grading: Strategies and Solutions*
Activity 21: When Grades Don't Match the State Assessment Results
Activity 22: Merging Local and State Assessment Systems
Activity 23: "Is This Responsible?"
Activity 24: A Self-Analysis for School Leaders
Activity 25: Connecting Assessment *for* Learning to Other School Improvement
Initiatives

Applying the Skills: Resources

Resource 1: Using Test Results to Self-Assess and Set Goals
Resource 2: Student Self-Assessment and Goal-Setting Activities
Resource 3: Implementing the Written Curriculum
Resource 4: How Principals Can Support Learning Teams
Resource 5: Conducting an Assessment Audit
Resource 6: Rubric for Grading
Resource 7: A Standard Cover Letter to Parents
Resource 8: Guidelines for Test Preparation and Administration

DVD Presentation

New Mission, New Beliefs: Assessment for *Learning*